PATHFINDER PIONEER

PATHFINDER PIONEER

The Memoir of a Lead Bomber Pilot in World War II

Colonel Raymond E. Brim, USAF (Ret.)

CASEMATE

Philadelphia & Oxford

Published in the United States of America and Great Britain in 2016 by
CASEMATE PUBLISHERS
1950 Lawrence Road, Havertown, PA 19083, USA
and
10 Hythe Bridge Street, Oxford OX1 2EW, UK

Hardcover Edition: ISBN 978-1-61200-352-8
Digital Edition: ISBN 978-1-61200-353-5

Cataloging-in publication data is available from the Library of Congress and the British Library.

Printed and bound in the United States of America

For a complete list of Casemate titles, please contact:

CASEMATE PUBLISHERS (US)
Telephone (610) 853-9131
Fax (610) 853-9146
Email: casemate@casematepublishers.com
www.casematepublishers.com

CASEMATE PUBLISHERS (UK)
Telephone (01865) 241249
Fax (01865) 794449
Email: casemate-uk@casematepublishers.co.uk
www.casematepublishers.co.uk

CONTENTS

To my beloved wife, Patricia, who made me who I am today with her love, her inspirational courage, and her intellectual curiosity. During the 33 years of our Air Force career she was a devoted and tireless wife and companion, tolerating countless reassignments. With each move she not only created a warm secure home for our family but also enriched our lives, from so many military installations in the U.S., to Japan, to Washington D.C., to Germany, and for decades after we retired. While Pat passed away in 2007 her love and guidance continues to be with me every moment of every day.

FOREWORD

A British Perspective

At 4pm on a foggy December day in 1944, an English farmer stood aghast as an American bomber, returning home from a mission, plummeted to the ground in flames before him. All nine airmen on board were killed in the resulting crash and explosion. One of the nine had not seen his family for two years. He would not return to his grieving mother who never recovered from his death. He would not see his 23rd birthday on Christmas Day, nor would he ever meet his son, born a month later to an English girl named Doris. This man was my grandfather, Staff Sergeant Robert (Bob) Lennes Burry from Detroit, and until I was 19, I had never even heard his name.

When my father was two years old, Doris married Alex Searle, my grandfather, who subsequently adopted my father. The past was buried away, silenced, and their lives moved on together as a new family. Doris never once spoke to my father about his American parentage; it must have been easier for her that way. It wasn't until my father was 10 years old, while building a chicken coop in the garden with Alex that he learned the truth.

"You know I'm not your real father, don't you?"

An awkward, one-line revelation from Alex, a responding nod from my father, and the matter was settled and never raised again. There had been clues, enough to raise a young lad's suspicions: gifts from a "Mrs. Amalia Burry", from America, who had once visited, and monthly insurance cheques from the American Embassy. Doris kept Amalia, Bob's mother in Detroit, updated on my father as he grew, sending letters and photos; but contact gradually became less frequent, until after Doris' death at the age of 45, it stopped entirely.

On my father's 50th birthday, when I was 19, everything I thought I knew about my father and my family history changed forever. I had always been interested in learning about the past, bugging family for stories and information. I knew that on my father's side, we were a typical local family; ties with the small town in Cambridgeshire in which we still live stretching back through the generations. Back in the 1990s, before the town grew, everybody knew everyone else; who was related to whom, and all their business besides. It came as a massive shock then, as we raised our glasses for a birthday toast, to hear our father reveal the secret he'd kept from my siblings and myself our whole lives. It came as an even bigger shock when the realisation dawned that everyone else in the family already knew the secret and had been complicit in the duplicity. Now though, after over 20 years, my father had finally found his American family and it was time for us to learn the truth.

I will never forget the first time I visited my grandfather's grave at the American Cemetery in Cambridge, less than an hour from home. It was the absolute silence which made the biggest impression. My grandfather is buried right at the back of the cemetery; in the most tranquil spot, overlooking the woods and fields below. As I knelt by the marble cross, the empty space I felt inside and the unanswerable questions gnawed at me. On that day, I began my journey on a path to find my grandfather, the person behind the face in the black and white photographs. Initially, there was very little available information, but piece by piece, gradually at first then slowly gaining momentum, I moved towards knowing my grandfather. Each discovery added more colour to those black and white images and helped me to see beneath the picture to my lost grandfather beneath.

Bob and Doris met and fell in love while he was stationed at RAF Alconbury, in Cambridgeshire. Despite the distance of 30 miles from his base to Doris' home, they tried to do all the things usual for courting couples: visits to relatives, the cinema and the local photographers. Bob came to spend most of his furloughs in our rural little market town of

March. He became a regular visitor at Doris' parents' riverside home, in one of the narrowest and oldest streets in town. I often wonder what the boy from the bustling metropolis thought to such a peaceful old fashioned place and I like to think that it provided him with a welcome refuge and escape from war. Doris' brother, John, who was a radar man with the RAF, told me about the Bowie knife Bob fashioned at their bungalow from one of two swords Doris' mother bought at a local sale. When reading the inventory of the items returned home to his mother after his death, it is the poignant entry of: "Bowie knife" therefore, which imparts the sweetest recognition. In time, Bob wrote home to tell his family he had met a girl and they were going to be married. Doris also discovered she was pregnant. After reluctant agreement from her parents, it was decided they would marry after his last mission in December. Bob and his crew had recently transferred to another unit in the hope of finishing up their missions more quickly and were now stationed much further away in Northamptonshire. Doris, eight months pregnant, was now faced with the prospect of infrequent visits; left counting down the days until his missions were over and she could be sure she would see him again. I know Hershel's wife received a visit at work from two officers, informing her of Hershel's death. However, as they weren't yet married, I don't know if Doris was afforded the same consideration. Bob had only been with his new outfit two weeks. I have no idea how much his new commanding officers knew about my grandmother and their future plans. I don't know how long my grandmother waited before she discovered it was in vain, that she would never see Bob again. The sadness of that desperate hope before learning the inevitable and horrific truth, haunted me; fueling my hunger to seek out more of my grandfather's story.

Robert Burry was the second of 10 siblings. By the late 1930s, the Burry family was suffering great financial hardship and Bobby was encouraged to leave school and seek employment after just two years at high school. This proved more difficult than anticipated and he eventually applied to serve in the Civilian Conservation Corps (the CCC) after turning 16, lying about his age. He arrived at camp in Illinois at only five feet tall and weighing 110 pounds. His dental records show he arrived devoid of his upper front and lower front two teeth; hinting at the already emerging boxer he was to become representing the Air Force. He is described in his camp records as a "good man", a patriotic individual who enjoyed reading and athletics. Bob would spend the maximum two years with the CCC, gaining new teeth, four inches in height and 40 pounds in the process. His love of camp life probably influenced his decision to enlist into the Air Force, at the first available opportunity – in Detroit on 27 January 1942. His stature marked him out as perfect for the role of ball turret gunner. In August 1942, seven months later, he arrived in England, with the 92nd Bomb Group, at RAF Bovingdon.

The internet has proved itself to be an invaluable, almost magical resource for me, leading to so many discoveries: reports of missions Bob flew while on loan with the 303rd Bomb Group and an eyewitness report of their plane, flying low over Daventry High Street, just minutes before their fateful crash. Albert Fitzpatrick, one of the waist gunners from the crew, later gave a sworn affidavit of their final journey together. He recounts how the plane had been severely damaged by flak and how they were lost in the fog. The crew doubted their ability to make base. Lieutenant Harris, my grandfather's last pilot, passed word upon reaching the coast of England, that whosoever felt inclined, should bail out. Albert was the only one to do so. Over the years, the question of why my grandfather didn't jump has been foremost in my mind. One which I think I have finally answered.

The internet also led to lasting friendships with Brian Francis of the 8th Air Force Historical Society, and Romer Adams, a representative of Sywell Aviation museum, who excavated the crash site two summers ago. A deeper understanding of the crash arose, as I learned, that despite the damage to the plane, it was the fog that proved their undoing. In the poor visibility, the pilot was unable to get a clear visual, turning too late to prevent the stay of a radar mast from ripping the wing from their plane, resulting in their crash. On 23 August 2015, the sacrifice of the crew was commemorated with the dedication of a memorial, commissioned by Daventry Council, which my father and I unveiled. I was honoured that both Brian and Romer gave their time and support and were such an important part of the day.

Grandad's brothers had told me about his prowess as a boxer. There was a family legend about a match between Bobby and the man who "fought Joe Louis", with Bob winning a silver ring as a result. I knew he had won medals and belts, but as none of his things survived the families' several house moves I didn't know what for. The internet had answers for me once again, which I found in the Stars and Stripes newspaper archives. There were several references to boxing matches featuring my grandfather, and even a report of an entertainment evening laid on at the Mostyn Red Cross Club in London with showgirls. Further digging unearthed a Pathe newsreel of one of the matches, dated November 1942. At 2am, my poor husband Richard, jumped out of bed, convinced that my scream as I caught a glimpse of my grandfather on film meant something dreadful had just occurred. The pride I felt was immeasurable.

As I discovered, my grandfather had spells with various Bomb Groups during the war, but completed most of his missions with the 482nd Bomb Group. The time he spent with them, a year and a half, was a blank in my research. I had no idea who his pilot was, who was on the crew or how many missions they flew together. Two years ago, Bob's sister, my Aunt Diane, contacted Maxwell Air Force Base requesting the records from the 482nd Bomb Group, which we hoped would provide some answers. A disc arrived two months later, packed with a file of over 1,000 scanned microfilm images. I spent the day eagerly scouring the pages for any mention of my grandfather. I didn't know how much I would find as, unless there had been an accident, it appeared only the pilot's name had been recorded for each mission. Abruptly, I stumbled across an entry of an aircraft which had crashed on the runway, returning to base. The entry listed the entire crew on board, and suddenly, I was in possession of the name of the man who had been my grandfather's pilot for a year and a half, Ray Brim. Starting again from the beginning, I re-read the pages, looking for Ray, hoping to uncover further details about any of their missions. There were many and I learned about the pioneering and brave work of Ray, his crew, and the rest of the 813th squadron. It was evident from the records that Ray and the crew had been instrumental in creating the Pathfinding process at its very inception. By this point, I was desperate to speak to the hero who had brought my grandfather safely home from 20 missions before returning home to America; the man who could tell me things I had only ever dreamed of knowing.

Fortune favoured me once again, as within 10 minutes of searching, I had a telephone number.

I spent an agonising day waiting (because of the seven-hour time difference) until a suitable time to call. My husband tried to steel me against disappointment, but I wouldn't be dissuaded. I wouldn't let it cross my mind that it would be a wrong number, or that Ray wouldn't remember my grandfather. I didn't think about what I was going to say. I simply remember my stomach dropping like a stone as I told the gentleman who'd answered the phone that I was the granddaughter of his ball turret gunner from WWII, and holding my breath while I waited for his response. What I received was an introduction to the most wonderful and modest man I have had the pleasure to call a friend. Further contact created mutual areas of interest and forged friendships with Ray's two daughters, Christine and Celia. I became part of an extended family, with a bond stretching across the ocean and spanning 70 years. Amazingly, when I speak to Ray, he says it is him who is the lucky one. He cannot understand why he is so special, and is so gracious and overjoyed whenever I call. I have tried to tell him he is a hero, that I am honoured to have made his acquaintance and am so lucky to have his friendship, but Ray will just say how lucky he was in his crew. It is humbling to hear of their faith and trust in one another to fulfil their roles, working as a team to make it through each mission. I am not sure how I would fare in such a situation.

Speaking to Ray, I finally understand why my grandfather decided to stay with the plane and not bail out on his final mission. He recounted all their hairy moments as a crew, where they thought they wouldn't live to see another day. On several occasions, he gave leave to the crew to bail. They never did. On 15 December, 1944, just a few miles from their base, my grandfather made the decision to stay with his team, his family. He felt a duty to them, and did not want to let them down. He had faith in them and trust their luck would hold, that they would see it through one more time, as they had always done before. If it wasn't for the fog that day, his faith would have proven correct once again.

When we visited the crash site with Romer, we were gratified to discover a very special place; a beautiful cornfield in the middle of an idyllic English landscape. The farmer's dog accompanying us, took a liking to my father, chasing around him while running through the corn. The wind blew roughly and the sun shone. Above our heads, I tried to imagine the turmoil, fear and noise of the crash 70 years before. Instead, I felt at peace, picturing my grandfather and his friends soaring above me in the blue beyond the horizon.

Ray might not tell you he is a hero, but I can tell you he is. They all were.

Rebecca Saywell
February 2016

PREFACE

Like so many of my generation, my life changed after the bombing of Pearl Harbor and my enlistment in the Army Air Corps to become a pilot. Before all that, I was just a kid from the small mining town of Dividend, Utah. Afterwards, I felt I was a part of history. At the age of 19, during flight training school, I began to keep a diary. During the war I kept writing, keeping track of each mission in the form of letters, notes to myself and journals. The writing habit turned out to be a hard one to break, and I recorded my adventures, often accompanied by my wife Pat, from the Pacific Islands to Alaska to Japan, Europe, Turkey, and across the U.S. In later years I wrote down my fond memories growing up in the 1920s and 30s in the silver- and lead-mining town of Dividend.

During my 93 years, I have had many experiences—some bad, but many more good. Fortunately, I preserved many boxes of documents, photos, and notes from my long career in the Air Force. As a personal history, this book is based on the facts. The only exceptions are a couple situations where I used pseudonyms out of privacy concerns. All historical events in the book have already been reported in public sources, from newspaper articles to government reports.

It is my hope that future generations may be entertained and perhaps even learn something about a profoundly significant period in their nation's history from one man's life.

In closing, I always remember what my mother used to tell me when I was a child: "Don't say you can't do something unless you've tried it."

ACKNOWLEDGEMENTS

I would like to thank my darling wife, Patricia, without whom this memoir could never have been made. I never thought of myself as a writer and was never confident of what I had written unless Pat edited my work. Yet from the beginning, as an author and teacher of writing herself, Pat encouraged me to tell my story.

My daughters, Christine and Celia, have been invaluable as we worked together to compile, organize, and edit what I had written over the course of two decades. They researched and identified photographs, fact-checked, and did more background work than I can ever describe. I am grateful to Ruth Hadlock, my professional organizer, who became a close friend as she and I worked long hours managing the numerous drafts and documents required to craft a chronology of events that was logical and interesting. My grandson Daniel provided research on the Raddatz family in Durango, Mexico. It's also important to recognize the unbridled enthusiasm and support for this book project given to me by my granddaughters, Julia and Emily Straus, and my grandsons, Daniel and David Blau. My four grandchildren are my true legacy.

When Celia offered the "friends and family" version of this memoir to Casemate and it was accepted for publication I was thrilled and, quite honestly, surprised beyond measure. I am so grateful to Steve Smith, Casemate's Editorial Director, and David Farnsworth, Casemate's CEO and Publisher, for believing that my experiences might be instructive and entertaining for their readers. While Celia was the primary editor and point person on this version, the work of Eric Hammel, editor and author extraordinaire, added immense value to my words, particularly in the World War II section where Eric's expertise shows forth on page after page. I must also thank Libby Burden, Casemate's Production Editor, who took a hard copy manuscript and copy edited it into a digital book with patience, wisdom and infinite good humor. I also want to thank Hannah McAdams of Casemate UK who took over the editing of this book and was responsible for the placement and captioning of all the photographs. Her diligence, eye for detail and creativity made it possible for a 2016 publication and at age 93, every month counts. I am in your debt, Hannah, and forever grateful. And I will also be indebted to the enthusiasm, talent and marketing know-how of Tara Lichterman, Casemate's Publicity Director. Without Tara's deep understanding of how to make the public aware of an author's work, no one would know *Pathfinder Pioneer* existed. Tara, thank you from an old soldier who hesitates to talk about his war experiences unless asked.

I am indebted to friends and family who took the time to read early drafts of this work and share their thoughts, often making constructive suggestions that improved the overall work. Any errors still here are mine. And I am particularly indebted to Rebecca Saywell, the granddaughter of my brave Ball Turret Gunner, Robert Burry, who lives in March, England, only a few miles from Alconbury, our base during the war. Rebecca's painstaking research over a two-year period helped rectify and reconcile an old man's memories of the air war over Germany during 1943 and 44. Her attention to detail and her dogged persistence gathering primary source material on each of our crew's missions gave me the latitude to recreate my experiences knowing that if I mixed up a date or an event, she was there to correct me. Rebecca spent literally hundreds of hours retyping the original but badly faded microfiche daily debriefs by the pathfinder pilots and navigators of the 482nd so I could check my memories of each mission against the facts as they were reported just hours after a raid. Tragically, Robert Burry was killed in action on a raid in late 1944 and never got to meet his granddaughter or his five great-grandsons.

There is no way to describe the loyalty and deep respect that comes from serving in battle with others over time. I probably would not have survived my service in the Army Air Force during WWII without my flight crew—nine men who were a band of brothers for 25 missions over France and Germany—and the maintenance crew that supported us. For the rest of my career in the United States Air Force, I had great respect for the officers and airmen who worked for me. Their loyalty and professional qualifications made our joint endeavors successful. I have always been grateful.

I will always be thankful for the wisdom, values, and guidance of my parents, Raymond and Flora Brim, and my older sister, Katherine.

PART I

DIVIDEND, UTAH, 1922–1941

CHAPTER 1

A TOWN CALLED DIVIDEND

I grew up in the tiny mining town of Dividend, Utah, in the 1920s and 1930s. When I tell people about those years I know it sounds as though my childhood was bleak, hard and "bare bones", but I don't remember it that way at all. We had few luxuries, but at the same time there was a rough-and-tumble environment in this small desert mining town that gave me the freedom I needed to grow into a self-confident young man. The reason I bring this up now is because there were a lot of demands made on those first American pilots in World War II—those of us who trained and flew with the Army Air Forces in 1943 and 1944. We were guinea pigs for much of the training, and later on, air war strategy (those of us B17 pilots chosen to experiment with the Pathfinder technology is a prime example) as the United States got up to speed. Somehow I managed to complete my missions and come home in one piece. A lot had to do with luck, but I have to figure that some of my resilience, resourcefulness and sense of responsibility to others had to do with growing up in Dividend and that seminal summer I spent working down in the mine.

Dividend was built by the Tintic Standard Mining Company, which was founded in 1907 by Emil Raddatz, the younger brother of my grandfather, Gustav Raddatz. Emil, Gustav, and their three brothers were born in Stettin, Germany, now a city in Poland (Szczecin) on the Baltic Sea. The Raddatz family emigrated to America in 1869 and settled near

St. Louis, Missouri. Three years later, in 1872, both parents died and the five boys were on their own.

In the latter part of 1874, Emil and his brother Gustav left Missouri and moved to Leadville, Colorado, to learn what they could about mining. In 1877 Gustav returned to St. Louis and married a woman named Catherine Guth. By 1880 Gustav had been hired by the Guggenheim Corporation to manage their interests in Durango, Mexico. My mother, Flora Raddatz, was born and baptized in Mexico as Florentina Josefina Catarina Raddatz. She called herself Lola.

Emil continued to work in mining in the U.S., and in June 1890 he married Catherine (Guth) Raddatz's younger sister, Emma Guth. Sadly, Catherine Raddatz, my grandmother, died at the age of 33, leaving my mother and her younger brother and sister in the care of their father, Gustav. My great-grandmother Guth went to Mexico and brought back my mother and her two-year-old brother Edward and infant sister Emma, and raised them in St. Louis.

After his marriage to Emma Guth in 1890, Emil moved to Stockton, Utah, where he worked as superintendent and manager for several mining interests. In July 1907, Emil, then manager of the Honerine Mine, made a trip to Ely, Nevada, where he met John Bestlemeyer, who had some claims in the East Tintic district. Tintic was the name of an Indian chief whose tribe had roamed this part of Utah long before the Mormons arrived. The Indians told stories of Spanish explorers, deserters from the Spanish army in Mexico, mining the area and becoming rich seemingly overnight.

It wasn't until September that Emil was able to examine the Bestlemeyer claims. The bold outcrops three miles east of other ore-producing mines, caused him to believe there was sufficient evidence of valuable lead and silver ore in the Tintic range. Mining men and geologists who had studied the eastern side of the Tintic range ridiculed his idea, calling it the "Raddatz Folly." Nonetheless, Emil sought investors for his mining venture, and in October 1907 he formed the Tintic Standard Mining Company. Bestlemeyer turned over his four claims for 75,000 shares of the 1,175,000 shares with which the company was incorporated.

Emil struggled to find investors, going back 19 times to his backers, but finally work was started on a 400-foot incline shaft. It showed interesting formations but revealed no ore. A vertical shaft was then sunk. From 1909 to 1916, only eight cars of ore were produced at the 1,000-foot level. Most men would have admitted defeat, but Emil persevered. In 1916, to everyone's surprise except his, he struck it rich.

At first, the mining site was called Standard. The name of Dividend was not registered until 1918, two years after the first rich ore was found and six years before my family moved there. In the early days, men housed themselves in tents and shacks around the mine, willing to make do with the crudest, most primitive living standards imaginable. There was a spring for water, but it was about a mile away from the first shaft, so the water was hauled to the mine site in large barrels. Of course, there was no indoor plumbing.

The mine was always hard to work. After the shaft passed the 400-foot level, large quantities of carbon dioxide and other poisonous gases issued from the cracks in the rock and, as work continued at the 1000-foot level, rock temperatures became excessive. It was not uncommon to lower a candle into the shaft to test for poisonous gases. Mechanical ventilation—forced air—was the only solution, and it was very expensive to install. At times the heat became unbearable and it was impossible to continue work until the ventilation system had cooled the working area. There were entire days when no work could be done. In 1941 when I worked down in the mine, ventilation and heat continued to be a major problem; we had large tubes of canvas and tin to bring the air back to the working places.

The original shaft was in such a position that getting a railroad to the mine would have been very expensive. Also, one of the drifts of the mine had shown a higher grade of ore north of the original shaft, so another shaft was sunk about a quarter mile away. Once ore was found, additional miners—"tramp miners," men who would move from one mine to another depending on the wages and rumors of rich ore—arrived on the scene. By 1916, building bunkhouses had become a priority.

In January 1917, the Tintic Standard stock sold up to $1.25 and shot up to $1.75 during February, closing the end of June at $1.65. This was partly because it was the end of World War I; prices for silver and lead were on a rampage and stock went to $15 a share. From 1916 to 1921, over $1.5 million dollars (worth about $25 million today) was distributed to the fortunate shareholders.

Emil was very concerned about the miners and their families, perhaps the result of the hardships he'd encountered in mining towns after his parents died. Dividend's first eleven houses were built in 1918, in what was known as "New Town." The houses had three or four rooms with running water and, of course, the "two-holer outhouse." Rent for each house was $6.50 a month, to be deducted from the individual's paycheck. Another eleven houses were built on Post Office Street using the same design, then additional homes and a new schoolhouse were built on what many people called "Snob Hill." These homes were for the superintendent and four other members of the management team. The rest of the homes, all equipped with bathrooms, were built on Main Street. All of the homes were made of wood and set on pilings, which were necessary because the ground would shift from the mining underneath the town.

CHAPTER 2

A DIVIDEND CHILDHOOD

My parents

My mother, Lola Raddatz, had always wanted to be a nurse. In 1912 she submitted an application to the St. Luke's Hospital Training School for Nurses and was accepted, graduating in 1915 with "excellent" and "splendid" marks on her final evaluation. She practiced as a private-duty nurse in St. Louis for a year and saved up her money to move with her sister Emma to Salt Lake City. Emma had been put to work in a small lampshade factory in St. Louis after she finished grammar school. She had early symptoms of tuberculosis. Mother assumed responsibility for her and got her out of St. Louis and into treatment for the tuberculosis, and she supported them both doing private-duty nursing.

My father, Alfred Raymond Elias Brim, was born in 1899 at the family sheep ranch in Echo Canyon, Utah, the eldest of the five children who survived into adulthood. As the oldest, he grew up helping out on the ranch. He would tell us about riding his horse to school in the little railroad town of Echo. But he didn't want to be a rancher. Instead, he attended the two-year University of Deseret, which would eventually become the University of Utah. Upon graduation, he returned to Echo and became the only teacher for the same one-room schoolhouse in which he had gone to school himself. He was also elected as a county judge, running as a Democrat, which was as much a rarity in Utah then as it is now.

Lola and Ray met at the Saltair resort, located west of Salt Lake City on the edge of the Great Salt Lake. An electric train ran out to Saltair from the city. It was just after the great influenza epidemic of 1918 had run its course, and the resort, which boasted swimming, picnicking, and dancing, was a main destination for young people like my parents. It wasn't long before the schoolteacher asked the nurse to marry him, and she accepted.

After they married in April 1919, my mother joined my father at the ranch in Echo Canyon. Unfortunately, my grandfather had arranged for all five siblings to write checks on the ranch account, and my father had not been able to put a stop to the drain on their cash. Mother brought this to a screaming halt as soon as she discovered it, but very little was left in the business cash reserves and the family had to take out a loan to keep the ranch going.

In 1920 they bought a home in Salt Lake City because Mother was expecting their first child, my sister Katherine (who we called Kay). She had the baby at home with the help of her sister Emma, who had just graduated from nursing school. Dad continued to run the ranch, so he spent part of his time back in Echo Canyon. But in the early 1920s an economic recession hit the farms and ranching industries all across the western states, and the family had to declare bankruptcy. I had arrived in October 1922, and by the next spring Dad had no ranch, two children, and few prospects for jobs in the city. That was when Mother went to her uncle Emil, owner of the now very successful Tintic Standard mine in Dividend, to ask for a job for my father. In 1924, Dad became the bookkeeper for the mine and we moved to Dividend.

Our house

Our house was small, only about 700 sq. feet. We had two bedrooms, a kitchen, a bathroom, a closet, and the living room. There was a back screened-in porch and a front porch. The house was heated with a coal-burning range that Mother also used to heat water, cook and bake. In winter we had a coal heater that was placed on the back porch during the summer, next to the washer. When the heater was moved to the living room, a shield was placed beneath it to prevent the floor from catching on fire, and of course, the stove had to be reconnected to the chimney. Both stoves had to be cleared at least once a day of the clinkers that were formed from the burned-out coal.

Dad would cover the screening on the back porch with canvas to keep the snow outside. During the winter, the washing machine was brought into the kitchen because of the cold, and warm water was transferred from the water tap to the washer in the kitchen. The washer had a wringer made of two rollers that would squeeze the water out of the clothes. Mother once got her hand caught between the wringers of the washer and injured her fingers before she could reach the control to release the rollers. During the winter, clothes had to be dried in the house or they would freeze solid. I remember that twice a year, Mother would take down the curtains and drapes for cleaning. The wallpaper got so filthy from coal dust that it had to be cleaned with putty cleaner that turned black with soot.

When we moved in 1924, the new house had two bedrooms; years later Dad added a bedroom for Kay. Mother and Dad's bedroom was off the living room and had a brass double bed, which took up most of the space. They had a dresser and a large bookcase against the wall near the foot of the bed. There were two windows with roll-up blinds. The bookcase was filled with books including the only set of an encyclopedia, *The Book of Knowledge*, in the entire town. One thing that Dad loved was the front porch during summer. He had a large rocker and would read the newspaper, the *Literary Digest* and *National Geographic Magazine*. He would say about the magazines, "It's the only way I can travel." For all of this luxurious living, the Tintic Standard took $18 rent out of my father's monthly paycheck, including electricity. It seems inexpensive, but Dad was making only $100 a month.

My bedroom was the smallest, but I was happy in it. It had the door to the bathroom and to the closet. I had a window, a small chest of drawers and last but not least, the back of a refrigerator.

A new stove and refrigerator

Dad got permission to have the wall between my room and the kitchen cut out so the door of the refrigerator was in the kitchen and the back came through my bedroom wall. The white box with the coil on top did not add much to the decor of a young boy's room, but getting the town's first electric refrigerator was a big deal, especially since it came on the heels of an electric stove.

Mother was getting tired of telling us not to slam the screen door because it would cause her baking efforts to fail. I don't know what caused these failures; it could have been the flour, the yeast, or the uneven heating in the oven, but it was a problem. Baking was the only way we could enjoy fresh cookies, bread, pies and cinnamon rolls because the company store only had Wonder Bread, brought in once a week from Salt Lake City. There was nothing like walking into the kitchen and smelling the aroma of those cinnamon rolls as they came out of the oven.

It must have been around 1930 when electric stoves became available at the one and only appliance store in Eureka, another mining town about three miles west of Dividend. I don't remember the exact cost of the stoves, but it was a lot for families who were living on $100 or less a month. Somehow, Mother had put a few dollars aside that allowed she and Dad decided to invest in a new electric stove. This was a major decision.

They went to Eureka in our 1929 Plymouth and selected the new Westinghouse electric range. The oven was set to the left of the four burners. The stove was set on four legs that brought it up to a working level. Our dog, Pal, loved to crawl beneath the oven where it was nice and warm and protected him from being stepped on. As I recall, Dad had to get permission to have the electric stove installed because the rent for the house included the use of electricity and no one was sure just how much it would consume. Mother was very pleased with her new stove, which made it easier to keep the house clean, but we still had to have the coal bucket and I still had to fill the wood box.

The next improvement was to get rid of the icebox. The Dividend Trading Company had an ice-making plant, which for a small mining town was rather unique. Ice for most mining towns and small country towns came from the frozen lakes or reservoirs where men sawed blocks of ice into different sizes and stored in icehouses that were insulated with sawdust. As the sawdust became damp it became more effective as an insulator. This ice was used not only for keeping foods cool in the summer, but also to cool drinking water. I'll never know why more people didn't get sick, because this ice was undoubtedly contaminated; perhaps we had more diseases and just did not know the cause.

The wooden iceboxes were lined with tin and the ice was placed in the top of the box. As it melted, it cooled the food below that was in a separate section. One could not keep food very long as these boxes were not too efficient. In hot weather the ice would melt before a new block could be placed in the top of the box. Below the icebox was a tin pan in which water from the melted ice accumulated, and it had to be emptied. No surprise that it was also my job to empty the tin pan. In time, the icebox was placed on the back porch of our house. I cut a hole in the floor and, with the help of a little hose, the water drained onto the ground beneath the porch.

After investing in a stove, the folks made the decision that it was time to buy a new ice-making machine called a refrigerator, which also provided storage space for fresh vegetables and other foods. Space was at a premium in our home and to find space for the refrigerator, as mentioned, so my bedroom wall was cut out to accommodate the back. From the kitchen, you would not see that this new white box had a coil on the top that was the heat exchanger.

After it was delivered to the house, some of our neighbors came in to see this new-fangled ice-making machine. We were very proud to show it off. The space for making ice cubes was very small, about eight inches square, so we had to be satisfied with two ice trays. You have to remember that there were no frozen foods at this time and the freezing compartment was not separated from the rest of the refrigerator.

In 1941, we took this refrigerator and the stove to our new home in Salt Lake City, and the first frozen food we put into the ice-maker was frozen peas.

Next, a radio!

The first radio that I recall in Dividend belonged to the Watkins family who lived two houses west of ours. The radio was operated by large dry cell batteries that had to be recharged after very limited use, and in time the batteries had to be replaced. On top of the radio was the speaker which looked like a large funnel mounted facing forward, so you had to be directly in front of it to hear what was coming out. A long wire antenna was strung from a telephone pole to the Watkins home which made reception possible. Of course we envied this new contraption.

Jerry Spaulding, who lived next door, between us and the Watkins, bought a new RCA radio around 1932, which was the latest model without batteries and it too had a speaker on top of the unit. I talked Jerry into agreeing to let us tap off the speaker to his radio and run a wire from his home to ours where we had a speaker just like the one his radio had. The wire came into our house through mother and dad's bedroom and the speaker was in our little living room. Whatever Jerry wanted to hear was what we heard, but we could turn off our speaker with a switch. There were three radio stations that could be received in Dividend, depending on the weather conditions and interference from power lines in the area: KSL and KDYL from Salt Lake would come in most of the time, and once in a while KHJ or KNX from Los Angeles could be picked up. Several programs were available for children such as Little Orphan Anny, Jack Armstrong and Chandu the Magician. There was also Myrt & Marg, Helen Trent and her troubles, Little Theater off Times Square, One Man's Family and Amos and Andy. Of course the big event was the World Series every fall.

As usual I got in trouble with mother when I asked Jerry to tune in afternoon children's programs for us. She thought I was asking too much of a good thing and she was probably right but it was in my personality to push the edges of the envelope, and I was a huge fan of Jack Armstrong.

Winter

None of the company houses in Dividend were very well insulated. In fact, there was *no* insulation in the space between the wood covering the building and the wallboard that made up the inside walls. The homes were heated by a coal-fired kitchen stove and a coal-fired space heater in the living room. On cold nights a member of the family had to insure that the fire kept going. In the Brim household, it was Dad's job until I was old enough to take his place.

Wood for the fires was provided by the company. Some of it came from what was down in the mine that could no longer be used. Some wood came from railroad ties that had to be sawed to the right size to fit in the stoves and then split for kindling. Not everyone had a saw horse that held the wood to be sawed to the right length, so saw horses would be passed around from neighbor to neighbor. One of my jobs was sawing railroad ties and then splitting them for kindling. This kindling was stored under the back porch of our house and brought in for use every night. Another job was to fill the wood box no matter what else I might have wanted to do instead.

One day in the middle of winter, instead of filling the wood box with kindling, I took a short cut by putting a layer of snow in the bottom of the box and covering it with one layer of kindling. When the wood box was brought into the house that night, the snow melted and the wood became too wet for Dad to start the fire the next morning. It took him about two seconds to get me out of bed, dressed, and under the back porch to get some dry wood so he could start the fire. I was lucky to remain alive.

Every house had a coal bin on the backside of the house. The company delivered the coal, but you had to order it and pay for it. Sometimes the pieces of coal were so large that you had to break them up to fit in the stoves. After the Tintic Standard Mine purchased the Blue Blaze Coal Company, located near Helper, Utah, this was the only coal available.

The winters provided us with sufficient snow for sleigh riding, skiing and snowball fights. It was also the time when Saturday night dances at the amusement hall were most popular. Sleigh riding was the big event because we had so many hills. One year my folks gave me a Flexible Flyer sled for Christmas and I thought I was the king of the road. I was the envy of my friends. During recess at school, we pulled our sleds up what we called Bunker Hill and got four or five rides in before the bell rang and we had to stack the sleds against the school and return to class. The roads were slick because very few people had cars; we would spend hours on the sleds, riding down the hill and pulling them back up for another ride.

My first pair of skis was made from barrel staves. We tacked on a strap far enough back so that the front end of the stave was pointing up. We then waxed the staves with paraffin that was left over from when our mothers canned fruit in the fall. The makeshift skis were not very satisfactory, but we had fun. In time, my folks bought my sister and me some real skis. The new skis were very wide, and to be properly fitted, they had to be long enough that when standing, with your arm stretched out over your head, you could touch the tip of the ski. These skis had a leather strap that you inserted your shoe in to hold the ski on. We still had to wax them with canning paraffin.

Trouble was my middle name

I was a handful growing up, a mischievous, high-energy child who was always getting into trouble. When I was five, Lola's sister, Aunt Emma was visiting and she brought little gifts for Kay and me. Mine was a tie stickpin. Aunt Emma left her Ipana Toothpaste on the back of the water tank, and with my new stickpin I punched the toothpaste tube many times. When Aunt Emma attempted to use the toothpaste that night, the paste dribbled out of my handiwork. She took it to Mother and the next thing I knew, Mother had me by the ear and marched me to her bedroom where my piggy bank was. She emptied it out and told me I was to apologize to Aunt Emma and I was to go to the store early the next day with my money and replace the toothpaste. So much for the tie stickpin.

A couple of years later I managed to get the entire town of Dividend angry with me. I had been painting the outside of the house with watercolors and when my mother found me, she gave me a slap on the behind and told me to go in the house and get cleaned up. I went into the house and made up my mind that I would show her by running away from home. I took my toothbrush, a washcloth and my winter cap and put them in a sack. I waited until my mother and father were nowhere to be seen and then I ran out the back door and started down a canyon that was about a half a mile from the main road that led into the town.

In the meantime, my mother came back into the house and went to the bathroom to see how I was doing about getting the watercolors off my hands, only to find me missing. Soon both she and my father started looking for me. Then the parents of my friends started looking for me and it wasn't too long before the entire population of Dividend—200 people—were searching the area for the Brim boy.

Meanwhile after reaching the main dusty road, I noticed a car approaching and I put up my hand to show I wanted a ride. The car stopped and one of the two men in the car asked me where I was going. Until then I was not sure but I said I was going to visit some friends who lived on a farm near Genola. One of the men asked me if my family knew I was going to make this visit, and naturally I lied and said yes. They told me to get in the car and they would drop me off as they were going by Genola.

In fact, my family did have some friends living on a farm near Genola. It was called the Thomas farm. In about 30 minutes we approached the area where the farm was located and I got out. But before they drove off I thanked them for the ride. Even a runaway has to mind his manners.

I walked the few yards to reach the turn off to the Thomas farm. As I approached the farm, Mrs. Thomas came out of the house and was very surprised to see me without my folks. She asked where my parents were and my reply was "Oh, they're at home, but they said it would be OK for me to come and visit you." Mrs. Thomas thought this was very strange, but then the families had known each other for years so it must be all right.

About this time the five Thomas children came out and wanted to play. Now play at the Thomas farm meant sliding down haystacks, riding bareback on one of their horses, looking for eggs in the barn and playing in the water that was in the ditch that was in front of the house. The most fun a six-year-old boy could possibly have.

In a little while Mrs. Thomas called everyone to supper and told us children that we had to wash before we could come to the table. We went to the back of the farmhouse where the water pump was. It was hand operated so one of us would pump the water into a basin so another kid could wash and then we would change places, each one washing off the dirt, straw and whatever we had picked up in the barnyard. Then we all sat around a big round table and had lots of mashed potatoes and gravy and peas and corn. Mrs. Thomas had fixed a bed on the couch and I was sound asleep in just a few minutes, not a care in the world.

By then some of the good people of Dividend thought I have been kidnapped since Emil Raddatz, who started the mine, was a relative of my mother's and very wealthy. Others thought I had fallen down one of the old abandoned mineshafts that were in the hills around the town. The postmaster had his two bloodhounds sniffing around the area in an effort to find some trace of me, but to no avail.

Several hours went by when a young couple drove into town and inquired what was going on. When they heard the story the lady said, "I think we saw him riding a horse alongside the road near Genola." The doctor in Dividend said he thought I might have gone to the Thomas Farm and he would get in his car and find out. It took him about 30 minutes to get to Genola. By then it was late at night and so when he knocked on the door, it took Mrs. Thomas a little while to open it.

She was surprised to see the doctor, and when she heard the story, she was very upset. She told the doctor that she should have checked with my parents, but I had told the story in such a convincing manner that she had just accepted it. They got me up and found my toothbrush, washcloth and winter cap and put me in the doctor's car.

When the doctor and I arrived home and stopped in front of the only house with the doorway partly painted with water colors, a cry went up from the crowd of people. My mother ran to the car and picked me up and gave me a big hug and started to cry at the same time I started crying. She was so happy to have me back that instead of being punished I got milk and cookies and went to bed.

School

Dividend had a four-room schoolhouse built on the same hill on which the mining officials lived. The school only went through seventh grade. We had seven boys and two girls in my class. One girl moved away and the other dropped out after the seventh grade to have a baby. There was a softball field in the back and two swings in the front, built on a slope. We would swing as high as we could and then jump to see how far we could land up the hill. At lunchtime, when the company's whistle blew, we all walked home for lunch except the Mexican kids, who lived too far from school and brought lunch with them.

Ralph Davis, the principal, made $90 a month. Before a stoker was installed, Ralph would have to get up an hour before school to fire up the furnace during the winter. After the stoker was installed, he had to be sure the bin was filled with coal. It did not have a timer on it and I remember him working on a system using an alarm clock that, with a long string, would pull the switch to start the stoker. I don't think it ever worked, but it was a great idea to avoid the cold mornings by just turning on a switch. The company provided Ralph with a job during the summer months to supplement his salary when he was not teaching. Besides teaching and keeping the schoolhouse warm during winter, Ralph was the janitor. He also taught the fifth and six grades. One course he taught was some basic math that included how to balance a checkbook. This practical day-to-day math was important because some of the students did not progress beyond grade school.

We had three other teachers, all unmarried women. When they stayed in Dividend, the teachers had rooms in one of the old bunkhouses (the same bunkhouse where the doctor's offices were located). I'm sure they were happy to go home on weekends. They made $60 a month.

Potatoes to card sharks

How county lines were drawn had an impact on how much money one school district received and where children went to school. The Tintic Standard mine was in Utah County and provided a tax base for the Nebo chool District, sufficient to pay for most of the schools in the district. This financial windfall forced the students of Dividend to attend schools in the Nebo District even though the schools in Juab County were much closer. To continue our education beyond seventh grade required that we be bussed to Goshen, where a junior high school was available. The distance from Dividend to Goshen was about 12 miles and to Payson for high school approximately 22 miles. To get to school we had to be ready to be picked up around 8 a.m. each morning.

The bus driver was Chris Christenson. He was a very special person, quiet and soft spoken, who got along with everybody. I do not recall his ever being out of sorts with the kids. He waited at each stop to be sure we all made the bus for school. He honked the bus's horn a couple of times if someone was missing because he knew each and every one of us.

The bus was garaged in a barn-like building overnight and on weekends, near the Dividend schoolhouse. I remember Chris starting the bus and waiting until the temperature gauge showed that the engine was warming up before he backed the bus out of the garage. In the winter he turned on the bus heater, which was rather small. It did a great job in the front of the bus but left something to be desired from about halfway back. The girls sat in the front and the boys took over the back half.

The trouble that happened on the bus started in the back where the boys were seated. At one of the stops, I stuffed a potato into the exhaust pipe, leaving the engine unable to function properly. Chris lifted the hood to see what was wrong, then closed it and attempted to drive on. About the third time he stopped the bus, one of us removed the potato and, all of a sudden, the problem was resolved. We did this several times before we were caught.

It was always a challenge to keep from getting bored while riding the bus, especially later when I was in high school. By then I had a job at the Dividend Trading Company on weekends and holidays, so I had a little extra cash compared to the other guys. One day I thought of an easy way to pass the time. I started a couple of penny games of twenty-one. We were fairly quiet and I was making some profit. We were told to stop playing cards but that had little impact on 16- and 17-year-old boys, so the games went on. The next day I was reported to Mr. Bates and was kicked out of school until my father appeared with me in hand. After the meeting (Dad had to get off work to get me back in school), I gave up managing card games. I tried to clean up my act and in my junior year was elected class president.

Junior Year

Being class president didn't keep me entirely out of trouble. The town of Dividend had an amusement hall that consisted of two large rooms. One was a hall where dances were held on selected Saturday nights; the other was a movie house. In addition to showing movies in this room, school plays were presented there, and on Sundays the Mormons would hold their church services in the room. The mining company provided the movies, which were shown on Wednesday nights for free.

The seven boys in my class and all the other boys in town always sat on the right side of the movie house. When we were all together, there must have been twelve to fifteen boys. No one else seemed interested in sitting with the boys, and of course the girls were seated apart from us whether they wanted to be or not.

I was taking all the classes I could to meet the requirements to go to college. One of the classes I took was chemistry. One day in the laboratory we mixed hydrogen sulfide that produced a horrible smell. The windows were opened but the smell went through all the classrooms on the second floor of our school. I put a small amount of the first element, a liquid in a test tube and corked it very carefully. The other element was shavings of iron, some of which I put in a small bag and took home with me.

It was the night of the movies and I thought it would be funny if I mixed these elements during the movie to see what would happen. I had to have a container to put the elements in so I took a jar cap that Mother used when she bottled fruit. In those days the caps had a glass insert and you had to use a rubber gasket to seal the bottle. The container had to be small enough that I could hide it after I mixed the two elements.

Shortly after the main feature started I mixed the elements in the jar lid. It was easy to do since my seat was next to the wall and everyone was busy watching the movie. As soon as I mixed the elements in the jar lid, I placed it on the floor and put my foot over it.

It wasn't long before people started to look at each other and to whisper to each other. Within a minute, some people were laughing and as the smell spread throughout the room, the noise became louder. All of a sudden the movie stopped and the lights were turned on. Someone opened the three double doors to the movie house, hoping the smell would dissipate. Most of the people were laughing but the grade school principal, Ralph Davis got up and walked to the front of the hall and said, "Whoever was responsible for this should be identified and should be barred from coming to the movies from now on." No one was identified and I just looked innocently around at the rest of my friends.

In a few minutes, the wind had cleared the smell out of the hall and the movie continued. It was after the movie had run for some time that I reached down on the floor, picked up the jar lid and placed it back in the paper sack.

I had gotten away without being identified as the bad guy—so my chemistry class was not a complete loss. Little did I know that H2S, the formula for rotten egg gas, would play such a major role in my life as the ground breaking radar technology for the Pathfinder planes I would be flying in just three years' time.

CHAPTER 3

DOWN IN THE MINES

You had to be eighteen to work down in the mine, but when I graduated from high school in 1940, I was just seventeen. I had known I wanted to go to the University of Utah and, fortunately, Mother and Dad had saved enough money for me to attend my freshman year, 1940–1941. To make extra money, I worked as an usher for university events at $1 per event. Although it was a struggle, I still had a lot of fun. Most of my friends were faced with the same money problems.

The summer between my freshman and sophomore year I was finally old enough to work down in the Dividend mine. The company had a policy that dependents of employees of the mine could be hired during the summer months, or whenever they were home if they were attending a university. It worked out well for us because the Depression was still going on and jobs were difficult to find. Mother and Dad were very concerned about my working down in the mine. After all, it was not the safest place to work and they had both witnessed the results of accidents. I later learned that whenever I worked the midnight shift, Mother waited up until she heard my footsteps coming into the house.

Before I could start work I had to buy a hard hat that held the lamp so we could see what we were doing. The lamp was battery-powered with the power pack attached to my belt. This was a great improvement over the old carbide gas lamps in which water dripped on the carbide to form a gas that was then lit by a flint sparked by a small steel wheel that was built on the reflector of the lamp. We had a lot more light to see by with the new lamp and it was much safer. In addition to the hard hat, we had to buy steel-capped safety shoes to protect our feet from falling ore. These purchases came out of our first wages.

I started work in the Dividend mine at the beginning of June 1941. It felt a bit strange to have grown up there and seen the miners go to work every day of my life, then suddenly to finally be one of them. I'll admit that I was pretty nervous starting out. Little did I know what was ahead of me that first day. My first shift started at 4 p.m., called the midnight shift because it ended around midnight. I walked to the changing room with my new hard hat and safety shoes and there I was assigned a locker. We all had a lunch bucket. I could tell the new workers by the brightness of their buckets, but very soon those same buckets would be dented and take on a dull black color. I was a mucker, the lowest type of miner. My job was to back fill where ore had been mined.

After changing into work clothes, we proceeded to the check-in building to pick up the battery pack and light and to place a brass tag on a hook, which told the management who was working that particular shift. (I still have a brass tag which has stamped on it "Tintic Standard, 169, M:CO".) In case of an accident, it was important to know who was working down in the mine. In addition, the numbers were recorded and sent to the payroll section of the office so we would be paid for the shift we worked. Once we had our lamps, we went to the cage that would take us down the mine. It held six men.

We entered the cage in order, depending on what level of the mine we were to be working on. This, by the way, was the same cage that would bring up the ore cars during the shift. The first thing I experienced as I dropped down the shaft was the sudden change from daylight to darkness. Then, as I descended into darkness, there was the sudden rush of wind going around the cage. During these first few days on the job, it seemed to me that we dropped very fast and I found myself praying that the engineer operating the cage knew what he was doing and that the cage would remain intact.

If we were going to one of the lower levels, we would see a flash of light from the working stations as we passed by them. On my first day I asked one of the experienced miners what would happen if the cable broke. He said that large hooks on the top of the cage would extend and grab on to the timbers that made up the shaft. If the hooks didn't work, well, then it did not matter since we were on our way to the bottom of the shaft. It was difficult to take much comfort in that explanation.

Our station was on one of the lower levels, a large room, maybe 40 sq. feet. It was next to the shaft of the mine. This is where the ore cars to be taken to the surface were placed and where the electric mules were lined up to have the batteries recharged.

During these years, mules—first live animals and later, when I was a mucker, electric mules—were essential in mining. A barn and stable were built not far from the mine entrance. The mules were used to move ore cars on the surface as well as down in the mine from different drifts to the shaft so the ore could be brought to the surface. In the old days, the animals were kept underground for the rest of their lives, serving the same purpose as electric ore cars.

To get a mule down the mine, it was taken to the shaft where it was blindfolded and its legs tied together. A harness was placed around it with a large hook on the harness that would be attached to the bottom of the cage. The cage was lifted just enough to lift the mule off its feet and suspended it over the opening of the shaft. The cage was lowered to the work station where they wanted the mule. When the cage stopped early enough to swing the mule out, the poor animal was pulled out to the ground floor of the station, where it would remain. Each level of the mine had a small area where the mules were kept and used to pull the full cars to the shaft and the empty cars back into the mine. I once saw a dead mule in the mine. It was on a cart that was being pulled by a team of horses to the company's dump in the canyon so the carcass could be destroyed.

The station was well lit and comparatively cool. We all put our lunch buckets on a shelf at the station and would come back to this spot to eat our meal. It was here that the shift boss assigned us our work for the next eight hours. The miners and their assistants went to tunnels, sometimes called drifts, where new ore was to be mined. The muckers and all other new employees were assigned the drudge work.

My first day

That first day I was paired with a friend of mine, Curtis Butler, who had the same amount of mining experience as I had (practically none). We were sent back to an old area of the mine to back-fill where ore had been removed. This back-filling was necessary to prevent cave-ins of the mine. Even with back filling, there was considerable movement and shifting of the mined-out areas. The rocks used to back-fill sometimes came from the surface and were brought down to the different parts of the mine in ore cars that were later used to haul good ore back to the surface.

The shift boss led us back to our work area. The farther we got from the station, the hotter and darker it became. In the top of the tunnel was round flexible canvas tubing that brought fresh air to the work areas. Alongside the air tubing were small electric lights, placed at approximately 100-foot intervals, which made it possible to find our way out to the station and also see the ore cars filled with the rocks you were expected to unload. Of course, on the ground, we had to walk over the tracks the ore cars used, which made progress difficult. We learned to walk with our head down so the lamp on our hard hat would show us the obstacles we had to miss.

The shift boss led us to where some wooden planks had been laid out on the ground at the end of a tunnel, with two mined-out areas on either side of the tunnel. We were told to dump the rocks that were in the ore cars onto the planks and shovel them as backfilling into the mined-out areas. As we filled up the areas, we were to place the planks on the side to keep the rocks in place until we filled the area to the top of the tunnel. To put it simply, our job was to fill a twelve-by-twelve room that was eight feet high with rock. When this room was filled, there was another one just like it waiting for us. As he was leaving, the shift boss said, "By the way, a regular shift of two men will empty that ore car in an hour. That means eight cars a day, fellas." With this guidance, he said he would see us in about three and a half hours at the main station at that level, when we ate our lunch.

It was more than daunting: two lights on our hats pointed to the ore car filled with rock, and when we turned, the lights pointed to where we were to shovel this rock into the back fill. We looked at each other. There was nothing to say. We pried a rusty bar loose from the back of a car so that some of the rocks fell out onto the planks. Then the two of us went to the back of the ore car and lifted it so the rest of it tumbled out. After we pushed the car out of the way, we started shoveling.

Neither of us had any experience with a shovel, and to our dismay the rocks fell off our shovels half the time. We started throwing the larger rocks into the back-fill by hand. Soon, however, we realized that we had to use our bodies as levers to get the rock to stay on the shovel. It seemed to be getting hotter with each shovelful and we had to get the rock to the back of the fill area, which made it even more work. Naturally, the more rock we shoveled the higher we had to throw it into the fill area.

I don't know how long it took us to get the one ore car of rock shoveled, but we were about halfway through the second car when lunchtime arrived. We foolishly did not have gloves and our hands were getting very sore. I had blisters from all the shoveling.

At lunchtime we walked out to the station where it was much cooler, the electric lights welcome. We turned off our lamps to save the batteries. The miners who were working on this level were already sitting around on benches or whatever was available, eating their lunch. We were asked how we were doing and when we said that we were still working on the second car, they gave us a very hard time. Several miners made comments that all the university education in the world would not make muckers out of us, which in all probability was true.

It was hard to go back to work. Just standing up made our legs and arms ache. As we approached our work area, it seemed to be much hotter than when we had left it. The air was not coming out of the tube as it had been. We attacked the pile of rock and in time had the second car shoveled. We were both getting very tired, so we took our time pushing the third car of the day to the planks on the ground. It took us the rest of the shift to unload and shovel the third car. Our hands were so sore that each time we picked up the shovel we were in pain.

When we reported that we had only emptied three cars, we were given a really hard time by the old hands. We learned that some of the air had been diverted from our area, which was in part why it had gotten so hot where we worked. I always thought this was part of the initiation of two college boys to the world of working underground.

When we returned to our work area and were looking at that damn fourth ore car that was waiting to be emptied, the lights in the tunnel suddenly flickered a couple of times, then went out. With only the two lamps on our hard hats, this tunnel became the blackest of black places I had ever been in. Curtis and I did not know what to do, so we started to walk or feel our way back to the station with just our battery lamps. The lights came back on just as suddenly as they'd gone off. We turned around, went back to our area and set to shoveling. When we talked about it while waiting for the cage to take us back to the surface, the other miners said that they didn't experience any problems with the lights and it must have been our imagination. Here again, I think they were just jerking around two young muckers.

Once I was in the cage moving up to the surface, I was only too happy to see the stars shining. We turned in our lamps so the batteries could be recharged, turned the brass tag to show we were out of the mine and headed for the shower room.

The shower room had maybe 12 showerheads, which meant that no one had privacy and several men would be showering at the same time. Sometimes someone would turn the hot water off on the shower next to him and the response was very vocal. By the time we had cleaned up, hung up our work clothes on the chained hook to be aired out and walked home, it was 1 a.m. in the morning. I had survived my first day as a mucker, and for this I was paid five dollars.

A seasoned mucker

I could hardly get out of bed the next morning. I was so stiff that even the slightest movement hurt. My hands were covered with blisters. After breakfast, I hightailed it to the company store and bought some work gloves. That night we went through the same procedure, going back to the same place to work. It seemed easier the second night and the air kept us cooler, but it was still hot and dirty. I don't think Curtis and I ever got eight ore cars emptied on our shift, but we tried.

Later on in the summer I was assigned to work with a miner. The miners had gained experience over the years of how to extract the ore. Their pay varied depending on their time with the company, but it had a range of seven to eight dollars a day. Miners knew how to timber the tunnel to prevent cave-ins, how to place the drill holes to break loose the ore, how to cut the fuses to the caps so the dynamite would go off in the right sequence, how to recognize and follow a vein of rich ore, how to shovel, and most relevant to me, they knew how to teach the mucker to do his job.

Timbering the drift required knowledge, time, and skill, not only to make the area safe for mining, but to protect the workers. The timbering was done with wood pillars that were about ten inches square and planks that were two inches thick, twelve inches wide, and twelve feet long. It was somewhat like framing a house with the planks making up the roof. While we did use nails, we also used wooden wedges to hold the timbers in place against the walls and ceiling of the drift because the surfaces were so uneven.

It was much more interesting to be working with a miner who knew his stuff than with another mucker. The miner checked the board on the wall at the station to see what the previous shift had reported. It was the responsibility of the miner who was on the earlier shift to report if all the blasting dynamite had gone off. If one of the holes had not been counted as going off, then it had to be recorded so the next shift would know to be cautious when removing the ore. If your shovel hit a fuse that had been placed in the dynamite, it could make it explode.

When the area where we worked was clear we went to another part of the mine, most often to an area I had never been in. The first thing we had to do was shovel the ore into the cars that the previous crew had blasted from the face of the drift. Most of the ore was on the planks, but the large pieces had to be broken up into smaller pieces so we could put them in the ore car. We used a pick or, if that didn't work, a sledgehammer to break the rocks into pieces and put them in the cars. The cars would be picked up by an electric mule and hauled out to the station to be lifted to the surface in the cage.

Our next job was to drill new holes for the dynamite charges. This was done with a jackhammer powered by compressed air, very much like the ones you still see being used during street-repair work. Jackhammers must weigh at least 125 pounds. While this weight was an aid when working on streets, in a vertical position, it was challenging when drilling horizontally into the face of a drift. We also had to change bits often, depending on the ore being drilled.

The kind of ore we were dealing with was one of the factors that determined the number of holes we drilled. If it was an ore heavy with lead and silver, we would have to drill more holes. The higher the holes were the more difficult they were to drill. The mucker (me) would have to hold the bit of the jackhammer against the face of the wall to get the hole started. This was not easy because the vibrations of the jackhammer caused the bit to jump around. The miner had to determine how deep each hole should be, inasmuch as the depth made a difference in how the ore came off the face of the drift when the dynamite went off.

When the holes were all drilled, I went to the station to get the blasting caps that had been attached to a black-powder fuse. The fuses were all about ten feet in length. We had to be very careful not to drop them since the blasting caps could explode. While I went for the caps, the miner would get the amount of dynamite he wanted and we would meet back at the work place. It was against all the safety rules to store the blasting caps and the dynamite in the same area of the station. One person wasn't even allowed to carry the two items together.

Next, the miner poked a hole in the stick of dynamite with a nail and inserted the blasting cap. He then wound the fuse around the dynamite a couple of times to prevent the blasting cap from falling out, and very carefully inserted it into one of the holes we had drilled. Then he used a long round stick we called a tamper to push the dynamite and the fuse to the end of the hole. Sometimes he would put another stick of dynamite in the same hole, but it would not have a blasting cap. Finally, he tamped some dirt or rags into the hole to prevent the dynamite from blasting outward from the hole.

When all the holes had been filled with dynamite, the miner cut the fuses to different lengths; he did not want them all to go off at the same time. In this way, the ore from the face of the drift peeled off in layers. The miner then lit each fuse and we made a quick retreat to a safe area. We waited for the explosions to begin and counted each one to be sure we knew of a possible misfire. If we drilled ten holes, we wanted to hear ten individual explosions. If by chance we heard only nine explosions, the location of the workplace and the fact that only nine explosions had taken place was recorded at the station. Firing the dynamite always took place at the end of the shift because, afterwards, it was impossible to go back into the work place because of the dust and dirt flying around.

The union

By working down the mine, I was under considerable pressure to join the Miners' union. The union represented the majority of those who worked down the mine, but I was in a little different position than most of the workers. I had been given 100 shares of stock in the mine by a relative and was also related to the family who owned the majority of the stock. Basically, I had a conflict of interest. But what bothered me more than anything was that the fee to join the union was $25. That meant I would have to work for a week just to join the union. I knew I was not going to make mining my livelihood and that this was just a three-month job.

At the same time, I also knew that I was taking advantage of what the union had made possible for all their members, such as better working hours and higher daily pay. The union had threatened a strike over a 25-cent-a-day raise that brought up the pay scale I was receiving. The company finally gave in to this demand and averted a strike.

One shift I worked was the same one the union recruiter was on, and one day when I came out to eat my lunch, my lunch pail was on the ground and the thermos had been broken. No one said anything, but I always felt it was part of the pressure to get me to join the union. I never joined.

Each day in Dividend started with a loud company whistle that announced the start of a shift down the mine, as well as the other work required to keep the mine going. It sounded every morning at 8 o'clock, and the town came alive. This also gave mothers an hour to get their children ready for school. The whistle sounded again at noon to herald the start of the second shift, and again at 4:30 a.m., the end of the second shift and the start of the final shift down the mine. Three shifts filled out the day.

If an accident took place in the mine, the whistle would sound three times, telling everyone in town that something had gone wrong. The mine had a safety team that went down—or attempted to go down—the mine in an effort to rescue injured miners. As the only registered nurse in town, Mother immediately went to the doctor's office, where they would stand by. The doctor was on a retainer fee from the company at around $200 a month, which was considered generous.

The Tintic Standard had worked out a medical plan with the union that each employee would pay 50 cents a month for medical coverage that included an insurance policy that covered hospital care in Salt Lake. In addition, the company had two doctors under contract, Dr. Floyd Hatch and Dr. Martin Lindon, both in Salt Lake City, to take care of the serious cases. There were also two doctors in nearby Eureka who were on call in case of a major problem down the mine or in the town. We had no drug store in Dividend except for the limited medications such as iodine and Band Aids sold at the company store. The closest drug store was in Eureka, three miles away over narrow dirt mountain roads.

Once the whistle had blown its three-note warning, the safety team took a wire litter, which was in the shape of a man but a little larger, on the cage that normally hauled ore from the mine, to the site of the accident. In the meantime, the wives and families waited at the surface for any information the company could or would provide. As uninjured miners were brought to the surface, there was always a cry of relief by some of the families.

When the safety team came to the surface with an injured miner in the basket, he was immediately taken to the doctor's office, which was about two blocks away from the shaft. The families followed the injured miner to the old bunkhouse, where the doctor's offices were located on the top floor.

The doctor treated the injured miner on site if at all possible. Sometimes first aid was all that was necessary, and the miner would stay in one of the rooms above the boarding house. If the injuries were beyond the scope of treatment available in the doctor's office, the miner was placed in a car that had been modified to accommodate that same wire litter, and was taken to the hospital in Salt Lake. It was about a two-hour ride and the little towns between Dividend and Salt Lake provided some escort to speed up the trip. The first 15 or so miles were on dirt roads and 40 miles per hour was top speed.

Three months of this work down the mine was enough and I was happy to see the school year arrive. I am glad I had the experience. I came away with great respect for the men who make their living working in such an environment. But the most important thing it taught me was that I did not want to make a living in mining unless I owned the mine.

CHAPTER 4

THE BLIND DATE THAT CHANGED MY LIFE

If someone asked me the question "What attracted you to Pat?" this would be my reply: When you are 17 years of age and you see a beautiful girl, it's easy to dream of being with her in all kinds of situations. I was not the exception. She was beautiful, had a wonderful smile, was extremely intelligent, was an accomplished classical pianist, could dance, and had a personality that would melt you away. Our first date at Rowland Hall School for Girls was different from anything I had ever experienced. It was just the beginning of our love affair of almost seven decades.

I was at the University of Utah in my freshman year and was living in a boarding house on the corner of 13th East and 2nd South. Housing for out-of-town students at the university was very hard to find. I lived with two fellow graduates of Payson High School in one large room. We each paid $30 a month for the room and board, plus two meals per day taken across the street at another boarding house where we ate in the basement dining room.

It must have been the first of October of that first year at the university when I was called to the phone at the boarding house. It was Mother's first cousin Pearl Pearsall. She asked me if I would be interested in going to a dance at a private girls' school, Rowland Hall. Pearl went on to say that her daughter Peg had a friend who was looking for someone to go to a dance with. If I was interested, she would have me and Peg's class-mate over to their home so we could meet. An opportunity to meet a new girl was not to be dismissed. I agreed immediately.

Patricia Condon

A couple of days later, Pearl had set it up that I would come to their home to meet Pat Condon. On the night of the meeting, I walked over to the Pearsall house. The Pearsalls had a lovely home; it was very large and, to me, very impressive. In a little while Pat arrived and we met for the first time. She had dark hair, hazel eyes, and a smile that melted me right away. The three of us (Peg, Pat, and I) went downstairs to dance to the music of big band leaders like Glen Miller and Tommy Dorsey. Peg had a collection of records such as I had never seen before of the popular bandleaders of the time. After a little while we all had sodas and Peg drove us home in her baby blue Desoto convertible. When I walked Pat to the door of her home, she asked me if I would like to go to the Halloween Dance at Rowland Hall, and I of course accepted.

On the night of the dance, we double dated with Peg and her date. When I went to the door of Pat's home, she met me and, of course, I had to meet her mother and father. I think I was more impressed with them than they were with me. After the dance, I asked Pat if she would like to go to a get-acquainted dance at the university. These dances were held Friday afternoons and were a lot of fun. She said yes and I told her I would call her later. I couldn't summon the courage to kiss her good night, but I sure wanted to.

At Christmas, Rowland Hall had a candle-and-carol service at the school chapel and I was invited to go with Peg's folks. We picked up Pat and went to the school for the service, which was lovely. Unfortunately for me, the offering plate was passed and all I had was a silver dollar in my pocket. I was seated next to Peg's wealthy father, Dr. Pearsall, and he put in folding money. I did not want him to think I was not going to contribute, so I put in the dollar. I had planned to take Pat to the College Inn for a soda, but that was impossible now.

After the service, the Pearsalls dropped Pat and me off at Pat's home. Pat prepared hot chocolate and we ate some cookies her mother had made. While we were on the coach, I got up nerve enough to kiss her. I did not know it, but the girls in Pat's class would call her to ask if I had given her a kiss yet. We had been dating for three months.

During Christmas break at the university, I returned to Dividend to see my folks. I also worked down the mine to make a little money for school. We had very limited phone service in Dividend, but on Christmas day I called Pat and we talked for three minutes, until the operator came on and said my time was up. I blurted out to Pat, "I love you." The phone went dead and I hoped Pat had heard it and that the operator did not think I was talking to her. Pat later told me that she had heard my message.

We dated steadily through the winter and spring of 1941. Then, the same summer I was working in the mine, Pat had her ankle fused on her leg that had suffered polio and she had a cast up to the knee. She had been stricken with the disease in 1926 when she was three years old, and she often had a brace or a cast when she was child and later in high school. Her parents had also used massage and exercise as therapy, years before Sister Elizabeth Kenny introduced this method for polio survivors. Pat was determined to be as active as her friends. As a result, she could do almost everything her schoolmates could do, including going to dances—preferably with me.

I made several visits from Dividend to see her, and one time I took the family car, drove two hours to get to Salt Lake, spent 30 minutes with Pat, and then drove back to Dividend. I did not tell my folks where I had been because I knew they would have been unhappy with me being on the road for four hours for such a short visit. But I was in love.

It was also during that summer that Glenn Miller brought his swing band to Saltair, an amusement center near the Great Salt Lake, the same amusement park where Dad courted Mother in 1919. This time I got permission to take the car, and Pat and I went out to hear Glenn Miller. By then, Pat had what was called a walking cast on her leg. While we danced a few times, we spent most of the time just standing in front of the bandstand, enjoying the music.

PART II

THE WAR YEARS, 1941–1944

CHAPTER 5

ENLISTING IN THE ARMY AIR CORPS

My contemporaries all know and remember where they were and what they were doing the morning of December 7, 1941. The bombing of Pearl Harbor changed our lives even though we were thousands of miles from the event. I had just turned 19, was a sophomore at the University of Utah, and was not getting along with the love of my life, Pat Condon. Pat had graduated from a girls' school and found many more men available at the university than when she was in high school and dating me.

I had always wanted to go to dental school, but after Pearl Harbor it was simply a decision of *when* I would go into the war and into what service. I did not even have a draft number. My exposure was through World War I movies and the struggle that army personnel had to put up with—mud, gas, and charges over open ground—did not thrill me at all. On the other hand, I was not a good swimmer, and the probability of having to swim, if I joined the Navy, left me with very little choice other than the Army Air Corps.

The Army Air Corps had just lowered its age limit to 18 and no longer required two years of college for pilot training. Knowing that there would be a need for additional pilots to fight a war, General Hap Arnold, the chief of staff of the Air Corps, announced this change in the minimum age requirements. My problem was convincing my parents that joining the Air Corps made sense. In time they relented, and Mother signed the paperwork for me to take the physical and the qualifying tests.

I took the physical and the tests right after Christmas, and was told that I had passed both and that if I wanted to become a pilot, I had to sign up at once. With the paperwork in hand, I signed on the dotted line, withdrew from the university, and awaited the notice to report in. January 24, 1942 was the big day. Of course I was excited, but my folks had many reservations and concerns. I had never seen my mother cry but at the train station on that cold day in January tears were streaming down her cheeks. She had witnessed the return of her brother who was gassed in WWI and was petrified something equally bad or worse was going to happen to her only son, but I am sure both Mother and Dad were proud at the same time.

Williams Field, Arizona

The orders read that we were to go by train to Chandler, Arizona, where we would be trucked to Williams Army Air Base. My family was at the train station to see me off, and Pat came with a couple of mutual friends. One of them, Joe Henriod, bid me goodbye and said, "We both have missions in our life. You are going into the service and I'm going on my church mission." I met some of the other cadets who were to be in my class aboard the train. Spencer Hunn, Dee Johnson, Ted Peterson, Hal Gunn, Dick Haight, and Allen Randle are a few who I remember. We were all excited about being in the Air Corps and could hardly wait to get started.

When we got to Chandler we were met by a second lieutenant who tried to instill some order into this gang of young bucks. We were all in civilian clothing and had been permitted to bring one bag with personal belongings. In time, a truck arrived and we piled in the back with our worldly possessions.

Williams Field was not at all what we had expected. After getting out of the truck, we were lined up and told that if we wanted to sleep under cover, the tents were over there and we were expected to erect them. With some supervision, the tents were put up over some wooden platforms. We were then issued army cots, four to a tent, with bedding to go with them. I did not realize how cold it could be in the desert. The next day, each tent was wired to have one electric bulb hanging from its center, and provided with a potbellied stove.

On our first day at Williams Field we learned how to march. We must have looked like a ragtag army, because we still wore the civilian clothes we had arrived in. But march we did. Left turn, right turn. Halt; eyes right, eyes left. Halt; to the rear, march. At ease; fall out.

Williams Field was also being used to train Chinese cadets who lived in barracks and had everything we had thought we would be getting. We were permitted to use the mess hall for our meals only after they had been served, and this produced some bitching. We were also permitted to use the showers and latrines in the Chinese barracks.

When we were not marching we were in school, learning about what it took to be a pilot. Our courses included Morse code, air dynamics, conduct of an officer, maintenance of aircraft, whom we were fighting and why, aircraft identification and weather. Besides the schooling, we were tested again and again to see if we were really qualified to be aviation cadets. We also started the shots that were to keep us from getting any disease wherever in the world we were assigned.

It was at Williams that I learned about a "square meal." The background of the cadets was so varied that the eating habits of some needed improvement. In an effort to make these changes, we all had to eat what was called a "square meal." The food on the plate, once on the fork, was to be brought up vertically from the plate to the height of your mouth and then pushed directly into your mouth. Moving the fork back to the plate, the procedure was reversed, making a square.

After one week at Williams, we were issued our first set of coveralls. One size fit all, and while we did start to look something like a military organization, we still had a long way to go. I sent my navy blue suit home and I'm sure it could have stood by itself with all the dust and dirt that had accumulated on it during our week-long marching program.

Santa Ana, California

About the end of the third week at Williams, we were told that we would be going to Santa Ana, California, for additional training. We were ready for the move—anything to get out of our tents and away from the dust kicked up from marching. The train trip took us to Los

Angeles, and then we were transported in the back of a truck to Santa Ana. It had been raining; when we jumped off the truck we landed in sticky black mud. The two-story barracks we were to live in had just been constructed. In line with General Arnold's guidance, all new airfields were to be of temporary construction to last for the duration of the war only, and these barracks at Santa Ana conformed to his guidance. Covered in tarpaper, with an open bay and latrines at one end of each floor, they were ugly but still better than tents. Each cadet was assigned a bed with a footlocker and one shelf at the head of the bed. The floor was covered with sawdust, but that did not matter because we had tracked in enough black mud to cover it. Of course, it was just a matter of time before a sergeant arrived and we were on our hands and knees cleaning up the floor.

Someplace between Williams and Santa Ana, all our shot records as well as the results of the testing had been lost. Thus, the first order of business was to take the tests again and start the series of shots all over. We were not a happy bunch of cadets. Retaking the tests was just a pain, but the shots were something else. The needles were large and dull after so much use, and we all knew that if we passed out while taking the shot, our cadet days were over.

Our days started early with "falling out" at six in the morning and marching to breakfast. This meant we were to be up around five so the bed could be made with square corners neatly secured. Nothing was to be out of place, period.

I have to say, to my genuine surprise the food was actually good and there was lots of it, which was fortunate because many of the cadets had never had such good food. But then most of the cadets, including me, were hungry teenagers and still growing, so most anything would have tasted good. After breakfast, we were marched to classrooms and the same subjects were reviewed over and over again. It was the old deal of telling the student once, then telling him again, and just to be sure, telling him yet again. We also had to qualify with rifles, which at least got us out of the classroom and onto the shooting range. I had had a BB gun as a child, but this was a new experience. I was not a very good shot; I had joined the Air Corps to fly, not fire a gun. But somehow I qualified and we did not have to go out to the range again.

The only thing that disrupted our busy schedule was the weather. It rained every day and that just made the mud so much deeper. We still had the coveralls we had been issued at Williams, so our dress code was simple—wear the coveralls we were issued until further notice. By the second day at Santa Ana we were taking off our shoes before entering the barracks and cleaning them in the latrine.

We were soon issued cadet uniforms. This was the biggest moment of our cadet career so far. We were jettisoning our filthy coveralls for real uniforms that made us look as if we really were somebody. Maybe the girls would pay attention now that we looked like officers, or something close to it. The first weekend after getting our new uniforms, some of us went to Los Angeles for the big USO, where we could meet some of those girls, dance with them, and stuff ourselves with cake, cookies, and all the other food donated by the people of L.A. The USO was also a place where we could write a letter to our folks and, if we could get a long-distance line, even call home. The USO had a photographer on site, and of course, we had to get our picture taken in our new uniforms.

In our class of 1942 iA (which I was assigned to) everyone was white, middle class and most were my age, nineteen or a little older. Today my class would have been called "white bread" although we had a number of Jewish and Catholic men. I would say ninety present of us didn't have a college degree but were like me—they had left college to enlist. We were all children of the Depression yet I was struck by how comparatively lucky I was compared to some of the more ragtag fellows. In isolated Dividend, we had managed pretty darn well it turned out. But what brought us together now, no matter who we were or where we came from, was a deep sense of patriotism and the urge to "get over there and do our part." In our few free moments, when we could find a radio, we were glued to the latest news from both the European and Pacific fronts. At that time Hitler was winning and the Japanese had taken over most of the Pacific so the news was usually bad, which just made us, and certainly our instructors, more motivated to get us through the training and overseas. Frankly I didn't spend much time worrying about my future, not just because I was nineteen and therefore death seemed impossible to fathom, but also because I was so involved in the daily challenges of learning how to fly. It was also a fact made clear to us from our first day that we'd have no control over where we would go or what we would be doing, so why waste time worrying about it was my attitude.

The following week we learned that we were to receive orders to our Primary Flying School and that our class would be known as 42-1. It was April 1, almost four months since most of us had enlisted, and we were all itching to start flying. Enough with the marching.

CHAPTER 6

LEARNING TO FLY

I was assigned to Rankin Aeronautical Academy in Tulare, California. I had never heard of Tulare and no one had any knowledge of the academy. It didn't matter; we were on the way to becoming pilots and winning the war. Those of us assigned to Rankin were trucked to Tulare. When we arrived at the academy, we were faced for the first time in our lives with upperclassmen who taught us, as we lined up for their inspection, the "brace"—coming to attention with your chin tucked as far as it could go into your neck, shoulders back, eyes straight ahead, no facial expression of pleasure, arms straight with fingers pointing at the ground. As they inspected us, the upperclassmen told us how dumb we were, calling us Dodos and other terms not printable in this memoir.

After absorbing considerable abuse, we were assigned to our rooms. We got our luggage and marched double time to our new quarters. What a change from Santa Ana. Two men to a room shared a bath with another room but had a washstand of their own. There was a bed with a footlocker for each cadet, and a closet.

My new roommate was George Lemen, a staff sergeant who was going through the flying program to become a pilot. George had "been around"; he taught me a lot about keeping our room in order to get by the inspections. One of the things was to do everything you could the night before, because when we were awakened in the morning, time was critical. For example, our footlocker had to be ready for inspection at any time. A diagram was pasted to the top of the footlocker showing where each item of clothing was to be placed. This meant that the socks had to be rolled so that the top of the sock had a straight line across the top of the roll and placed in the tray of the footlocker in the assigned place. Shorts and vests were to be folded in such a way that they were all the same size and placed in the exact position shown on the diagram. It did not take long before I got rid of anything that was not absolutely necessary.

We had just started to settle in when we were called out to the field for more abuse by the upperclassmen. After an hour of standing at attention, we were marched to the auditorium for our first lecture about the use of a parachute. When the chief of the parachute department took the stage, we all stood up at attention until he gave us permission to take our seats. The one thing I remember this fellow telling us was, "If you cadets should pop your cookies and it gets on my parachutes, plan to clean it up to meet my standards and plan to clean the airplane as well."

After the parachute lecture, we were marched at double time to the dining hall for our main meal of the day. We were assigned to tables. At each underclassmen's table there was one upper classman who had complete control, including that we eat according to the "square meal." If someone did something the upperclassman didn't approve of, the cadet had to hit a "brace" in the seated position and wait until he was given permission to resume eating. We had to sit at the table with our hands in our laps until everyone in the dining hall had finished eating. Then, with one command, we all stood up and filed out of the dining hall, table by table, with the upperclassmen leaving first.

The following morning, we woke early, polished up the room, and marched to breakfast. No exceptions were made by our upperclassman at our table regarding eating manners. The food was very good but if you took the food, you ate it. Luckily, I was way ahead of this game because my mother's clean-plate policy at home was exactly the same—if it was on your plate, it went into your stomach.

Following breakfast, we were given a few minutes back in our room. There, George insisted that we polish everything and then *back out of our room*. He was of the opinion that if we made a good impression the first day with the upperclassmen and the officers managing Rankin, we might not be inspected a second time that day. And he was right.

Flight Training

The means of enforcing the rules at Rankin was with a demerit system. Depending on the infraction, we would be awarded demerits, and after so many we were given extra duty or walked the demerits off by marching with a rifle on the weekend. Cadet officers as well as military officers could award demerits. I remember once getting a demerit during an inspection of our room because water was in the bottom of our washbasin. From that time on, we turned the tap off as tightly as we could and plugged the outlet with toilet paper.

Our class at Rankin was broken up into four companies with a cadet commander and a cadet staff for each. Two companies flew in the morning and went to ground school in the afternoon. This schedule would change every other week.

We were introduced to our flight instructor, and in my case it was a civilian by the name of G.J. McKee. He had four cadets to inspire and risk his life in order to teach them to fly. Cadets Wilson, Brim, Cisne, and one other who washed out were his charges. He was all business. We were the second class he had instructed at Rankin. I liked him. After our introduction, we went out on the flight line and walked around the airplane, a PT-17 made by Stearman. The PT-17 had a wood frame covered with fabric that had been covered with lacquer to make it non-porous. It was a bi-wing plane with guide wires running from one wing to the other. The engine had to be cranked to get it started. It had two cockpits, one for the cadet and the rear one for the instructor. I had never been this close to an airplane before. My experience with airplanes had been going out to the Salt Lake Airport and watching them land and take off.

Right from the beginning, I had trouble landing that Stearman. The air work seemed to go okay, but when I got close to the ground, I panicked, afraid I would ground-loop the plane, not keep it on the runway, come in too fast, or come in too slow. It was a nightmare for me; I worried that I might wash out. McKee seemed to be taking over control of the plane time and time again as I attempted to make a landing.

The army had a policy that cadets had to solo within a certain number of hours of instruction. My hours were up and McKee felt I was not ready to solo, so he put me up for a check ride. Historically, cadets who went up for check rides automatically became members of the "Hugo

Club", which meant that your pilot days were over and you were eligible to go to navigation school or to become a bombardier. Thirty-three percent (72 cadets) of our class washed out at Rankin, and I think this was just about normal for all the flight schools.

Problem days

There was a lot of pressure to get pilots into the war and so there were adjustments made to accelerate the program to train pilots and deploy them as fast as possible. We were living in an open bay barracks at the time. When a fatality occurred among our ranks we'd often hear about it second hand. No time for a formal announcement, a memorial service or, heaven forbid, halting our training to pay respects. If a cadet was missing or killed in an accident a Sergeant would enter the barracks, clean out all of the cadet's personal things without saying a word to any of us, and leave. And that was that.

However, just because no one mentioned fellow cadets who died during training exercises, didn't mean we weren't afraid the same thing could happen to us. And yet I think I was more worried about washing out than being killed. For me, the fear of crashing was strongest when I was landing the plane because of my eyesight. Needless to say the Army Air Corps required that all of us have 20:20 vision. I was slightly nearsighted and knowing that, I had memorized the eye chart before my eye exam during the intake process. But it wouldn't have mattered much since the Sergeant who gave me my eye exam started with the bigger letters and then just stopped halfway through. If he was suspicious of my missing a letter or two, he let it pass. Just another example of how eager the military was to recruit.

For a short time I kept a diary during my problem days at Rankin and I will let the notes speak for themselves:

Diary: Learning to Fly an Airplane

April 24, 1942

Upper class is leaving. I finished the mathematics and the navigation classes today. Flying is continuing to be a challenge. I beat out an army check ride yesterday but am still having trouble landing the plane. Received a letter from Dad yesterday.

April 25, 1942

I'm up for an elimination ride with the civilian flight commander. I don't think he likes me because I passed Capt. Page's check ride. A lot of pressure. I am sure if I get the chance to get some experience by myself, I can master it. Went to Tulare tonight and had my picture taken while I'm still a cadet. Great life I lead. New student cadets arrived today.

April 26, 1942

Not a very happy day for me. I failed the civilian instructor's elimination check ride, so have to go up with the army tomorrow. I went to Sunday school and church at a Baptist church in Tulare this morning. Then went to a show—the third one in three months. Then went to the USO and had cookies and orange juice while waiting for a bus to take us back to the base. I talked to Mother, Dad, and Aunt Emma on the phone. Reversed the charges. It was good to hear friendly voices.

April 27, 1942

I started new classes today—engines and meteorology. Went for my washout ride with Capt. Page and he told me to come back so as to have another officer ride with me. I will probably wash out today and Capt. Page just didn't want to do it because he soloed me in the plane earlier. I am both depressed and nervous. I don't want to wash out.

April 28, 1942

Not much doing around here. A windstorm came up, so only one flight went up. So I didn't take my check ride because of the storm. So it ended up being just another day to worry about it. I just hope I'm on when I do take my flight. It may be my last flight.

April 29, 1942

Guess what? I passed the army check and had an hour and 25 minutes solo! I was very happy to think I was able to do something that no one else has done so far here at Tulare. Now to get my head out and prove to them that I wasn't a bad investment. It was a real thrill, and I did the following maneuvers when up by myself—power-on stalls, power-off stalls, spins, crossroad S's, and everything I could remember doing during the check ride. A very happy day.

April 30, 1942

Well, I am still flying and sure hope to keep flying. Shot stage landings and received a grade of 86 percent on them. Am to solo three hours tomorrow so as to catch up on my time. Have my 20-hour check ride coming up soon so must practice.

May 1, 1942

I'm still flying and, after three hours in the air, I'm tired. I was told I would have my 20-hour check ride Monday. Sure hope to pass it. Went to town and had a couple of drinks and then came home after a game of bridge at the USO. Got in about 2 a.m.

May 2, 1942

Stayed in bed until noon; then went to a show. Went to the USO and played some more bridge and came home. I went to bed early to prepare for my check ride. Sure hope to pass it.

May 4, 1942

Passed my army check ride again. That puts my record up to four army rides and I am still flying. I am enjoying flying more and more and only hope to "Keep them flying".

May 5, 1942

Shot my 180-degree approaches. Didn't do it too well. Flew three hours, so I am rather tired. Have an engines test tomorrow. I wrote home today.

May 6, 1942

I was up just two hours today. Had a play dogfight and put the plane through a damn good workout. Received a letter from Mother today.

They are clamping down here at Rankin and Capt. Bradley is sure in his glory when he is able to put us cadets in braces.

May 7, 1942

Just flew a while today. Shot my 180-degree overhead approaches and received a grade of 80 percent. My instructor showed me loops, snap rolls, slow rolls. I tried a snap roll and fell out of it, ending up in a split-S, which is against army regulations. I received a letter from Kay today. I am wondering if my old friends in Salt Lake have forgotten me. They sure don't write or answer my letters, especially Pat.

May 8, 1942

Flew for a couple of hours. Not much doing around here. Have a paper to write on engine-control systems. I received a package from home today. What a treat. I sure wish they would pay us. Up to date, they owe me about $200. I must write Mother and thank her for the contents of the package, especially the cookies. It is so great to get something from home.

May 9, 1942

I flew for a couple of hours and we got a weekend pass. Went to Fresno and mixed up with a Jr. Chamber of Commerce fellow who was having a party. Saw a heck of a lot of drinking and, as for me, I had enough to make me feel good. Came in at 3:45 in the morning.

May 10, 1942

Went to Sequoia National Park and saw what we could. It was so foggy we could not see too much, but it was a nice ride. We went up to the snow line and saw the biggest redwood tree in the world. Came home and cleaned up my room a little. We start everything an hour earlier tomorrow morning. That means I get up at 4:50.

Nothing written from this point on. I wish I had kept up with it.

When I retired from the Air Force in 1975, I had more than 4,000 hours of flying time and had flown 15 different aircraft. I would like to think that Captain Page, who was responsible for my first solo flight, would say, "I made a good decision regarding Brim".

CHAPTER 7

THE BT-13 AND THE AT-6

We had each accumulated 50 hours of training as pilots and had survived the upperclassmen's treatment, only to become upperclassmen ourselves and dish it out to the next batch of new Rankin cadets. We were on our way to basic training to fly BT-13 Valiants. Our class would be split up going to different training bases, and I was one of the cadets selected to go to Lemoore, California, which was about 30 miles southwest of Fresno.

The living conditions were not up to what we had just experienced at Rankin in terms of privacy. It was back to the open-bay barracks. We were underclassmen again, but by now we were better conditioned to this lowly status. The instructors were all military officers and demanded more military discipline. One of the nice things about the BT-13 was that it had a radio we could use to communicate with the tower regarding takeoffs and landings. In addition, it had a canopy over the pilot's head that had to be cranked to close and open. We had to leave it open for takeoffs and landings in case of an accident, because it would be easier to extract the pilot and his instructor. I remember chasing cattle in an open field by buzzing them in the plane. It was also during this time that I lost my wallet while doing slow rolls with the canopy open. I failed to button the pocket of my flight coveralls and gravity took over.

Ground school was expanded to include subjects like weather, navigation, and Morse code (which was useless for pilots). We also had to learn the jargon of using the radio. We added words like roger and wilco to our vocabulary. While at Lemoore, Jerry Beem from Omaha, Nebraska, and I became very good friends, and we spent our weekends in Fresno at the bars chasing girls. We were both 19, but our cadet uniforms were enough identification that we were not challenged at the bar. Jerry was later killed in an explosion of a B-17 over Montana, brought about because an additive to the gasoline rotted the fuel lines and the gas sprayed on the engine.

It was at Lemoore that we had our first experience flying formation. The key to good formation flying was picking a spot on the plane you were flying off of and keeping it in relation to your own plane. I enjoyed flying formation, but it demanded your attention from the time you joined up until you broke off. It was at Lemoore where we lost the first cadet due to a training accident. Graduation from Lemoore was on July 26, 1942.

The decision regarding our going into multi-engine or single-engine planes was made just prior to graduation. I have no idea who made the decision, but I was selected to go to Luke Field to be trained as a fighter pilot. The idea of being a fighter pilot was the best news I had had in some time. Being in control of your airplane and fighting the Luffwaffe one on one or the Japanese Zero had been drilled into us from the day we joined up as the ultimate in assignments.

Luke Field is west of Phoenix, Arizona, and the months of August and September were very hot. We arrived by bus from the Phoenix railroad station and again were met by upperclassmen. In retrospect, it seemed to me that with each advancement from Rankin to Luke, the upperclassmen became more demanding, if that was possible. After getting out of the bus and gathering our luggage, we were doing push-ups on the hot cement in front of our barracks. The physical conditioning programs at Rankin and Lemoore had prepared us for some of this drill, but the heat of Arizona added a new dimension of endurance. The barracks were again open-bay and underclassmen moved into the hot top floor. Air-conditioning consisted of open windows. Cadets arrived from different basic flight schools all over the country and each of us claimed we were from the very best. This resulted in long debates with nothing ever being resolved.

The first morning at Luke, we marched to the flight line and were introduced to our new instructors. Lieutenant Hanna was my instructor, and he showed us the AT-6. The difference between the AT-6 and the BT-13 we had flown at Lemoore was that the AT-6 was faster and its landing gear could be retracted. After a couple of hours in the AT-6, the four cadets assigned to Lieutenant Hanna had soloed and we were attempting to fly by instruments.

You may be impressed by now about how short these training sessions were. The Army Air Corps needed pilots flying planes against the enemy as soon as possible, so training was kept at a brisk pace. There weren't enough instructors and there wasn't enough time. More than 50,000 men were trained as pilots in that first year and a half. Over time, more than 15,000 young men were killed in training accidents and more than 52,000 were injured.

We had to get 10 hours of instrument training to graduate. It was here that we had our first experience "flying the beam", which was an aid to locating an airfield. Sky Harbor, Phoenix's municipal airport, had the only beam in the area, so we had to watch out for other cadets also attempting to fly using instruments. Also, it was at Luke where we were introduced to the Link trainer, another instrument-training device. We now had more freedom to fly the AT-6 on our own, but the required check rides were all part of it. On one occasion, Lieutenant Hanna took his flight of four cadets on a cross-country hop to the Grand Canyon, and naturally we had to buzz down in the cavity before returning to Luke.

Silver wings and gold bars

A popular song at the time was "He Wears a Pair of Silver Wings." Going into pilot training was considered as "good as it gets" for war assignments, so needless to say my graduation from flying school was critical. Not only would I get my silver wings but also the gold bars of a second lieutenant and an increase in pay from $75 a month to $225. We had hit many braces for upperclassmen, walked off demerits, in my case survived check rides in primary training, and passed the ground-school courses covering subjects we had never thought about prior to becoming cadets.

I had hoped to fly P-38s, but one day Hanna told us that in all probability we would be flying P-39s or P-40s. The demand for these two aircraft in Africa and the South Pacific was greater than the production of the P-38 and we had to take what we were given.

We graduated from pilot school on September 29, 1942 and were waiting our orders when we learned that West Coast Training Command had new orders for us. When we picked these up I was heartsick. It appeared that the powers that be had gone down the graduation list and every other person had been assigned to become a copilot on B-24s or B-17s. So instead of piloting a fighter, I was destined to be a co-pilot on a B 17 bomber. There was nothing I could do about it, but I was damned disappointed I can tell you that.

CHAPTER 8

BOMBER PILOT

I was to report to the 34th Bomb Group's 7th Squadron at Geiger Army Air Base, Spokane, Washington, no later than October 15. The only good thing about this assignment was that I would be going through Salt Lake City and would get to see my folks and friends en route. A friend of mine who had gone through training with me had a car and was going to Salt Lake as well, so I joined him on the trip home. Since it was a permanent change of station, he had no trouble getting gas-ration tickets. He was lucky enough to be assigned to fly P-40s and we all were envious of him.

Stopping off in Salt Lake to see my folks was wonderful, but the one person I really wanted to see was Pat. She had not written me often while I was a cadet, but when I appeared at her front door in my uniform with the gold bars of a second lieutenant and the silver wings of a pilot, she suddenly had a different, far more enthusiastic, attitude. When I offered her my pilot's wings to pin on her blouse, she seemed to melt. All of a sudden I was acceptable and could be shown off on the steps of the University Park building. I think I saw her every day and part of the night before leaving for Spokane, Washington.

Geiger Army Air Base

I left Salt Lake City by train and arrived at Geiger the second week of October 1942. As a second lieutenant, I was eligible for a single room in a barracks. The room was furnished with a G.I. bed, one chair, and a closet. It was the first time since Primary training at Tulare that I was not sleeping in an open bay with 20 other cadets. I could now go to the officers' club. I no longer had to get permission to leave the base to go to Spokane. I was being saluted and I was a pilot.

After getting settled, I went down to the flight line to see a B-17 for the first time. When I compared it to the AT-6 that I had been flying, the B-17 looked like a monster. It featured four engines, a wingspan of more than 100 feet, and machine guns protruding from all sides. I crawled inside to look over the cockpit and again was amazed at the number of instruments and the dual controls. For the first time, I learned that the crew would be ten men: four officers, one engineer, one radio operator, and the rest gunners. What a change from the single-engine AT-6.

After checking in at the 7th Squadron office, I was scheduled to fly this beast. On October 12, I made my first flight and I remember how stiff and slow the B-17 responded to the controls compared to the AT-6. Just keeping it level and headed on course required planning, and when it came time to land, the engineer read off the airspeed aloud on the final approach. I learned that this was going to be a team effort if we were going to make a success of the transition from the AT-6.

However stiff and slow the B-17 felt, it was a strongly built airplane that could sustain incredible damage and still fly crews home safely. It had four Wright Cyclone 1,200-horsepower radial engines. It could fly up to 35,000 feet and deliver about 6,000 pounds of high-explosive bombs to a target. When you think of hundreds of these Flying Fortresses in a formation over Germany, you get a sense of the power at our disposal.

The twin 50-caliber machine guns in the top and ball turrets operated mechanically, guided by a Sperry aiming mechanism that allowed the gunner to lock into a fighter and shoot the plane down with amazing accuracy. The gunners using single 50-caliber guns had a much more difficult time hitting those agile Germany fighter planes. For high-altitude bombing above 25,000 feet nothing was better than the B-17. Of course we would soon learn that high-altitude bombing didn't necessarily translate into accurate bombing.

My records show that I flew only six hours before being assigned to a crew as the co-pilot. I also had several hours logged as an observer where I stood between the pilot and co-pilot watching the different procedures.

The Lloyd Eves crew

Just how the crews were selected will always be a mystery, but one day at the squadron, posted on the operations board, was a list of officers and enlisted men who were assigned to a crew. I was now the co-pilot on the Eves crew and, as the day wore on, I was to meet these fellow warriors. Lloyd Eves, the pilot, was a first lieutenant from New York; Walter Haynes, the navigator, was from Florida; and Ray Hatfield, the bombardier, was from Missouri. The enlisted crewmen were Langford, the assistant engineer; John Allen, the radio operator; Richard Vaux, the ball-turret gunner; William Klein, waist gunner; Chester Willing, waist gunner; and Shorty Cromack, the tail gunner. These members of our crew had just finished training schools, as I had, and were all eager to learn more about each other as well as the plane we were going to fly in combat. I don't think we had a clue of what we were getting into, but that's part of being young.

Special Orders No. 298, dated October 30, 1942, Geiger Field Washington, assigned Combat Crew 18, our crew, to Casper, Wyoming for additional training. We were originally ordered to fly to Casper, but these orders were canceled and we were sent by train. No one knew where Casper was located until we got a map and found it was almost in the center of Wyoming.

We were assigned to the 331st Bomb Group's 462nd Bomb Squadron in Casper. What a place. The airfield was about five miles from the city and was situated in the most isolated place it could be. Mountains were to the south, and sagebrush surrounded the base. Wind seemed to come from all directions and at speeds that penetrated the barracks, the hangars, and every flight jacket. During one of the windstorms, our planes that were parked outside were sandblasted with such force that they had to be grounded and cleaned up. The officers' club was under construction, so we ate our meals in a common mess hall with the enlisted men. Officers had reserved tables at one end but everyone ate the same food.

When we were not flying or in ground school, we would go to town and find a bar, which Casper was not short of. It seemed to us that some of the friendliest people in the world were in Casper, and they appreciated what we airmen were trying to do. The main gathering place was the Gladstone Hotel. It not only had a bar but also a dance floor with a live band. The round mirror ball suspended from the ceiling over the dance floor provided moving lights throughout the room. A beautiful young Native American girl was the vocalist and received plenty of attention.

Captain Anderson was our squadron commander. He and several other officers assigned to Casper had been flying B-17s on anti-submarine patrols out of Panama and had accumulated many hours of flying. We would be scheduled to fly different training missions—cross-country, gunnery, and local missions, shooting "touch-and-goes". Since we had a limited number of planes and more crews than expected, we had time to go to ground school and learn more about the B-17.

I flew one low-level gunnery mission over the sagebrush of Wyoming with targets placed in remote areas. Lloyd Eves wanted to fire the .50-caliber machine guns we had in the back of the plane and Ray Hatfield, the bombardier, came up from his position in the nose of the aircraft because he wanted to try his hand at flying. We were moving over the range at about 160 miles per hour. The range varied in elevation, so the targets would appear suddenly and the gunners had little time to aim and fire. All of a sudden, we were getting very close to the ground and I added power and pulled back on the control column. The people in the back of the plane were tossed around and made some very unkind remarks about "who in the hell is flying this plane?" Lloyd returned to the cockpit and we headed for home. I often wondered what the jackrabbits thought about the .50-caliber projectiles stirring up the earth around the targets. In retrospect, this was not very good training, except for making instant decisions on whether or not to fire the guns. It was always fun to buzz the countryside, but in a big airplane you had to plan ahead.

One time we were on our way home to Casper, after a cross-country training mission, when one of the crew said he could smell gas. It wasn't long before the rest of the crew noted the same odor, so we declared an emergency over Cheyenne, Wyoming, and asked for permission to land. The fire trucks were alongside the runway when we got the plane down on the ground. We shut everything off, and departed the B-17 as quickly as we could. We were lucky in that the very same problem that had killed my friend Jerry Beem had occurred on our plane. The additive that had been mixed with the aviator gasoline had rotted the rubber hose on one of the lines to one of the engines, and the hose was spewing fuel.

After calling Casper and telling them of our problem and turning the plane over to a United Airlines maintenance crew to replace the hoses, we went into Cheyenne to find a place to sleep. Ray Hatfield knew a dentist there who was very helpful in getting us a place to stay. He took the officers to dinner and I remember him telling us that he was on the fuel rationing board for the Cheyenne area.

It got colder and the wind was more penetrating as winter approached. Horizontal snowstorms were common, and the snow often piled up against the hangar doors. The poor maintenance crews worked under these most trying of conditions and earned the respect of everyone. Flying was canceled during these storms. The pot-bellied stoves in the barracks were going full blast, and keeping them going with coal was a duty we all took very seriously. With the high winds, snow usually found a crack and drifted into our barracks—not a lot, but just enough to remind us that nature was in charge. Our heavy winter flying clothing became our regular uniform of the day. But despite the weather, the Eves crew, as we were called, was accumulating hours of training in the B-17 and we were advised that we would be going overseas shortly after Christmas.

A visit from Pat

Pat and I had been corresponding on a regular basis, and when I could get a phone line I called her. I don't remember if it was in a letter or a telephone call that I asked her to come to Casper. Lloyd and his wife Margaret had found a small house which they shared with another couple. They had said that if Pat came to Casper, she could stay with them, so I passed that invitation on to her. I was not hopeful, but I could dream. Frankly, I did not think her parents, her mother in particular, would even consider this proposal.

To my great surprise, Pat told me she had gotten permission and that during the Thanksgiving break at the University she could come to Casper. This required her to take a bus to Rawlins, Wyoming, and then another small bus to Casper. Of course, it was snowing and she was the only passenger on the small bus to leave Rawlins. I was at the bus station waiting when she arrived in Casper and gasped at how beautiful she was.

She told me she had slept most of the way from Rawlins, but her main problem was keeping warm.

We had a great time, going to different places, dancing, going to dinner, going to the Riverside Club. The entertainment at the Riverside was a black woman who sang off-colored songs such as "I didn't like it the first time, but oh how it grew on me." By then the officers' club was in full swing. Since it was a holiday, the crew was given some time off and I spent it with Pat.

Each night I deposited Pat at the home of Lloyd and Margaret, which was not what I had hoped, because rooms were available at the Gladstone. But it was there that I asked Pat to marry me, and she accepted. This was my dream come true and one of the happiest times of my life. Her problem was going to be explaining to her mother and father that she wanted to get married. That was to be a challenge.

CHAPTER 9

GOING A.W.O.L.

Pat left Casper by bus, reversing the trip she took to get there. I had her Rowland Hall ring and went to the only jewelry store in Casper to order another ring the right size. Pat had said she wanted the ring made of platinum so it had to be ordered from Cheyenne. She also told me she wanted to be married on New Year's Eve, because her parents had been married on that date. I would have agreed to any place or time. I just wanted to be with her.

Training continued when the weather permitted. We were advised that the 100th Bomb Group in Rapid City, South Dakota, was forming and that we might be assigned to it. I called Pat and told her I might be gone by the first of the year and could we be married earlier. This of course caused all kinds of problems for her, withdrawing from school, buying a trousseau, notifying friends of her plans, and all that goes with getting married. The date was set, December 7, 1942, one year after Pearl Harbor, and in St. Mark's Cathedral in Salt Lake. There was just one problem – I couldn't get the leave.

In the *Officers Guide*, it says that an officer getting married required the permission of his commanding officer. I went to the headquarters and asked to speak to him. After saluting, I told him my plans. He asked how long I had known Pat and, when I told him about two years, he made some comment that most of the people getting married had only known the bride less than two months. Fortunately, he did not ask me when the wedding was to take place or where.

How was I to get to Salt Lake for the wedding and get the time off as well? Leaves were not being approved because the crew was on standby to be reassigned to either a new combat group or as a replacement crew. I talked it over with the officers on the crew and they said they could cover for me. As time drew near I "developed" a sudden sore throat and went to the hospital to get treatment. It was necessary to have a fever to be grounded and confined to either the hospital or your quarters. With a little help from the hospital heating system, I developed the fever. I was confined to quarters and told to report back to the hospital the following Monday.

The wedding

I was already packed but had to pick up the ring and catch the bus to Salt Lake. I was officially AWOL, but young men with drives and priorities take chances, and I took that chance. I depended on my crew to cover for me. It felt like the longest bus ride I had ever taken.

Pat's mother had invited my folks over for dinner Sunday so we could all be together the day before our wedding. I gave her the engagement ring out in the kitchen shortly after I arrived. It was the only place where we could be alone. The next morning Pat and I, along with Dad, all went down to get a marriage license. Dad had to go along because I was 20, not 21. In Utah, a woman could marry at 18 but the man had to be 21. I was a commissioned officer and co-pilot about to go into combat, but I couldn't marry without my parents' consent.

The time was so short that we couldn't send out wedding invitations, so Pat and I called all our family and friends in Salt Lake and invited them personally, with just a few days' notice. Pat also called Mrs. Jones, headmistress of Rowland Hall, to ask her to come and perhaps to let a couple of Pat's good friends who were still in school come too. Instead, Mrs. Jones dismissed the entire school and marched them down the two blocks to St. Mark's Cathedral for the wedding, in their school uniforms, of course. Most of them, all the younger ones and the lower school, didn't know us at all, but they were thrilled to get out of class for an hour to go to a wedding. Because our invitations were so impromptu and haphazard, the church wouldn't have been more than half-full. But with all of Rowland Hall there, it was completely full.

Pat wore my pilot's wings on her wedding suit, to pin her veil in place. The dean of St. Mark's Cathedral married us. My sister Kay was Pat's only attendant, because none of her best friends from high school were in town that early in December.

We were married on December 7, 1942, at high noon. As we came out of the church, the bells were ringing and a very light snow was sifting down, although the sky was blue and the sun was shining. It was the best thing that ever happened to me.

Panic for a honeymoon

We left by train that night to go to Cheyenne, where we were to catch another train to Casper and planned to arrive Tuesday, one day late for the hospital recheck. It did not work out that way. The only air raid that Salt Lake had during World War II took place that night. It was a false alarm, but the train pulled off on a side track, all the blinds were pulled, and we sat there for several hours waiting for the all-clear signal so the train could proceed. This meant we would arrive in Cheyenne too late for the connection to Casper.

Panic took over. I was more than just a little concerned that in my first week of married life, I would be in a military jail for being AWOL. I called Lloyd Eves in Casper and explained that I could not get back until Wednesday. We got a hotel room very close to the railroad station and I started checking ways to get to Casper. I considered taking a taxi but due to gas rationing, this proved to be impossible. I remembered that Ray Hatfield's friend, the dentist, was on the gas-rationing board in Cheyenne and called him, but he could do nothing without the support of the rest of the board. I then called Lloyd for the second time and learned that the pressure was off. The weather was so bad in Casper that flying had been canceled. In addition to weather problems, one of the gunners was sick. We would not have to fly until Thursday. There was only one bus scheduled to Casper, and I bought two tickets for Wednesday morning. What a way to start a new life with a new bride.

As soon as we got settled in at the Gladstone Hotel in Casper, I called Lloyd again and was assured that all was well. I had tested the system beyond the norm but if "crew integrity" meant anything other than when flying, it had saved me from all kinds of troubles. In the meantime, I went out to the base and checked in at the hospital, and for some unknown reason my cold was much better and I was cleared to fly.

Pat and I found a small three-room furnished apartment over a garage. The landlord, by the name of Burns, had a son in the service and felt sorry for us. The Burns family were wonderful people who basically adopted us. How lucky we were.

CHAPTER 10

FINAL DAYS IN THE STATES

My flight log shows that I flew 60-plus hours during the month of December with flights to Denver, Rapid City, El Paso, and Scotts Bluff. This amount of flying left little time to be with Pat. She was rapidly learning the joys of being an Air Force wife. She did keep busy with the other wives of the crew and that helped some. We did not fly on the 24th through the 26th of December, which made it possible to be together on our first Christmas away from our families. I gave her a gold bracelet and we had a little Christmas tree.

Then in mid-January the crew received orders to go to Salina, Kansas, the replacement center for B-17 crews going overseas. We had to make a decision as to whether Pat would go home or come to Salina. She wanted to go to Salina, saying she could travel with the other wives on the crew. Ray Hatfield, our bombardier, had married his college sweetheart shortly after Pat and I had been married, so along with Lloyd's wife that meant that the three wives would travel by train from Casper to Salina.

The crew flew to Salina, but according to the wives, the passenger train car they came on had been last used shortly after World War I. The seats could not be adjusted, so they had to sit up straight for the whole trip. In addition, the lights were on very small chandeliers and gave off just enough light to see the aisle. So little heat was provided that the three of them wrapped themselves in all the winter clothing they could get their hands on. It was a miserable trip but they survived.

We had a hotel room in one of the few hotels in Salina but could stay for only four days. This meant that we had to find other accommodations, so we both went room hunting. We found a room in a very old home that had three bedrooms upstairs, one rented to an enlisted man and his wife, and one rented to another officer and his wife. We were the lucky couple who ended up with the last bedroom. One bath was shared by all.

On the main floor, the landlord and his wife had one bedroom, and two young ladies who worked at the air base had the other. We were to share the living room but had to go out for all meals. We cheated on this part of the conditions in that we had a footlocker we used for a table and Pat prepared our breakfast on it.

This was an interesting experience in that the landlord was a bootlegger and also had a land-office business. Kansas was a dry state and he went out of state to get his supplies of liquor. How he got away with selling liquor and not getting caught had to be because of the war. He must have paid someone off.

In addition to the liquor-distribution business going on at this address, the two unmarried girls were very active in bringing men to their room. We had a gas heater in our room and one morning I went downstairs to get some matches that we had seen in the living room. When I opened the door, I noticed that clothing was strewn around. Only after entering the room did I see the couple asleep on the couch. I got the matches as quickly and quietly as I could and got out of there posthaste.

Smoky Hill

We were assigned to the 1st Bomb Provisional Group's, 16th Airdrome Squadron, Smoky Hill Army Air Field. My flight records show that we made our first flight on February 14, 1943. It must have been around the 16th that some members of the crew came down with measles. I had had measles as a child, so I was not confined to the hospital or quarters.

It was during this time that I met Captain Dick Ezzard, who had already flown in the Pacific as a pilot of a B-17 and was now assigned to Smoky as an instructor pilot. We were assigned a new B-17 that we thought would be our plane for fighting the war. Lloyd Eves was not able to fly because of the measles, so I flew with Dick and his friend Captain Fred Crimmins. My records show that I flew about 36 hours while at Smoky.

One of the navigation aids that we were able to convince the maintenance people we needed was a drift meter. This instrument made it possible for Walt Haynes, our navigator, to determine the impact of wind on the plane as we flew from one point to another.

On February 28, 1943, Special Order Number 59 sent crew C-23, ours, on its way overseas to combat. Just where we were to go was classified, and we would not know until we had the orders and were on our way. This was only the first of many times that we were scheduled to leave for overseas, only to return to Smoky.

I packed my B-4 bag time and time again and said good-bye to Pat, only to return home later in the day. This was not all bad because we were still together, but it was difficult for Pat. She did not buy her train ticket to Salt Lake until I had left for sure. The big day came on March 9, 1943, and I had to say goodbye to my wonderful wife. She had been so understanding, tender, loving, and supportive during the three months we were together. I knew I had a diamond.

We were now part of the Crimmins Provisional Group going overseas. The "powers that be" sent Dick Ezzard along with us. I liked him very much and he proved to be of great assistance on our flight over. He had an 8mm movie camera and recorded most of our trip on film. We departed Smoky Hill on March 9, 1943.

CHAPTER 11

OVERSEAS

Our orders directed that the Eves crew proceed to Morrison Field, West Palm Beach, Florida, to an undisclosed destination. We were to give our friends and relatives our address as APO 3650, c/o Postmaster, New York, New York. The orders also read "In lieu of subs [subsistence] a flat per diem of six dollars ($6) per day is authorized for travel by air."

Once we got to Morrison, we assumed that our destination was either North Africa or England, rather than the Pacific, but all we were told was that we would be advised as to our final destination at a later date. With weather conditions preventing our departure for two days, there wasn't much to do but check out the bars, or, in the case of those of us who were newly married, try to call our wives.

Long-distance telephone calls were difficult to make. If you wanted to make a long-distance call, you had to place a request ahead of time. When your turn came up, the operator would call you back and allow you just so many minutes for the call. They would not accept calls from the base, so one night Ray Hatfield and I rented a hotel room in West Palm Beach, just to be able to call our wives.

For this trip I was the Class B Finance Officer and had been issued $1,000 and a money belt (I still have the belt). The money was to take care of unforeseen contingencies and to pay the crew for travel expenses.

U.S.A. to England, via Trinidad

We were going to England, but not by any direct route. On the contrary. No one in their wildest dreams would have conceived of the convoluted journey we took to get there. On the morning of March 25, 1943, at four in the morning, we started to taxi out to the runway when one of the engines fouled up. For a while we thought we would have one more day of putting our feet up on the brass rail, but to our great relief the problem cleared up and we were soon on our way to Trinidad, the first stop. Our course took us over Puerto Rico, which looked very inviting from the air with all its green fields.

We decided to stay beneath the cloud build-up. The ocean was a bluish green with a few whitecaps. Before we reached Trinidad, we were down to 1,000 feet above the water. To get to the airfield, we flew down the coast and then turned northwest to land. It was then that we could really see the natural beauty of the island. The jungle was very dense and dark green, the only break being an occasional rusty roof of a hut. From what we saw, it was pretty primitive living for the natives. We could also see many birds flying over the jungle, which added to the beauty of the island. Even though the airfield and facilities were still under construction, after nine and a half hours of flying, it looked good to us.

The barracks we were assigned to were built on pilings and screened in to keep the bugs away. It seemed to me that all the bugs God ever created were trying to get into our rooms or were already in there and trying to get out. It was very hot and sticky. The fact that we were still wearing our heavy pink-and-green uniforms did not help the situation. Even after a shower, we looked as if we had been working in the fields. Our clothes were always wet with perspiration. Nevertheless, the heat and sweat didn't keep us from testing the local rum that night, and afterwards we were able to get some sleep even with all the bugs. Shell Oil Company was operating the base and doing the construction work on the airfield. We were told to be very careful with all our belongings because the Trinidadians would steal anything they could get their hands on.

The following morning, we took off at 8:45 for Belem, Brazil. We were all happy to get into the air, where it would be cool. Walt had plotted our course so that we would fly over Devil's Island, the famous

French prison colony. Dick Ezzard had his camera ready and we all planned to take a quick look.

The intertropical weather front was between Trinidad and Belem, and we had to get through it. As we approached from our altitude of 9,000 feet, we could see it would be impossible to fly over it. Another B-17 had tried but had given up at 30,000 feet and come down to go underneath instead. Dick Ezzard had experienced a similar condition and recommended going under. We weaved around through the clouds, letting down all the time, until we were at 200 feet, where a cushion of air that sits above the water would provide clear flying. It was during this time that we missed Devil's Island. There was little comfort in Walt's claim that we couldn't have missed it by more than a mile.

The rest of the flight was in and out of rainstorms and over more jungle. It was brought home very clearly to us that if we had to make a forced landing in the jungle, it would have been next to impossible to survive. What might have looked like a good place to land was generally nothing more than a swamp covered with moss.

Belem, Brazil

The airfield at Belem, developed by Pan American Airways, had just recently been taken over by the U.S. Army. The approach to the field was over the Amazon River, which was easy to identify because of its size and the amount of silt it deposited into the ocean. We touched down at 3:40 p.m. and were happy to have this leg of the trip behind us.

Once again, our quarters left something to be desired. While the building was a newly painted white house, it too had screens all around it. And of course the weather was just like it had been in Trinidad, if not hotter and stickier. The air had a strange smell of mold. Besides the insane number of bugs trying to get through the screens, there were all kinds of spiders in our rooms. We were warned to be careful putting on our shoes and be sure no spiders or scorpions were inside.

We took a quick shower, and it had to be quick, because when we were all soaped up and shampooing, the water was turned off. Our hosts had forgotten to tell us that the water was on for only a few hours each day. I had never seen so many avocados in my entire life as were in the mess hall. I must have consumed a half dozen, but they were so good I just couldn't help myself. After our meal, we went back to our room and tried to sleep with one eye open to watch for the bugs and spiders.

We were scheduled to depart for Natal, Brazil, the next morning but a weather forecast of rain and thunderstorms forced a delay of at least one day. The five officers decided that it would be great to see the city of Belem. We changed into clean clothes and took off for the big city. As there was no transportation to the city, we started to walk. It wasn't too long before a local taxi picked us up and we had a wild ride into Belem with our driver using both sides of the road and honking at other cars, people, and animals that happened to be on or near the road. Once we arrived in Belem, the taxi driver drove down the streetcar tracks which were much smoother than the cobblestone roads.

The Grand Hotel was the center of American activities. We were told that Pan Am had spent $50,000 refurbishing it to bring it up to standards they considered acceptable. The old residential section had both old beautiful homes and entire blocks of tin and wood shacks. Also in this area were the docks and warehouses. Here we saw the extreme poverty of the Brazilians. There appeared to be hundreds of unsupervised children running around, dressed in tattered filthy clothing and appearing malnourished at best. The newer section of Belem contained modern structures built by the American oil companies and other businesses. We spent most of the day walking around the city, taking in the typical tourist sights.

That night, we had dinner at the Grand Hotel. I had a history of having to be careful of foods, so I was suspicious of the menu. But luck was on my side. Actually, I don't think anyone had a reaction to the dinner, and afterward we all went on a tour of the local red-light district to observe the action. I want to emphasize the word "observe". We had been told that the local girls were about 85 percent infected with venereal disease. What came as a shock, though, were the children who were offering themselves. We returned exhausted to our quarters, but sleep was almost impossible with the heat and the bugs.

The next morning, the weather forecast was much more encouraging. We were cleared to take off for Natal. We didn't regret leaving Belem. Our B-17 got us airborne at 8:00 a.m. on March 28.

Yet again we flew over jungle and were reminded of the problems of an emergency landing if it became necessary. We flew low enough to observe the scarlet-and-white birds flying over the dark green of the jungle. And yet again we could see the rusted roofs of native homes miles away from any sign of civilization. One of the nice things about this leg of the trip was that we knew we could always turn east and find the ocean and then follow the coast to Natal. This wasn't necessary, and we landed at another Pan American field at 2:40 p.m.

Inasmuch as the next leg of the trip would be over water, we had planned a couple of extra days for servicing the plane. Sergeant Maynard, our chief engineer, was in charge of this effort with the help of contract people who worked for Pan American. We slept in tents, which proved to be better than the houses we had at Belem because the breeze passed through the tent sides and cooled everything down.

We were told that, because a couple of sailors had been knifed in the city of Natal, it had been put off limits to all American military personnel. This being the case, we took off for the beach each day we were there. My reward for swimming in the ocean was an ear infection. While we were on the beach, the locals brought pineapples, coconuts, and watermelon to sell to the "rich Americans." With my propensity for stomach ailments, I had to be careful of what I ate, but avocados from Trinidad and pineapples from Brazil seemed to agree with me.

The mess hall at the base was a large tent and the waiters were local residents who left something to be desired as far as being clean. In time, we learned that if we wanted second helpings to hold up our plate and call out "mice," meaning "more." When I first heard the word, I was not sure that we weren't being served these little critters on rice.

We left Natal at 5:10 a.m. on April 3, 1943, and headed out for a small dot in the Atlantic Ocean called Ascension Island. We were the lead ship for three A-20 light-attack bombers since they did not have a navigator and therefore were following us. A-20s cruised a lot faster than our B-17, so following us presented a problem for their pilots.

Ascension Island

Ascension Island was a British possession with a few Brits living there, but the assignment must have been like a prison sentence. An inactive volcano had spread itself to about seven miles in diameter, covering most of the island. The U.S. Army had built an airstrip that started over a very sheer cliff going uphill at first. It gave the impression of a very short runway as you approached the field. The last three quarters were downhill. You landed and took off in the same direction, no matter what the direction of the wind. We landed after the three A-20s at 3:40 p.m.

We were assigned a tent on the side of a hill and were told that, because of the limited available water, we each could have a canteen full for drinking only. This was one way to encourage crews to spend as little time as possible at Ascension. We left the following morning, April 4, at 8:10 a.m. headed for Roberts Field in Liberia.

The flying weather was bad, with many thunderstorms. In fact, we heard later that a couple of A-20s were lost that day trying to get to Roberts. When we arrived at 2:00 p.m., the first place we went to was the mess hall, where we had the best food on the trip so far and didn't worry about "mice."

After getting settled, we learned from the operations people assigned to Roberts that, if we wished, the locals would take us for a river trip in their dugout logs to a native village and to the Firestone rubber plantation. The locals were only too happy to paddle the "rich Americans" up the river and show us the village. We had three boats with one person rowing each. In short order, we were at the village, which was rather small and only on one side of the river. It could have been set up for visiting Americans, but it was interesting. The villagers were half-naked. The men were sitting around idle while the women were pounding poles into a container making mush of some kind. The children were around, but they seemed to be afraid of us. The houses were made of bamboo poles placed together upright to make the walls and then covered with mud. The roofs were made of interwoven bamboo with leaves placed on top. Upon learning that the word "boy" meant friend, we used it a lot on this boat trip.

Farther up the river was a Firestone rubber plantation that was comparatively new and not producing yet. But with the need for rubber to support World War II, I'm sure the Firestone people were hoping for an early yield of rubber latex. The dock on the river was fairly large and would have handled a lot of rubber once it was available. The Firestone people had nice quarters, but the plantation was isolated from the world.

It did not take long to come back down the river to the airfield. We paid off our guides with money and candy, and again we had a good meal before retiring for the night. I was so tired that bugs—or anything else—couldn't have kept me awake.

Dakar

We took off for Dakar the next morning. Our flight plan took us out to sea and we basically flew up the coast. It was an uneventful flight. We could see how rough and yet beautiful the surrounding area was. We saw a few small boats, but that was about all we did see as far as activity in the area.

As we approached Dakar, the jungle thinned out to a gray desert. Dick Ezzard wanted to make the landing, which was bumpy to say the least, so that once on the ground we had a great time kidding him about going back to flying school. The runway was made of pierced steel mats, the first we had landed on. The mats made a terrible humming noise during the roll of a B-17 on the runway.

We were met by a Free French Army officer. After some communications challenges, we piled onto a truck and were taken to our so-called quarters. Upon looking over the quarters, Dick and I decided to sleep on the plane's wing, where we would be out in the clear air and also able to watch over the plane, even though a French sentry was stationed to guard it. We did take a shower at the quarters, changed our clothes, and inquired about going to the city of Dakar. We learned with some difficulty that since we were not stationed there, we were not permitted in the town.

After a short discussion among the five officers, we thought it was worth a try to go downtown anyway, claiming we did not understand the restriction. As soon as we got off the base, we hired a taxi and, following another harrowing ride, we were in the city of Dakar.

One of the sights I wanted to see was the site of the battle between a British fleet and Vichy French ships and shore batteries that had been fought back in 1940, plus the remains of French ships that had been scuttled to keep them out of the hands of the Germans. We walked down to the dock, but, instead of seeing the navy, we were met by a couple of French military police who asked us to leave. They were armed, but being cocky and curious we ignored them and went on ahead into the city.

Dakar was somewhat cleaner than the cities we had been in on this adventure. Still, it seemed to me to be very old and in need of attention. The open cafes, where you could eat outside, added a new dimension to traveling in a foreign land we had not seen before. They had good food and excellent wine. We were approached on the street by vendors, all of them trying to sell us special items. It was here in Dakar that I bought a beautiful ivory bracelet for Pat. I argued with a vendor about the price of the bracelet and in time got it down to what I wanted to pay.

The next day at the base it seemed to me that the local residents were much poorer here, as indicated by the way they dressed. They wore anything from an inverted sack with holes for their legs to layers of dirty cloths. Sand covered them until they looked more gray than black. They seemed to be everywhere and would come from all directions if they thought we would give them a handout. It was not uncommon for them to sleep among the bushes surrounding the base. To indicate that someone was guarding the airplane, I fired my .45-caliber pistol at a stump in the brush away from the plane, and much to my surprise a young man dressed in rags, about halfway between me and the stump, came out screaming and waving his arms in the air. The sound of a shot got a lot of attention from these poor people.

These same people knew that if they helped around the plane, just loading luggage, they would be rewarded with candy, gum, a few cents, or some other little thing. The trouble was that there were too many of them and they did not understand the dangers of being around the plane when the engines were started. The French sentry put up with them for only so long and then he fired a couple of rounds in the air and they scattered back into the bush for a while.

Prior to our early morning departure from Dakar, we filled our water containers, got a box lunch put up at the French mess hall, and of course checked out the plane very carefully. The operations officer asked us to take along a general and his two aides on our next leg of the trip, to

Marrakech. We refused because we felt we already had a load. Following a hurried clearance, we took off rather than face the general's wrath.

We were flying over barren country marked only by sand dunes, so this leg of the trip turned out to be the biggest test of Walt Haynes's navigation abilities. Checkpoints were not to be had. Walt had to depend on "dead reckoning," which was nothing more than flying on a heading for a set time and then making a turn to another heading. Along the way, there was a mountain of rock named Zedness, which stood out and which we were all glad to see because it was shown on the maps. Unfortunately, a G.I. had backed a truck into the radio beacon at Tembutes that day, putting the beacon out of operation. This checkpoint was to have helped lead us through the Atlas Mountains.

Our route took us on a course that required our climbing to 12,000 feet just to pass through a valley. We were not alone; 11 other planes had left Dakar that day and found the same problem. One B-17 was lost on this leg of the trip and seemed to have just disappeared in the desert. Walt had some doubts as to our exact location and, as we turned towards the mountains, clouds covered them and appeared to build up for several thousand feet above them. It was late in the day and we were concerned about the fuel we had left. We decided to turn toward the coast and find a place to land. As we let down and got out of the clouds, we came across farms and small villages, which provided us with a sense of security. The little fenced-in fields at the base of the mountains were really beautiful. From the air, they looked very green and orderly. The villages reminded me of Pueblo Indian homes, some being built on top of each other and made of rock and mud.

Flying on a westerly heading, we finally reached the coast, and the whole crew became more relaxed. We knew that if we couldn't find a field. we could land on the beach. Turning north, Walt found a checkpoint and a French city about 30 miles away.

As we approached the city, we saw an airfield and made a short pass over the runway to look it over. The runway looked very short. We noted that a new one was being built but was still not ready for use. I was surprised to see four P-38s and a couple of A-20s parked off to the side of the runway. This was the best news yet since it meant other Americans were nearby.

The trailing antenna on the B-17 would not retract, so we had to go out over the ocean and cut the wire, which let a lead weight and about 175 feet of copper wire drop into the ocean. It was about dusk when we made our final approach. Because of the short runway, we knew it would be tricky. We decided to land just short of the runway, wait until we were on the hard surface to apply the brakes and unlock the tail wheel, which would allow us to turn and take advantage of the largest part of the field. All worked out as planned, and one happy crew was on the ground and safe with no damage to the plane.

What a welcome those French gave us. I guess there were 150 Frenchmen running around our plane, waving their arms and calling out to each other. We were the first B-17 ever to land at this field and they wanted us to know how great it was. We didn't tell them we were very happy to see the field and how glad we were to be on the ground. We had arrived at Agadir.

One of the French officers wore the wings of a pilot and could speak some English. He had many beautiful ribbons on his uniform and I inquired about them. He told me: "The first one I received in the last war for shooting down a German; the second medal I received from the French for getting two English planes over Dakar; and the last one, my newest, I received for shooting down an American while I was fighting for the Germans." He was now training new French cadets with American planes for the Free French. I'm not sure how accurate he was in this report, but it made a good story.

It was from this officer that we learned that the Americans had a rest-and-recreation hotel downtown. He said that if we would show him and some of the other officers our plane, he would provide transportation downtown. As the guns on the plane seemed to provide the most interest, we gave several rounds of .50-caliber ammunition to a couple of the officers. This little gift insured that we would have guards posted around the plane. Before we left for the city, two guards with rifles and fixed bayonets were marching around the plane.

The French officer's offer of transportation must have been nothing more than a telephone call to the hotel, because in time an American sergeant arrived in a jeep and gave us information about the hotel. The officers were to ride there with him. A truck was on the way for the rest of the crew and the luggage. This all sounded too good to be true, but as we pulled in front of the hotel, a Red Cross lady came out to meet us. This alone confirmed our good luck. What a great way to end our day after the long flight and the concern for our lives.

The hotel, built right on the beach, had been taken over by the U.S. Army. The Red Cross lady told us it had been built in 1936 and was considered one of the finer hotels in the city. We were each given a room with a bath and, after cleaning up, changing clothes, and relaxing with a drink, we realized we had been very lucky. This was the first time we found ourselves with Army Air Corps people who had been fighting the Germans and the Italians.

What delicious food we had that night! We could eat all we wanted. It seemed like something out of this world. With the wine, which seemed to go down without any trouble, it was by far the best meal we'd had since leaving the States.

I met a couple of classmates from flying school at the hotel. They were flying P-38s and loving it. I envied their assignment to flying fighters. We started to discuss other classmates, and it was then that I learned that a friend, Dee Johnson, was last seen going straight down, his plane ablaze. Another classmate, George Brittin, was missing after a dogfight over the desert. Later I heard that George had bailed out and been found by the Arabs, who collected reward money from our government. George got home in one piece however.

Dick and I went to the market where I bought Pat a small silver sword pin and a couple of bracelets. It was fun, and yet a challenge, to be in the marketplace because you were continually being asked to buy something. If a vendor did not have a small stall to show off the merchandise, it was spread on the ground. One of the things that upset me was the meat markets and all the flies covering the meat. Sheep heads as well as other parts of the sheep's carcass hung on nails in the back of the butchers' stalls. Only when someone showed an interest in buying some meat would the butcher sweep the flies away.

Some of the enlisted crew went to local "social" houses. It seems that the wife in some households made the living and if she could entice a man to go to bed with her she would take him home. The husband would clear out when he heard them coming. It was here that Maynard was rolled and lost his wallet. That husband must have stayed around.

We spent two days in Agadir. Being with other pilots who had been in combat was extremely interesting, especially the ones who had seen combat against the Germans. They all had great respect for the German fighters and the planes they flew. They had been fighting with the 15th Army Air Corps in Africa and we listened to their every word.

We had to wait while the French refueled our plane. They had a 500-gallon fuel truck filled with gasoline that had only a hand pump. In addition to the slow pumping process, the gasoline had to be pumped through a chamois to extract water. We pumped gas all morning with a lot of Frenchmen looking on.

When it came time for takeoff, we had an even bigger crowd than had been there to welcome us. It took us awhile to taxi out and check the engines. We taxied as far as we could with the tail of the plane just about touching the fence. Lloyd ran up the engines to maximum power and released the brakes. When we came up to the runway, I dropped some flaps to give us additional lift. As we ran out of runway, we became airborne as each of us recited his own silent prayer. We were on our way to Marrakech for the second time.

Marrakech

As it was a very short trip, we took the most scenic route along the coast. Once north of the Atlas Mountains, we saw snow on some of the highest peaks. The mountains were much more rugged than we had been led to believe, now that they were not covered with clouds and could be seen.

The Marrakech field was a lot better than the one at Agadir. The landing strip was much longer, but it was covered with gravel which, upon landing, kicked up enough to put holes in the elevators. The parking area was filled with B-17s and some Free French Air Force planes. We learned from the operations people that a bomb group was training there; it was also a transit depot for crews and planes for both the England and the North African war effort.

As there were no quarters on the base, we were assigned to a hotel downtown. To get there we had to ride in a French bus that must have been built about 1927. We would be going along fine, when all of a sudden the engine would hiss and a great cloud of black smoke would appear. We were told that the gasoline was of such poor quality that we were lucky if it ran at all. We arrived at the hotel we had been assigned to and found that it was fully booked. A second hotel was also booked up, so we ended up staying at the Casino Club. Because of the war, the club was unfinished, so our army took it over and installed bunk beds in one wing for the enlisted men, and canvas cots for the officers in another wing. Our biggest problem was the lack of bathroom facilities.

There were also no eating facilities at the casino. We had to go back to the largest hotel run by the army for our meals. At one time, the dining room had been a beautiful place to eat. The hotel staff still used white tablecloths, which was a nice change after some of our previous mess hall environments. Both the food and service were the best we had experienced, even better than Agadir. It seemed to us that we each had our own waiter. They took care of us as if we were important dignitaries. The red wines were outstanding and we tried to consume all that was available.

Whenever we left the hotel or the casino, we would be assailed by local people, all asking to be our guides. Some would show a letter purportedly from some American saying they were outstanding guides. Others would just grab your arm and pull you away. Because of the shortage of gasoline, horse or donkey power was used to get us around in anything from a wagon to a car with the engine removed. The driver sat on the top of the car, his feet swinging back and forth in front of the windshield.

One day, with a small Jewish boy for our guide, we made the mistake of going on a tour of the marketplace. The Arabs were furious, pointing out that we had a Jew for a guide. They screamed all kinds of unknown words to us and at the poor kid. They then told us he was stupid and did not know anything about Marrakech. It reached the point that I was afraid that if we did not get our young guide out of the marketplace, he would be chased out and perhaps killed. It was my first experience of the hatred between the Arabs and Jews. We went back to the hotel and paid him off for his help. It was sad. Here we were, going to war, as we thought, to make a better world, yet at this moment in Marrakech a young Jewish boy was being treated as if he were a pariah, and there was little we could do.

The marketplace was a combination of small stalls and open displays placed on a blanket on the ground. The displays of food were colorful, but the flies made you appreciate how much more careful we were at home. Some of the streets were very narrow, with stalls on each side while branches crossing overhead provided some shelter. What bothered me was the filth around the shops and in the street. Human excrement was in the gutters and children were urinating whenever and wherever they wanted to. Filthy beggars with tin cups were everywhere. The stench was overwhelming.

While in the market, if you stopped to look at something the Arabs surrounded you and tried to sell whatever they had. You had to be prepared to bargain about the quality and the price. If I wanted something, I soon learned to bargain and walk a few steps away. The price would drop, and if I really wanted it, we had a deal. Sometimes the whole family of the shop owner would get into the act. I did buy several silver bracelets from a shop that was making them out of thin sheets of silver and molding them into what I thought was a beautiful design. I'm sure I was taken with each purchase, but it was fun at the time and what the heck, I was on my way to combat.

The replacement depot finally gave us orders to go to England as one of the first replacement crews in the 8th Air Force. We were scheduled to take off from Marrakech at 1:00 a.m. on April 11. All the crew arrived on schedule except Sergeant Maynard, our engineer. We sent Sergeants Allen and Klein back to his barracks, but Maynard was not there. We had no choice but to take off without him, so our actual takeoff took place at 01:55 a.m. Sergeant Klein served as the engineer in Maynard's place.

After takeoff, we headed west over the ocean for many miles before turning north toward England. This course put us out of range of the German fighters stationed in France. It was a long flight. We finally landed in England at 10:50 a.m. in a rainstorm. Our navigator, Walt Haynes, told us afterwards of his incredible joy and relief when we arrived.

The trip had taken us seventeen days, from our departure at Morrison Field, Florida on March 25, 1943, to our arrival at St. Ives, England, on April 11. The total flying time was 60 hours and 10 minutes.

CHAPTER 12

ENGLAND AT LAST

Up to this time, we had thought we would keep the same airplane for our combat missions. We were disappointed that, instead, "our" plane became one of many to be distributed to different groups that needed replacement aircraft. We had become very attached to this B-17, Tail Number 42-5406. I have often wondered what group received our B-17 and if it survived the war.

My first trip to London

Our home base would be Alconbury, but from St. Ives we went to Bovingdon Air Station in south central England for final training. We were not pleased with the assignment to Bovingdon, but we were only there for a couple of weeks. We had been training for combat from October 1942 to March 1943. Our confidence in surviving combat was unlimited. Later, when exposed to incoming German fighters, flak, and 20mm projectiles exploding into our plane, our inflated confidence quickly evaporated and fear became a great motivator. We were told at the first meeting at Bovingdon that, even with the additional training we would receive, we only had a 50 percent chance of surviving the 25 required missions. With this encouragement, we thought we should at least see London once.

The trip from Bovingdon to London took less than an hour on the train. Upon arriving at Paddington Station, we found that we were among many American servicemen, all looking for a place to stay. We took a taxi to Columbia House (a hotel that the British government had taken over and made available to American servicemen), where we got a very simple but clean room. As I recall, the W.C. was down the hall, but no one was complaining.

Columbia House was very close to Marble Arch and across the street from Hyde Park. Dick Ezzard and I walked around London, sightseeing and taking in places like St. Paul's Cathedral, the Parliament building, Westminster Abbey, and various stores. Of course we saw the damage to buildings by the German bombing raids. Up to this time, I had no idea as to the extent of the damage that could be done with bombs. I had seen the movies showing London aflame, but, like so many things, the actual sight of the damage was incredible and extremely depressing. So far, we had only dropped blue 100-pound practice bombs filled with sand on some target in the sagebrush-covered lands of Wyoming.

Simpson's-in-the-Strand and an air raid

Dick and I went to Simpson's-in-the-Strand for dinner that night. What a beautiful setting. It was so formal. White tablecloths, more silver and crystal at each place setting than I had ever seen before, and waiters standing around watching every move we made. We did not know that we were expected to tip the special waiter, the carver who served the meat course, and so did not understand why he stood around waiting and watching us while we enjoyed our meal. We did know enough to tip on the total bill.

It was dark when we left Simpson's, and we were in the Piccadilly Circus area when the air-raid sirens went off. Here we were, our first night in London and we were caught in an air raid. It was interesting how fast the streets cleared. As Dick and I continued down the street, a white-hatted British air raid warden told us we had to get off the street. We didn't know where to go, so he encouraged us to follow him down some steps. As we were in uniform, he must have felt free to take us into a control center, where we watched many people moving small planes on a large table. We were watching the German air raid in progress and the defense the RAF was making.

We did not hear any bombs going off while we were in the shelter, and after about an hour, the all-clear signal was given and we were permitted to go upstairs to the streets. We decided that it was best to go back to the Columbia House for the rest of the night.

Upon entering the hotel, who did we run into but Major Crimmins, with whom Dick had served in the Pacific and I had met in Salina, Kansas. Crimmins had been on a raid the day before and told us he was most impressed with the Luftwaffe and the defense it was putting up. In fact, he said he had never seen anything like it in the Pacific.

We inquired the next day about damage from the raid and asked if we could go see what the Germans had done. It was made very clear that in no way were we to add to problems by being on the East Side of town where the bombing had taken place, so we stayed away.

The other officers on the crew did not want to go, but Dick and I were able to get tickets to the symphony that was to be held that afternoon in the Royal Albert Hall. It was interesting that even during the war, the British carried on social and cultural events under very trying conditions. Royal Albert Hall had not been damaged as far as we could tell, and it was beautiful. The royal box was on the first level above the main floor, very close to the stage. Everyone in the audience continued to look toward the box to see if some royalty would occupy it. But no one used the box at this concert.

Sir Adrian Boult was conducting, and how I wish I had saved the program. I do remember that the last piece played that afternoon was "God Save the King." Years later, I was able to contact Ms. Jacky Cowdrey via a friend in England who gave me Ms. Cowdrey's email address. She was at that time the archivist for the Royal Albert Hall. She sent me the program for the evening, which featured the London Philharmonic Orchestra conducted by Sir Adrian Boult, with piano soloist Leff Pouishnoff. The music was as follows:

Prince Igor (Borodin)
Suite for Swan Lake (Tchaikovsky)
Concerto in F minor, Op. 22 (Glazounov, with solo by Pouishnoff)
Symphony No. 5 in E minor (Tchaikovsky)

During the next 14 months, I was able to get back to London several times, but never was I as impressed as I was during my first visit there.

CHAPTER 13

ESCAPE AND EVASION TRAINING

While we thought we were prepared for combat, it was clear that Germany had some fundamental advantages. The defender gains the advantage of odds. German fighters were over their own territory, so they could refuel and rearm quickly and return to the attack. German pilots, if they were shot down unharmed, were safe; Allied pilots became prisoners of war. Also, German gunners on the ground had access to unlimited supplies of ammunition. When a raid was over, they could rest. German radar sets could pick up Allied bombers at great distances, including the sound of a radio being tested on a runway before a raid.

Allied bombers had to fight their way to the target and then fight their way home after dropping their bombs. They faced bad weather and landing crashes because of tired crews and damaged aircraft.

Flak and formation flying

We were told that, because of formation flying, there was nothing we could do about the flak. We could see it, but we couldn't take evasive action because above all, we had to keep the "integrity" of the formation. This was essential to our survival against fighter attacks by Luftwaffe pilots who, we were told, were very experienced and daring, which we soon enough came to find out was true. They would dart and weave through a formation to isolate a bomber so they could better attack it. They would come barreling in, swooping in from 12 o'clock high and blast fire into the flight deck, killing the pilot and co-pilot. All we could do against the flak was endure it. Our only recourse to avoid it was to fly and bomb from a greater height. The problem with that approach was that we had trained at about 16,000 feet. We were taught that if the bombardier couldn't hit the target at that height, just fly lower. But once we started flying missions over Germany, we found that to avoid flak we had to fly at 25,000 feet, where the temperature was minus 40—too high to see the target and too cold to avoid frostbite. But I'm getting ahead of myself.

While we were at Bovingdon Air Station Replacement Center, we were given a briefing about escape and evasion. This briefing was part of the indoctrination program to prepare crews in case they were un-lucky enough to be shot down on one of the raids. A British army major, wearing what we called an Eisenhower jacket, had spent some time in France evading the Germans, and he told us some of the things we should do. He started his briefing by asking for a show of hands of how many spoke German and then asked the same question regarding French. Very few hands were raised. He said "typical Americans! You have just reduced your chance of escaping by 75 percent by not knowing the language of the people you will be flying over."

If we were shot down over Germany, our chances of not being caught were very slim, but that we should try anyway. Depending on what part of Germany we were over would impact our decisions and our actions. If we were in the Berlin area and could not keep up with the formation because of battle damage, we were to head for Sweden, but we could count on German fighters attacking until we were over Swedish territory. Our chances of sur-vival were a lot better if we bailed out over Germany rather than over the Baltic Sea. The water was so cold that we could die in a matter of minutes in the Baltic. If over southern Germany, say near Munich, we could consid-er trying to get to Switzerland. But here again, German fighters would be attacking until the last minute. If we bailed out near Switzerland, we were to work our way south, making sure we were in Switzerland before talking to anyone. But the countryside all looks the same.

Keep calm and carry on

If our plane was shot up, we should try to head for France. Our chances of survival and escape were much better there. Aside from the most of the people being sympathetic, the French were better organized with their underground efforts than any other nation in Europe.

We found out that one of the most difficult things to do was to keep calm. Of course since this was a lecture, most of this advice fell on deaf ears. We would have to experience combat to fully understand the importance of these words. If we were in a difficult position, we could improve our chances of making contact with the right people if we remained calm. The shock of being shot down, bailing out, and surviving the landing would be very traumatic. We were to get our bearings and hope that our navigator had given us some indication where we might be before bailing out. As a general rule, we should head south.

Depending on where we were, we should travel at night and trust no one until we had observed them for a while or they had approached us. The French would know if a plane had crashed nearby or if aircrews had bailed out over their countryside. The French had to be very careful, but many of them would help crewmembers escape.

The first thing we were to do once on the ground was to hide the parachute. We were to dig a hole with whatever we had and get rid of the chute. It was important to try to remember where we had buried it, because the French would go back and get it. Another thing we were to do was cover our shoes with mud. All American shoes were easy to identify because they were different than the French or German ones, and this covering of mud might help avoid detection.

If possible, we were to move away from the area where we landed as quickly as possible. Forests were not always the best place to escape to since, in all probability, the forest would be the first place the Germans would look. We were to leave as few tracks as possible and to use hedges to our advantage. If we got into a building, we were to be sure there was more than one way out. While it might not always be possible, we were to put ourselves in a position to observe the people around us or those entering or leaving a facility or area at all times.

We learned to identify the Big Dipper constellation at night to give some indication of direction. Everyone was to have a compass in his pocket or in the escape kit attached to his parachute. We carried different kinds of compasses. There was the regular compass which was approximately 2 inches in diameter and could fit into one's pocket. Then there were two buttons that, when one was placed on the other, there was a small pin in the center, which turned out to be a compass. The smallest compass was less than a quarter of an inch in diameter and could be hidden in many places on one's body or clothing. (I still have all three of these compasses.)

We were to stay away from cities until we had been picked up by the underground. It would then be the underground's responsibility to help us around or through the city. If we had any rations, we were to stretch them out for as long as we could. We should drink water or eat snow as it was very important to keep liquids going into one's body. We were told not to eat in public places because American eating habits were different than Europeans' and would be noticed by anyone who was interested in strangers. For example, we used our knife and fork as separate tools while most other people in the world used them together for getting food on the fork.

Even if we had a weapon, we were told, we should not try to shoot it out with the Germans. We would lose. We could use the weapon to obtain food, but we still would have to be careful when we used it so as not to attract attention.

Prior to going on our first mission, we had some photos taken in civilian attire. They were to be the size that could be used on the identification papers that are required throughout Europe. We had several different pictures with different coats and shirts so the people who made up our new identification papers would have one to meet the needs of the time. I still have several pictures that were taken for the purpose of making identification papers. Fortunately, I never had to use them.

After a question-and-answer period, the British major left with nothing more to say than "good luck." We all left with a better understanding of the problems of escape and evasion, as well as a hollow feeling in our stomachs.

I think people often forget how young we were during this time. I was commissioned at 19 and flew my 25 missions in combat at 21 and 22. We grew up in a hurry. We didn't have any other options.

CHAPTER 14

MOUNTING A MISSION

Mounting a mission was a complicated undertaking that took hours of preparation before we could actually take off in our Forts. Once a mission alert had been posted, the ground crews spent the night checking and testing the planes, everything from the radios to replenishing the oxygen bottles, topping off the fuel tanks, and checking the cameras for strike photos. The ordnance and chemical crew who handled the explosives and incendiary bombs began loading before dawn. Then the ammunition was put aboard and the turret gunners checked that they had enough. (Their attitude was: You could never have enough ammunition.) As a member of the combat crew, I was awakened and served a hearty breakfast following the mission's briefing. Trucks carried us to the plane and each of us made last-minute checks. The navigator studied the routes, the bombardiers their targets, the gunners their weapons, and the pilots their position in the formation and any special issues having to do with the mission.

After all this preparation, many of the missions were cancelled—or "scrubbed"—because of weather, mostly. This didn't improve morale one bit, because it meant we couldn't fly one of our 25 missions after all the anxiety and preparation. Everything had to be done in reverse, bombs, guns, cameras all had to be removed and the fuel drawn off the bomber. Often, only a few hours later, the mission would be deemed a "go" and the whole ritual would begin again.

Other major challenges were the weather and the cold. Dampness permeated the aircraft and then turned to ice at 15,000 feet. When I was flying in 1943 and 1944, the congealed oil, due to freezing temperatures, caused the machine parts to break down. At 25,000 feet, bomb-bay doors wouldn't open, trimming tabs stuck, superchargers wouldn't work, landing lights burned out, glass covers cracked, and our oxygen masks became stiff with ice. The crewmembers wearing electrically heated suits and shoes soon found that these garments were not adequate by a long shot and they were always being sent home with frostbitten feet.

Joining the 92nd Bomb Group

After training at Bovingdon, we traveled as a crew to Alconbury by train where we were assigned to the 92nd Bomb Group, a premier unit. It was early May when we arrived. Our first living accommodations were half-round buildings made of tin, officers in one and enlisted in another. There was an enlisted orderly assigned to keep our quarters organized and clean. Our B-17 crew had spent many hours preparing for our first raid, but down deep in our hearts, we had hoped it would never come. While our crew was trained as well as any of the other crews, in retrospect, training prepared you to react but did not prepare you for the mental challenges that accompanied going into combat. We had talked to crews that had been on missions and we had read accounts of different crews who returned from missions, and so we had some idea of what to expect. But there was no substitute for the experience itself.

The experience of combat in the air war

I have been asked if the movies about World War II reflect the true air war. My answer is always that movies most of the time romance the war and do not reflect its horrors. For every person killed, there were probably nine wounded. There were terrible results: arms or legs blown off; gut wounds with entrails falling out; loss of sight because of head wounds. Every member of every combat crew was at risk of projectiles tearing the body apart.

Unique to flying bombers over enemy territory was the problem of attempting to care for the injured at 30,000 feet while under enemy attack. We had limited first-aid training. In fact, I was better prepared than most because of my Boy Scout training in first aid. We could not call for a medic for assistance. You felt so helpless. The crew had to manage the situation the best way they could, sometimes at minus 30 degrees. The cold did stop the bleeding in some cases. A fellow crewmember would attempt to care for the injured if the air battles permitted. As hard a decision as it was, saving the other crewmembers had priority. The emotional trauma of returning with your friends injured was beyond belief.

The first aid kits provided little if any help with major wounds. One of the most discouraging events was opening the first aid kit to find that someone had taken the morphine out for their personal use. This problem became so prevalent that a medical technician would remove the first aid kits from the planes and then replace them just before the raid. Morphine would be given to an injured crewman just to relieve his pain until we got home. Once home, removing the injured from the plane after hours of flight, completely exhausted, became heart-rending.

The firing of the red flare on final approach that notified people on the ground that you had injured aboard specifically alerted the medics, the ground crews, the ambulance drivers and all of the people who had been counting the planes that returned from the mission.

Perhaps the most upsetting was the smell of death and of the wounds. The dirt, sweat and blood; the cordite from the guns; the excrements from the body; and the clothing soaked in fuel from the plane all combined to make a sickening odor. Movies cannot possibly reflect that reality of war. A true picture of the human cost of war can only be appreciated by the many white crosses at the graveyards, at the military hospitals, and the knock on the door that brought the message that a loved one had been killed.

I was scared on all of the combat missions I flew, scared that I would not get back to home base; scared of the flak; scared of the fighters that fired 20mm cannon shells that seemed to walk towards you as they exploded; scared that I would not be able to bail out because of centrifugal force as the plane spiraled toward the ground; scared of fire in the plane with the potential of blowing us up; scared of being injured, and of dying. And most of all, once I was a pilot, afraid I wouldn't be able to get my plane and crew home in one piece.

According to the official historians, from May 1942 to July 1945 the 8th Air Force planned and executed America's daylight strategic bombing campaign. It suffered forty percent of the Army Air Force's World War II casualties: 47,483 out of 115,332, including more than 26,000 dead.

I was lucky. I survived. Many of my friends did not.

Our gear

The gunners wore blue electric "heat suits" under their overalls, but the pilot and co-pilot wore only our flight uniforms because we had hot air coming in from the floor of the cockpit. We also needed more flexibility to move around, from flying the plane to adjusting the super chargers and throttles. Other than in the cockpit there was no heat in the fuselage. The gunners had to have the windows open for their gun placements which meant the temperature could dip to forty below at the high altitudes in the main area of the plane. I started with "long johns," heavy underwear and then over that, the uniform of the day. The pants were called "pinks" because they were light grayish pink. Our jacket was a dark brown flight jacket made of leather with sheep's wool on the inside to add warmth. It was designed with a big collar that you could zip up to keep your neck warm, although some pilots sported scarves as well. I wore heavy gray wool socks inside my boots, which were made of the same leather as my jacket, lined with sheep's wool and with rubber soles.

I never wore a flak jacket as a co-pilot maybe because when we were being issued uniforms for those early missions Command thought we were immune to flak. After a couple of missions crews quickly learned that flak could penetrate any part of a Fort but it wasn't until after I'd completed my missions halfway through '44 that flak jackets were issued to all the crew members. I had a leather cap insulated with wool and earflaps. Our oxygen masks fit over our nose and mouth, buckled under our chin and were mandatory over 10,000 feet. I wore silk gloves that fit inside my leather gloves, which were made of a finer more flexible quality of leather than my jacket so I could manage the instruments. The gunners wore leather mittens with the trigger finger separate. Lloyd and I wore our parachutes on our backs, but the crew wore chest chutes because they had to be able to move around. My headset (ear phones and a mouth piece) fit over the leather cap.

We normally did not carry a weapon. I turned in my Colt .45 semi-automatic along with the two clips I'd been issued when we traveled over to England, to the Armaments officer. We were briefed that it was insane to try to shoot it out with the Germans if we were ever captured.

CHAPTER 15

PREPARATION

We were scheduled to fly our maiden combat mission on May 15 to Wangerooge Isle, off the coast of Germany, but unfortunately our first mission fizzled in one of the worst possible ways. Nevertheless, it may be instructive to describe the degree of preparation involved for each combat flight.

The briefing room

Before an upcoming raid, a list of the crews placed on alert was posted in the squadron operations office. It was then the pilot's responsibility to alert the rest of his crew. But in most cases, word spread throughout the organization in a matter of minutes. If a mission was scheduled for a morning takeoff, a sergeant came around and pounded on the door of your quarters and said it was time to get going. It would usually be around 2:00 a.m. when the pounding started. I always dreaded that knock on the door. After a special mission breakfast of fried eggs, bacon, toast, and a lot of strong coffee, the crew retrieved our equipment from the lockers, the gunners checked their electric cords in the heated suits, and the carbon dioxide capsule in their Mae West life vest. Temperatures in the B-17 could drop to as low as minus 40 degrees, so cold that your eyelashes froze. We next entered the briefing room, where we all waited for the final word as to where we would be going and where in the formation we would be flying. There were a lot of different formation patterns during that early phase of the war, a sort of trial-and-error process to see which ones gave the most accurate bomb drops and provided the best defense against German fighters. From planes flying in trail formation in a straight line led by a single plane, a standard eighteen-plane formation was adopted by the time we were flying. That meant there was a lead squadron, a high squadron to the right, and a low squadron 200 feet below to the left. Three groups made up a combat wing of 54 planes. A division was made up of a number of combat wings, depending on how many planes were available at any one time.

By far the most dangerous position in any formation was the outside plane in the low squadron, known as "Tail-end Charlie," because that plane was exposed to the maximum amount of flak as well as being an easy target for fighter planes to pick off.

A large map of Europe and England had been glued to the wall and was always covered with black drapes except when a pre-flight briefing was to take place. This added to the suspense of where the target was. Of course, we all were concerned about a raid deep into Germany, where we knew we would be exposed to prolonged flak and fighter attacks. Before the flight path was revealed, the crews put up a front of confidence and at the same time tried to guess where the target might be. Nervous tension ran high.

We had to wait for the group commander, Lieutenant Colonel Bascomb Lawrence, to arrive. After we were told to "carry on," the briefing of the day started by the black drapes being pulled back. Our tension would increase with each foot that the drapes opened. On this occasion, there was a sigh of relief when the target was revealed. It was not Germany. The colored yarn showed us leaving the coast of England and going to Holland. The operations officer started his briefing, standing beside the map with a very long pointer, telling us what our target was and pointing out the assembly areas for the different groups.

Since we were a composite group (made up of different B-17 organizations that could not by themselves field a full flight of planes), we had to assemble with other planes and watch for a particular flare that would identify the leader we were to join. Dark areas on the map were reported concentrations of antiaircraft batteries. Our route was mostly over water after leaving England. We were told to expect flak over the target, but I came to learn that operations people always understated how much flak would be encountered. In later raids, many of us felt that the antiaircraft guns shown on the map had been adjusted to avoid the route in and out of the target area. Or maybe our intelligence was not the best about the German gun placements.

The colored yarn showed the IP (Initial Point), where our bomb run would start. A yarn of a different color showed our route home. It all looked so nice and clean on the map.

A very short briefing by the weather officer, followed by one from the intelligence officer regarding the importance of the target, completed the process. He showed us a chart giving the time to start the engines, the taxi sequence, the take-off time, and the altitude we would be flying during the mission, and most important of all, the formation plan.

When I saw the chart, my heart started pumping faster. It was bad enough to be going on the raid, but our crew (Eves') was to be in the low squadron, in the last element and on the outside of the formation. This position was the most exposed place for fighter attacks and, being lower, for more flak. All of a sudden, I had a very tight feeling in my stomach. I said a silent prayer as a vision of all the things that could happen became very real.

A humiliating takeoff

On the May 15 mission, 10 planes, of which we were one, were scheduled from the 92nd Bomb Group. We would be the last of the planes to taxi out and take off. After hacking (synchronizing) our watches, the navigators (Walt Haynes represented our crew) were instructed to stay and get more detailed information on the routing of the mission, including where we would pick up the other planes in our composite group. With this final word, the commanding officer said "Good luck," and walked out, the signal we should be on our way to our plane.

Crews normally stayed together during these briefings and, as they walked to the trucks that would take them to pick up chutes and oxygen masks, all kinds of comments would be heard. For example: "If you believe there will be little flak, then you have holes in your head and the Germans put them there," or "The S.O.B. who picked the I.P. has never been on a raid."

At the personnel equipment shop, we picked up our chutes (mine was number 13) and checked to see that the pins holding the chute in the canvas bag were in place. (An open chute in the plane would cause many problems and greatly reduce the chance of success if you had to bail out.) The oxygen masks had been cleaned and, here again, you wanted to check them out to make sure the valves were clear. Once we were back on the trucks and our plane came into view, we knew our first mission was about to take place.

We were normally assigned to a plane maintained by the same four enlisted men. It was interesting how attached to each other the maintenance crew and the flying crew became. The maintenance crew helped us off the truck and did as much as they could to relieve our tension. By now they knew where we were going, and showed concern. When I became a first pilot, I always made it a point to be very considerate of the ground crew. In my mind, they were the unsung heroes of the air battle. When a plane came back from a mission, they would work around the clock to get it back in commission. Their changing of engines, repair of battle damage, and continual checking of every system that might impact the operation of the plane made it possible for the flight crew to fly the next mission. And, unlike us, they also knew they had to stay until the war was over.

Once the chutes were aboard the plane, each flight crewman had his responsibilities. The gunners checked the ammunition to ensure that it was in the right place to feed the guns when needed. They also dry-fired the guns (no ammo in the chamber) to be sure they were working right, and at the same time checked for too much oil, which could freeze at the low temperatures (minus 60 degrees inside the plane) of high altitude. Shorty Cromack, our tail gunner, always wanted more ammunition than was authorized. Somehow, he found room for more on this raid. Of course our radioman, Sergeant John Allen, spent his time checking out his radio and setting the right frequencies for the raid.

The bombardier, Ray Hatfield, checked the bombs in the bomb bay to ensure that each was hung properly from its shackle so that it would release at the right time. One thing the crew did *not* want to happen was to have an armed bomb hung up in the bomb bay over enemy territory. If that happened, it was the bombardier's responsibility to crawl back into the open bomb bay and work the bomb loose. This was not an easy job at high altitude; it would be beyond freezing, and he would have to be on a portable oxygen bottle, which would restrict his movements. He would stand on a 10-inch rail looking down into many thousands of feet of open space, working with the bomb until it fell clear.

Lloyd Eves and I walked around the plane to check such things as the control surfaces and flaps, make sure the fuel tanks were filled, check that the struts on each landing gear were about the same length, and we examined the superchargers on each engine to insure that they were all in good shape. The supercharger made it possible to fly at high altitudes by compressing the air to get sufficient oxygen to the engine so that it would run. This was a critical check. The supercharger was made up of many fins called buckets, and if one of the buckets was cracked or broken when you brought the supercharger on, it could come apart. Each bucket would be like a projectile hitting the other engines and the plane. Normally the crew chief was with the pilot and co-pilot during the walk-around.

By the time Walt Haynes arrived at the plane with his maps and the detailed flight plan, the rest of the crew had carried out its pre-flight responsibilities. The maps we used were provided by the Royal Air Force and were much more detailed than ours. Beginning with this first mission, Walt gave us a short briefing on what changes had been made in the routing. If Walt told us to fly 039 degrees, we attempted to fly 039 degrees. We never questioned his guidance.

Once aboard the plane, everyone had additional checking to perform. The most important check was the intercommunication system. Each crewmember had to be able to speak to the others. Survival could depend on getting information to all the crew. Oxygen systems were also checked to be sure each crewmember would be getting oxygen above 10,000 feet.

Checks completed, all we had to do was wait for a colored flare to be fired from the control tower, the signal to start the engines. Lloyd and I got all four going, one after the other. Now we had to wait for the other planes to taxi towards the runway. Since our position in the formation was in the low end, outside the formation, we were last to fall behind the other B-17s getting in position for takeoff.

In the process of taxiing out from the hardstand where our B-17 had been parked, a tight turn was required. The right wheel of the plane went off the taxiway and got stuck in the mud. We lowered flaps and tried to work the plane out of the mud, but the more we tried the deeper the wheel sank in. As the number-four propeller was getting very close to the ground, we decided to stop all the engines.

When the crew got out of the plane, we were met by many experts, none of them scheduled for the raid. The operations people wanted us to take a stand-by airplane, but it had a different type of oxygen system, and in all likelihood we would not have been able to catch up with the other planes, now long gone on the mission. The ground crew was less than happy with us because they had to unload the fuel and then place large bags under the right wing that would be filled with air to lift the plane from the mud. It was not until the plane was again on the hardstand that the bombs could be removed. This was not a very good start for the new Eves crew, and we were exposed to considerable criticism and ridicule.

On May 16, we learned that we would be flying on another mission on the 17th.

CHAPTER 16

MISSION ONE—LORIENT SUBMARINE BASE

May 17, 1943, 92nd Bomb Group—5:30 hours flying total—118 bombers over targets, 6 planes lost, 0 escorts.

This time we stayed on the taxiway and waited for a flare from the control tower to signal the lead plane to make its takeoff.

Our takeoff was normal. We then followed Walt Haynes's directions to rendezvous with the other planes that would make up our combat group. In time we spotted another small group of B-17s. A flare was fired, which indicated they were the planes we were to join on the raid. It was here that two of the planes from our group aborted the mission and returned to Alconbury. Somehow we did not move up in the formation and were still stuck out in the most vulnerable position—Tail-end Charlie.

I am pretty certain we were assigned the Tail-end Charlie position because of getting stuck in the mud two days before. We had screwed up and everyone knew it. Flying my first mission as the most vulnerable plane in the formation, easy pickings for Jerry, was not a great start, and to say I was nervous was an understatement. Plus, while we'd had some training in formation flying, this was the first time we were flying in a combat situation with a large number of planes and no escorts.

I did most of the flying since the plane we were in formation with was on our right and it was easier for the co-pilot to fly from that position. We flew off the left wing of another B 17. Flying formation demanded close attention and was extremely hard work. You had to continually adjust the throttles and fly the plane to maintain your position. Prop wash—turbulence—from other B-17s ahead of us bounced our plane around, making our flying even more difficult.

Keeping the formation tight insured some protection from fighters because of the concentrated firepower from all the guns in the formation. I always underestimated the strain of concentration hour after hour combined with the rush of fear and nervous energy the entire crew felt in combat.

We flew tight formations because it was the best defense against German fighters. Our wings almost touched the wings of the bombers to our right and left. The theory was, tight formations kept the Germans from picking off a bomber because they faced concentrated fire from the entire squadron. When Jerry attacked a group of bombers he had 75 machine guns aimed at him from 38 turrets. Another reason we flew as we did was to keep a tight bomb pattern. Each bombardier dropped his bombs when he saw the lead plane's bombardier drop his. The myth was that, thanks to the Norden bombsight, our bombardiers "could drop a bomb in a pickle barrel from 30,000 feet." But while everyone boasted that was true, it wasn't by a long shot. During my early missions I have no idea how often we hit the target but it wasn't often.

Combat!

We climbed to our assigned altitude by making wide turns and at the same time maneuvered into place with the other B-17s going on the mission. As we left England, we must have been at an altitude of about 26,000 feet. Once over the Channel, the gunners were told to test-fire their guns, this time with ammunition. The guns in the top turret fired about 18 inches above the heads of the pilot and co-pilot; I never got used to the noise from those "twin fifties."

On my first mission I discovered another challenge that I hadn't foreseen. From the ground looking up, our planes appeared as though they were flying smoothly, just cruising along. But in the cockpit we were bounced around like crazy. There was a 10-inch-wide ramp over the bomb bays that ran from the radio room to the engineer's position through the fuselage that the crew had to walk like a tightrope in the wind when we were in combat. The air was very unstable because of all the "prop wash" from the planes ahead of us and above and below, so making the journey was often dicey. Plus every time flak hit the plane it would rock back and forth. During these first missions we lost a number of planes because of mid air collisions with our own guys. The plane ahead of me would overrun our formation and I'd follow, then I'd get back into formation and hit prop wash and fall out, then get back in. During those early missions before we were leading formations as the Pathfinder there were times when the nose of my plane would miss the tail of the one ahead of me by two or three feet. It took every ounce of concentration and focus to keep in position with the sky filled with tracers, 20mm exploding cannon shells from Jerry, falling fighters and burning, crippled Forts. When we landed, I climbed out of the cockpit and for the first time since takeoff relaxed my muscles. I remember Shorty Cormak, after looking at the holes in the fuselage, wisecracking: "Gadzooks! Those Jerries used live ammunition."

It was a beautiful, clear day and it was not long before we could see the coast of France. Ray Hatfield had the best view of the area. He was sitting up in the nose of the plane behind the Perspex nose. He kept the rest of us informed about what was coming up and of course watched for German fighters. I do not recall any reports of German fighters until we got over France. It was about that same time that someone on the crew reported flak exploding in the area of the formation. I was so busy flying formation that I did not see much of anything except the other B-17s.

Walt announced over the intercom that we should be coming up on the IP and should prepare to start our bomb run. At this point, the bombardier would take over with his Norden bombsight. It was the pilot's job to follow the instruments reflecting directions that would put the plane in position to drop its bombs on the target. Ray opened the bomb-bay doors and, when the cross hairs on the bombsight met, the bombs would be on their way to the submarine pens in Lorient (this procedure was later changed so that the bombs were released when the lead plane released its bombs). Flak began to show up all around us. Flak was most concentrated around cities, and we *always* encountered flak on our raids. These exploding 88mm and 105mm shells filled the sky with hot metal that could cut through an airplane in a second and wound or kill an airman. You couldn't see the metal fragments in the sky until they hit your plane even though you could see them down below exploding upward as large puffs of black smoke.

The formation was rather loose following the bomb run. All of a sudden, someone called out over the intercom that a B-17 was on fire and going down. "Watch for chutes," was the next thing we heard on the intercom, but none was reported. Another crew of ten men killed in action.

We were still within range of the German fighters over the water when I noticed that the plane we were flying next to in the formation was falling behind the rest. They were having problems and starting to lose altitude. Lloyd and I discussed what action we should take and decided to catch up with the rest of the formation. This was much easier said than done. With all the power we could get out of the engines, we only very slowly closed the gap between us. When Ray Hatfield called out that he could see the coast of England, we all felt great relief.

Usually Royal Air Force Spitfire fighters came out to escort us back over land, but they had such a short range that they could only help a short distance from the shore. Within their range, however, they were a welcome sight to the battle-damaged stragglers who lagged behind. Finally, after arriving over England, our group formation broke up and we all headed for our home bases. The crew on our plane could not have been happier.

Lloyd landed the plane and taxied it back to the hardstand where we were met by the ground crew. We had been in the air five hours and ten minutes. It seemed much longer than that. The ground crewmen were just as happy to see us return as we were to be back. As they helped us out of the plane, it was discovered that we had some flak damage, but nothing critical. The flight crew was jubilant; we were pounding each other on the back. We had made our first mission and were back at Alconbury with no one hurt. The last to leave the plane, our Ball Turrent Gunner stumbled to the ground, then slowly unwound himself from the crouched position he'd had to maintain for the entire flight.

The ball turret gunner's position was by far the least comfortable. The ball turret was a steel ball with small windows on the side and between the gunner's legs. It was suspended from inside the fuselage so the gunner couldn't be in it for take offs and landings. Once we were in the air, the gunner would climb down into it and curl into a ball. There was no room for a parachute. There were two 50 caliber machine guns along the sides of his legs that could shoot 800 rounds a minute. Electrical motors powered the turret in a circle. But it got cramped in there on a long flight, particularly later on in the war when missions ran eight and nine hours.

We again boarded trucks and dropped off the chutes and oxygen masks on our way to the debriefing. Later on in the war, when we went into the debriefing room, we were given a shot of whiskey, but I don't think we got one after this mission. The debriefing consisted of one of the intelligence officers asking us about the mission, such things as the number of fighters attacking the formation, the amount of flak, the number of B-17s we saw go down, did we see any chutes, did we think we hit the target, the amount of damage to our plane, and anything out of the ordinary that had taken place. This had been our first raid, so we had no way to compare it to any others. As soon as the intelligence officer had filled out his forms, we were released to return to our quarters.

That night at the officers' club drinks flowed very freely. The celebration of just being able to have a drink with your own crew and with the other crews who had made the raid was rewarding. If anything, this raid on Lorient had confirmed to us that if luck was on our side, we could survive. It also made us more conscious of what the dangers of combat could be.

A matter of luck and inches

During the years since WWII, I have seldom talked about the sad part of the war, where you lose friends because of enemy action. I consider myself to be one of the luckiest people on Earth. I survived combat when the 8th Air Force was still in its formative stages, as we were one of the first replacement crews to arrive in England. We came over to England with a cocky, war-winning attitude. Perhaps we were influenced by the media, which presented a somewhat overrated picture of our air successes and understated the ability of the Luftwaffe. Still, for all our confidence, we were aware that the odds of not making it back from a full combat tour were, at this point in the war, no better than fifty-fifty.

The concept that well-armed bombers could fight off enemy fighters was being tested and the results were very questionable. The number of missions expected to be flown by one airman was set on the basis that you had a 50-percent chance of surviving. Twenty-five raids were established as a complete tour at first, but the average number of missions for a crew in early 1943 was actually six. The need for fighter support became more obvious with each raid. On our first, second, fourth, fifth, and sixth missions we had none.

Learning the hard way

Why didn't we have fighter escorts on those first missions since it was so obvious we were losing a huge number of B-17s and B 24s every time we went out? The Eighth Fighter Command started out in 1942 and early 1943 with fighters with small fuel tanks. The philosophy was that they were there to protect the bases in southern England and to fight in defense of our facilities on the ground. The doctrine was that there was no need for range-enhancing improvements such as auxiliary fuel tanks.

This doctrine was much like the RAF's, whose Spitfires could barely reach the Dutch Coast. This was a main reason that the British Vickers Wellington, the twin-engine bomber and the only British made bomber manufactured during the entire war, flew night raids to evade the German fighter planes as much as possible. When I first started flying missions, I felt lucky to be greeted by Spitfires halfway across the North Sea with the coast of England almost in sight. We'd come in over the Channel grey-faced and blue-fingered with German fighters just lining up for the kill and hear someone over the intercom yell, "The Spits! They're here!" and those Jerry vultures would turn tail for home. Trouble was, that in those early days when our fighters tried to engage the German Luftwaffe, they had little success. Fighter Command ran sweeps that Jerry simply ignored. Our individual fighters weren't going to do the damage against the Germans in the air that our bombers had the potential to do to their war machine on the ground; however, our bombers were easy targets. Basically the German fighters got real smart real fast and realized it wasn't worth engaging an enemy fighter plane when they could save their resources and take out B-17s during those bomber streams of 1942 and early '43.

This strategy was reinforced by the Eighth Bomber Command who believed that the B-17 and B-24 could always get through a mission because we were flying self-defending planes. All those machine guns had a purpose, and with so much firepower our Flying Fortresses wouldn't need fighters to escort them. When I think back on this philosophy I am yet again struck by how lucky I was not to get shot down, since the idea that we could take care of ourselves was tragically proven wrong with every mission during those early months of '43. The policy of having no escorts on our early missions cost us thousands of lives. Another myth was about the number of German fighter planes "shot down." It was highly exaggerated. This wasn't anyone's fault. Often one or two German fighters would take on a number of bombers flying in formation and be riddled by dozens of turret gunners, each of whom would then claim the victory. Our command most probably encouraged these hyper-inflated numbers because it kept up our morale and was good public relations back home.

There was one squadron of reconnaissance planes in the Fighter Command, consisting of long-range P-38s (and later on when our missions were deep into Germany, P-51s with drop tanks) which would go in at high altitudes after a mission to determine how successful our bombing actually was. But the true success of a mission was seldom shared with the crews. Better to let them fly their raids believing their targets were being severely hit.

Eventually, as our air war fighting doctrine improved with experience and sophistication, the US Fighter Command started outfitting our fighters with larger fuel tanks, and they would act as escorts to our bombing missions. At first they would meet us on our way home from a raid over the North Sea, but by the end of my missions they were escorting us all the way to the target and back. By then we were also targeting the factories that made the German fighter plane parts, the ball bearings plants for example. Fewer ball bearings factories, fewer fighter planes.

During these early raids, learning by experience was the way of doing things. So many planes aborted due to technical failures that the ordered chain of command often became unstructured. Officers sought enlisted men's opinions on tactical problems as well as equipment breakdowns. Our military manuals seemed completely irrelevant to what was taking place on the ground and in the air.

Wounded

Upon returning from a mission, if you had injured aboard you were to advise the tower of the condition, and as you approached the runway you were to shoot off red flares. The rescue team would attempt to be at your plane's side as soon as you shut down the engines. Even if I did not go on a particular mission, I would rush to the flight line when the group was returning to see who had made it and who was missing. During the first couple of months I was in Alconbury, it was one of those times when I had not gone on the raid that I witnessed an injured friend being removed from the plane. His name was Bosma, a bombardier.

In the early days of the 8th Air Force, each crew bombed the target using the American Norden bombsight. This time the target had been a submarine base in France that was used by the Germans and was highly defended with fighters as well as antiaircraft guns. Over the target, the flak had been very heavy and, as the saying went, "You could almost walk on it." During the bomb run, a bombardier had to concentrate on the target via the Norden bombsight and, in fact, he temporarily had control of the plane.

Shortly before bombs were to be released, a piece of shrapnel from flak somehow came up through the bombsight and entered Bosma's eye. The bombs were released and the navigator attended to Bosma. There was little that could be done. But because the target was on the coast, the pilot let down to a lower altitude as soon as he could and came straight back to Alconbury, our home base.

The rescue crew went aboard the plane and I watched them lower Bosma through the hatchway below the pilot's compartment. He was rushed off to the base hospital, where Major (Doctor) Schumacher made the decision to send him over to the general hospital that was not far away. I talked to the crew and of course they were very upset.

About three weeks later, I hitched a ride in an ambulance to the general hospital to visit Bosma, and what a shock. The impact of combat was brought home to me in a hurry. Just seeing different air crewmen who were able to get back to England and who had been badly injured was sickening. When I found Bosma, it was even a bigger shock. The doctors had removed what was left of the eye and part of his skull, leaving a concave section behind the eye. Bosma's morale was surprisingly good. After we had a short talk, the ambulance was about to leave and I had to go. I never saw Bosma again.

After this experience, I made up my mind that I would never go to a general hospital again unless I had been injured.

CHAPTER 17

MISSIONS TWO AND THREE— THE PICCADILLY PRINCESS

KIEL CANAL, May 19, 1943, 92nd Bomb Group—6:45 hours
flying total—103 bombers over targets, 6 planes lost, 0 escorts.

Two days later, May 19, we prepared for our second mission. By this time we had decided to name our plane "The Piccadilly Princess." A member of our squadron's ground crew had a talent for painting scantily dressed, good-looking women with long legs on the side of planes. Crews came up with names for their planes and he would be asked to interpret.

This time our mission was over Kiel, on the coast of Germany. The target was the turbine engine facility of the submarine-building shipyard. We flew with several other groups and this time we were fortunate enough not be in the Tailend Charlie position. We were awakened again around 3:00 a.m. When we took off there were no clouds and the weather was perfect. The 92nd was the third group to bomb with 250- and 500-pounders.

Bombing the turbine factory would destroy a factory manufacturing a critical component of the German U-boats. We flew in from the south beyond the target, turned around and slashed across German territory, dropped our bombs, and then turned right and retraced our path back over the North Sea. I noticed that on this second mission everyone was grimmer and more businesslike than on the first. Maybe we were pumped up before, it being our first raid and all, and then, having survived it figured there was cause for celebration. But this time the crew was subdued. We'd completed one mission but there were a good many more, twenty-four to be exact, to survive. Even Shorty Cormack, our tail gunner and a real wisecracker wasn't spouting his usual gallows humor. I hadn't gotten used to the top turret gunner test firing his guns and his initial "wham, wham" made me jump half out of my seat. But then, once we achieved some altitude our oxygen kicked in and I gulped in big breaths of the mix and relaxed a little. Still, in my mind, every time I heard firing from our plane, it was a sign that German fighters were trying to shoot us down.

We saw a B 17's engine catch fire and it left the formation. I immediately started scanning the sky for parachutes. Since we were over land and not the North Sea, I figured the crew stood a chance. Doctrine said that the pilot and the co-pilot were the last to leave the plane, like a captain being the last to leave his ship. When a B-17 engine caught fire there was a good chance it would spread to the gasoline tanks and the plane would explode, so if we saw six or seven parachutes but not all ten before it exploded we figured the pilots didn't make it. This time there were no chutes before the explosion. Everyone on our crew was angry and expressed it over the intercom: "Those f---ing Jerries..." and a whole lot worse.

There was a lot of teamwork between the pilot and the bombardier because there was only one set of conditions when a bomb could be released to hit its target, and these had to do with altitude, speed, direction, and so forth. When we were at about 20,000 feet, Ray Hatfield, our bombardier, called out "Bombs away." At this point, Ray's word was law. For pinpoint bombing, Hatfield always used the Norden bombsight, which enabled him to put the target squarely in his sight. As the plane advanced on the target, the crosshairs would move on the Norden and when they crossed, Ray opened the bomb bays and dropped the bombs. As the bombs left the plane, we jerked up due to the decreased weight we carried.

As with our first mission, we had no escorts, and this made the Germans feel like they had open season on us. They attacked us relentlessly—but cautiously—in groups of five or six from about 800 yards, sweeping through our formation, diving, and swinging in and out with their advantage of speed and maneuverability. They kept after us all the way into the English Channel. While our bombing was not as accurate as we advertised on this mission over Kiel, we managed to take out some ships in the harbor, but we also lost six planes with no parachutes seen.

ST. NAZAIRE SUBMARINE BASE, May 29, 1943, 92nd Bomb Group—
6:00 hours flying total—147 bombers over targets, 6 planes lost, 131 escorts.

This was the first mission I had flown where we had escorts. Our group had a total of 22 aircraft flying that day—15 B-17s and 7 YB-40s, armored upgunned B-17s used as a test for possible future escort duties. Two of the bombers and one YB returned early because of engine trouble.

Our target was the St. Nazaire submarine pens in occupied France. The entire formation was led by Major William S. Cowart, flying as air commander with Captain Fred A. Rabo of the 325th Bomb Group as mission lead. After our first two raids, this one seemed a little easier, although there was always the same grinding fear in the pit of my stomach as we crossed the Channel and headed toward the target, knowing that enemy fighters were waiting for our arrival. But this time there were no fighters, literally no fighter opposition anywhere over the targets. What there was was flak. I could see it hitting our planes everywhere I looked. It was so concentrated and accurate both for deflection and height. At first we were taken aback because we couldn't see how all that flak could miss us. Then it started hitting the plane.

As bad as the flak was, it led us directly to the Initial Point. All Walt Haynes had to do was follow the flak right in over the U-boat target pens. The 92nd group dropped a total of 25 tons of bombs, some of which hit the targets. I could see the smoke and flames shooting up to about two thousand feet. In all, just after 5:00 p.m., 147 of our 1st Heavy Bombardment Wing B-17s dropped 277 2,000-pound bombs on what turned out to be the impenetrable fenno-concrete roofs over the U-boat pens. Seven B-17s were lost with all hands, and one crash-landed at sea with nine surviving crewmen. When we returned to Alconbury, the Eves crew noted little damage to the plane and no casualties.

By this time I was chomping at the bit to have my own crew. It hardly mattered that I was just twenty and had only been flying a little over a year. I wanted to be in charge of the action. When I think back, each of us in our own way wanted to contribute the most we were capable of. Time and again, and certainly after this raid, I overheard gunners complaining that the lack of German fighters had been disappointing in that there was nothing to shoot at. But in the end, as a group, we were able to report to our superiors that the mission was successful. We had exacted a high cost on the German U-boats docked in those pens.

The maintenance crew

The maintenance crews were the unsung heroes of the 8th Air Force. They did not qualify for the Air Medal but they did get their hands covered with dirt, blood and grease. They were not subjected to debriefings following a raid, and they didn't share in a shot of whiskey, but they saw the damage to the plane and knew hours of work would be required to get it ready for the next raid. They guided the pilot to the hardstand and put the chocks against the tires. They helped the combat crew on and off the plane, hoping and praying no one was hurt. If one of the crew needed medical attention, they were the first people there to assist in any way they could. They knew they would be assisting crews until the end of the war.

There were just four of them assigned to a plane: the crew chief, his assistant, the engine specialist, and the armament specialist. Other specialists were available for such things as communications and instruments when we needed them, and of course there was the line chief who had overall responsibility for all the planes assigned to the group. Their pride in keeping the planes flying and ready for the next mission went beyond a sense of duty. If it required an all-nighter, so be it.

For the ground crews, the launching of their B-17 was the highlight of the mission until we returned. By the time the war ended, there probably wasn't a member of the ground crew who hadn't experienced the sorrow of their aircraft failing to return from a raid. They never knew the targets, but they could tell the length of the mission by the amount of fuel and ammunition we loaded aboard.

Imagine climbing into a cockpit, as one crew did later in our missions, where the co-pilot had his arm severed over Berlin and for maybe an hour had attempted to take over control of the plane, with blood shooting out in all directions before he died, and having to clean up this horrible mess. The maintenance crew had to treat this as routine, as part of the job, and get the plane ready for the next mission. The impact of death and injuries on the surviving flight crewmembers was devastating, but once on the ground they left as much as they could behind, knowing it would never be the same.

At this point, the ground crew had to take over and begin the process of setting the priorities of repairing the plane. If a projectile had entered the plane through the instrument panel and then hit the co-pilot, it required the removal of the panel and all the connecting wires on all four engines, the altimeter, airspeed indicator, and so on. Hours of essential, painstaking work. The damage to an engine could mean a removal-and-replace, which required finding a new engine. If a new engine was not available, or they couldn't scavenge one off a "hangar queen," the crew would disassemble the damaged engine piece by piece, in an effort to find the problem and repair it.

When it came time to patch the many holes in the plane, again, they had to decide where to start. If it was large enough in a control surface, such as an elevator or rudder, a replacement was installed. Small holes were covered with metal, riveted in place, like a metal band-aid. Just cleaning up all the brass casings from the bullets fired from the guns and left by the gunners was a challenge to make sure they did not jam the controls of the plane. Each member of the maintenance crew considered the plane they were working on as his own.

When I was going on a mission, as a co-pilot on the Eves crew or later on, when I had my own plane, I would always go out to the plane the night before and talk to the maintenance crew, just checking on the condition of the plane and what was left to be corrected. The crew chief and I would go over the Form 1, the record of previous write-ups, and what maintenance had been accomplished. I think he appreciated my concerns, as the rest of the crew did.

Many of us are here today because of their absolute commitment to keeping the planes flying.

Just lucky

On May 27, 1943, I rode my bicycle past the base operations tower to meet with the crew chief. I had just stopped when a tremendous explosion took place behind me. The crew chief kept the bike and me from crashing to the ground. We looked behind us and saw a cloud of smoke where several B-17s were parked. People were running in all directions.

A 500-pound bomb had exploded as it was being loaded into one of the B-17s. This caused several other bombs to explode. Four B-17s were destroyed, 18 men were killed, and 21 were injured. About a minute earlier, I had been within 150 feet of these B-17s. Body parts and airplane parts were found on top of the control tower and some were found behind some of the operational buildings. Eighth Air Force Headquarters canceled the scheduled raids for that day because of this accident.

MISSIONS FOUR AND FIVE— TESTED TO THE LIMITS

WILHELMSHAVEN SUBMARINE YARD, June 11,
1943, 92nd Bomb Group—6:15 hours flying total—
218 bombers over targets, 8 planes lost, no escorts.

Our first June mission was on the 11th on a raid against the submarine construction yard at Wilhelmshaven. This was our fall-back target after we discovered that the primary target, Bremen, was covered by a heavy layer of clouds. As part of 8th Bomber Command's largest mission to date, we had 14 bombers in our group flying, although two turned back early for technical reasons. This raid turned out to be the exact opposite of our previous one over St. Nazaire in that there was almost no flak but a great number of German fighters. We had no escorts. It is surprising, considering the odds, that we lost only 8 planes. This attack was led by Major Brousseau flying with Lt. Shaefer, and all twelve of the 92nd Bomb Groups planes returned safely with little or no damage. But it was still a harrowing raid.

The opposition came on extremely strong from the get-go. German fighters started coming at us over the coast on our way in and they didn't stop until we were about 35 miles out to sea on our return home. They were relentless. Once again positioned in the formation with a plane to my right, I was doing most of the piloting. The B-17's at the front of the formation were hit the hardest. The fighters darted in and out of our formation in pairs and singly from all directions. They were fast and regrouped 800 yards away, so it was difficult for our gunners to do much damage. Occasionally, one of the cockier Germans would execute a barrel roll through the middle of the formation.

We estimated there were about 100 German fighters, mostly FW-190s and some BF-109s and BF-110s. They attacked so rapidly over the target that we had little time to assess the results of our bombing. A smokescreen covered most of the targets, so it was hard to tell if our bombs hit the shipyards. We did see some fall into the town, but there was just too much fighter action going on to stick around. When we got back to Alconbury all I wanted to do was get the interrogation over with, get something to eat, and hit the sack. But as glad as I was to be home in one piece, I kept thinking… if I'm going to be doing most of the flying, I want my own crew.

I found out later that we lost 8 planes and 62 were damaged. Three crewmembers were killed outright, 20 were severely wounded and 80 were missing, the ten crews of the 8 planes that went down included a Major General who happened to be flying as an observer. A number of high-ranking Army Air Corps decision makers were forced to reassess the need for longer-range escort fighters just because of this mess of a mission. While we, as bomber crews, advertised that we could defend ourselves, it was a damned lie.

BREMEN—June 13, 1943, 92nd Bomb Group—6:30 hours flying total—122 bombers over targets, 4 planes lost, no escorts.

Following a day's rest, our 1st Heavy Bombardment Wing was dispatched to bomb the naval installations at Bremen. Bremen was a dreaded target because we had heard that you could expect a lot of flak. Of course, we weren't told that at our briefing, because that would have been a negative. Lieutenant Colonel Buck, with Captain Rabo from the 407th, led the mission. The 92nd BG had 16 bombers leading the attack, and we dropped 500-pound bombs on the target. There was a firestorm of flak—so much that I heard that every plane was riddled with holes, including the "Piccadilly Princess." Two crewmembers from Lt. Gurney's crew, the navigator and bombardier, were wounded by shell splinters. When I think back on it, it's amazing that we didn't lose more planes or have more casualties among our sixteen crews, the flak was so bad.

Dividend, Utah, 1942. This shows where people lived when Ray and his family lived there.

Flora Raddatz Brim, Ray's mother at the time of her marriage in 1919.

Tintic Silver, Lead and Iron Standard Mine, Dividend, Utah, 1937. Miner drilling in the face of the drift of ore to insert dynamite. On his belt is the battery cord that went up his back and over his helmet to power his lamp. Everyone had one of these.

Tintic Standard Mine, Dividend, Utah, 1941. Miners going down into the mine in the cage.

Santa Anna, California, 1942. Training at Rankin Air Academy.

Pat and Ray at their 'A.W.O.L. wedding'.

Rankin Air Academy, Tulare, California 1942. Ray in flight training at 19 years old, wearing a flight helmet. The rubber tubes coming down from the helmet over the ears were attached to the Instructor Pilot's mouth piece, so he could tell students what to do.

Alconbury, 1943. Passport photos taken to be used for identification if pilot is shot down. The photos were in civilian dress and were to be used by the French underground for fake passports if the pilot was so lucky to meet up with them.

B-17 returning home after a mission. The large letter "A" on the tail represented the First Air Division.

B-17 tail gun damage after being hit by 22 mm projectile fired from a German F.W. 190.

Salt Lake City, September 1942. Ray in uniform after being commissioned as a 2nd Lt. having completed flight school.

Ray's B-17 with the ball turret manned by Robert Burry and chin turret firing straight ahead manned by the bombardier.

Alconbury, 1943. 95th Bomb Group explosion of B-17s when a bomb slipped out of its cradle while being loaded and exploded, impacting other bombs. Three planes lost, men killed and wounded, Mission cancelled for the day. Ray was riding a bike on his way to talk with the maintenance crew of his own plane.

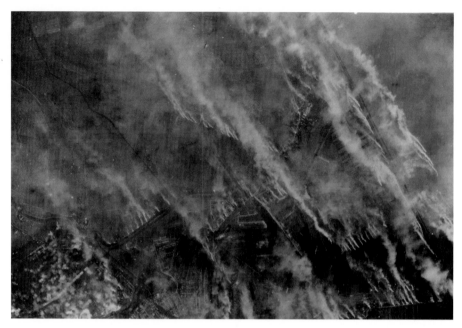

September 27, 1943. Bombing results.

Alconbury, 1943, Flight crew and ground crew of Brim Crew. Back row (l-r): Ray Brim, Nick Dear (bombardier), Fritz Hienze (co-pilot), Doug Cunningham (navigator). Front row: Sgts. Davis, Ford, Milton, Fitzpatric, Burry and Woods.

Alconbury, 1943. Ray with the Royal Air Force Officer assigned to base. US crews were flying out of Alconbury but the base itself belonged to the RAF.

Alconbury, January 23, 1944, returning from a solo night raid testing the Oboe equipment, Ray's B-17 had an electrical outage impacting on the hydraulic brakes and making it necessary for him to make an emergency landing that ended up in a rendezvous with a cement mixer.

1944. B-17 in formation with bomb bay doors open, dropping bombs.

The *Evening Huronite* and the *Salt Lake City Tribune*, Wednesday January 5, 1944, telling of Ray's 14th raid over Kiel, Germany the previous day.

Stateside, 1944. Ray piloting a B-17 after having completed his missions.

Alconbury, 1944. Ray with John Ford, his tail gunner, after having just completed their 25th mission.

Salt Lake City, 1944. Captain Ray Brim is being awarded the Air Medal by the U.S. Army Commanding Officer of Fort Douglass.

Stateside, 1944. Ray piloting a B-17, not on a mission. Note that the headset had a radio, a technological improvement over the headsets used during training at Rankin. Every crew member of a B-17 had this headset.

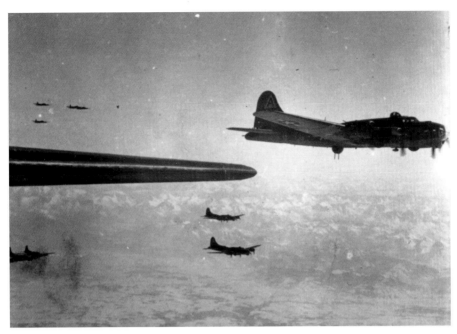

B-17s from 482nd returning to England after having completed a mission.

Inside of the German Aircraft factory, manufacturing the Dornier twin engine bomber that was successfully targeted by the 482nd on Ray's last mission.

Berlin, March 1944.
Bombing results.

Telegram addressed to parents telling them that Ray had completed his missions and was coming home.

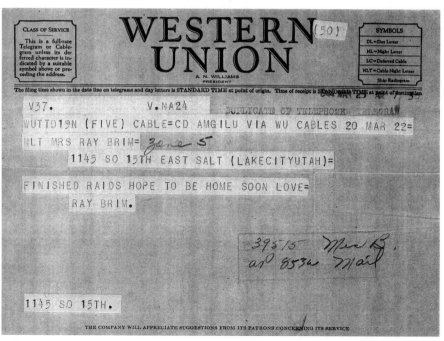

Tokyo, Japan, 1959, Director of Manpower with rank of Major.

Ray's quarters on Cape Air Force Base in Alaska, 1950. In the background is a rock shaped like a ship situated between the Arctic Sea and the Ocean. The black dots are quarters for enlisted men buried half-underground for heating purposes and to shelter them from winds.

Colonel Raymond R.E. Brim, 1972.

We started out early as usual with a 2:00 a.m. wake up. By six, we were in the air and crossing the North Sea. The sky was full of Forts, and it was a beautiful sight to see. What surprised me, as we were closing in on Bremen, was how few German fighters there were. The few I saw stayed up and away from the formations, hanging out to watch and wait for stragglers.

But then we began to experience the explosions. Once again, I was doing most of the piloting due to our position in the formation, and it took every ounce of energy and concentration I could muster. There is no way to describe the intensity and sheer noise of a mission when the flak is bursting all around you. The plane is rocking back and forth from the explosions, some of which are blowing holes in the skin of the plane, gunners were shooting up a storm, and the smoke was so dense I couldn't make out whether I was over the target or not. All Eves and I could do was wait to hear from Ray Hatfield that we were over the target and he was ready to open the bomb-bay doors and release the bombs. We hung on his every word over the intercom, even as chaos surrounded us on all sides. The smoke was so thick it was like a blackout. Once Ray said "bombs away," we had achieved our goal. We thought we hit the target, but between the ground haze and the smoke it was impossible to tell for sure.

When we returned to base our crew was pretty shaken up. It was definitely our roughest mission so far. Everyone was talking about what happened to the two crewmembers on Lt. Gurnay's ship. A burst hit beneath the nose and splinters flew into the plane. One big piece hit the navigator, 2nd Lt. Bryan Bosalma, between the eyes. The bombardier, Sgt Lewis Fletcher, picked up the intercom and called Gurnay to tell him what had happened, when another piece of flak hit Fletcher in both legs. There was still about four minutes left on the bomb run, so, forgetting his injuries, Fletcher stayed over the bombsight until he could call "bombs away" over the intercom. Fletcher then threw the switch to close the bomb-bay doors, went over to Lt. Bosalma, and made him lie down on the deck. By then, the intercom system had been knocked out—this happened all the time on our plane as well—so Fletcher took off his oxygen mask and crawled up to the pilot compartment to ask what else he could do. Gurnay said to give Bosalma a shot of morphine and make him as comfortable as possible. By this time, Fletcher was getting woozy from loss of blood and no oxygen at 20,000 feet, but he crawled back to Bosalma, covered him with a coat, gave him morphine, and attempted to keep him still. Later on, halfway home across the North Sea, when Gurnay had taken the plane down to 10,000 feet, he sent the engineer back to help Fletcher. When the engineer cut Fletcher's pants off, he found 30 holes of various sizes and shapes between his knees and hips. Both of the wounded men lived, and have told their story many times over.

On the same day we flew our mission, 72 Forts flew a diversionary mission over Kiel which was a total disaster. A staggering 22 bombers were shot down and 24 were damaged, one beyond repair. The losses were unprecedented: 213 crewmembers either missing or captured, no one knew which. Another screwed up mission that made our Fighter Command finally take notice about the need for escorts.

News from home

When we left Salina, Kansas, we were given an army post office (APO) number that was for mail sent to the overseas replacement depot, but we did not know that it was for Marrakech. Upon arriving at Marrakech, we all checked for mail, only to find out that it had been returned to sender because there was no record of our having been assigned to the base. I wrote to Pat, but our final assignment had not been made, so I could not give her the new APO number. Once we were in England and assigned to Alconbury, we had a new APO, which was just for that base.

The importance of mail should not be underestimated. Officers and enlisted men alike looked forward to mail call. The knowledge that someone from home had taken the time to write or send a package made being overseas easier. We all needed to be connected with our loved ones via the mails; that was all we had of home.

I don't remember how often I wrote home to Pat and my folks. I'm sure I should have written more. We were restricted as to what we could write for security reasons. I could describe a trip to London or that I was near Cambridge, but I couldn't give the name of our base or organization. Officers could censor their own mail and had to sign on the outside of the envelope that the letter had been censored. When crews were not flying and were off duty, it was part of our job as officers to censor enlisted men's mail. We had to cut out anything we thought might be of a classified nature. We also read some rather interesting notes regarding what the individual was going to do with his wife or girlfriend when he got home. We normally let these little tidbits pass the censorship. Sending mail home from overseas was free. The serviceman had to write "FREE" in the upper right hand corner of the envelope and initial below.

If someone received a package, it was assumed that it was food, so everyone stood around until the package was opened. Sometimes the contents were in a tin can, a wooden box, or just loose, but someone at home had tried to protect the contents from the rough trip across the ocean and the careless tossing of the mail bags aboard a big old army truck. Once Mother sent me a "man's cake," my favorite, in a tin container. While it was somewhat stale, it tasted marvelous. It attracted a group of fellows who were more than happy to help me eat it.

If you were a member of a combat crew, you always ate the goodies sent from home before you went on a raid. You did not want to leave any food should your luck run out and you were shot down.

Pat sent me cookies and anything I wanted if she could find it in the States and it was not rationed. I began to lose my hair and wrote Pat to ask her to go to Dr. Pearsall, a dermatologist and distant cousin, to see if he could recommend something to slow the process. For some reason, she went to her hairdresser and told her of my problem. Pat followed her recommendation and in time I received a package from Salt Lake. Not knowing what was in it, I was surrounded by the normal gang of hungry men away from home who could hardly wait until I had opened the package. They expected cookies, but when I unwrapped the package and found a bottle of sheep dip, guaranteed to cure everything including falling hair, I caught it from everyone and got comments like, "What does your wife think of you, sending sheep dip?" or "What are you going to mix it with?" and many more uncomplimentary suggestions directed at me. One morning, I got up early and went to the shower before anyone else was up and tried the sheep dip as a shampoo, but I only tried it once. It smelled like a railroad tie, and so did I.

We worked out a system that would keep Pat informed on the number of raids I had completed. In letters I wrote, for example, that I had been on a raid on June 11, 1943. Pat kept newspaper copies of all the raids the 8th Air Force made, and she went back to find the news coverage for that date.

The nose art painted on the planes usually showed some well-developed young lady wearing very few clothes, stretched out beside painted bombs that indicated the number of missions that plane had made. Pat had asked several times what our plane with the 92nd was named, and in one of my letters I told her it was called "Piccadilly Princess." She received the letter while visiting the Flat Rock Club in Idaho and opened it while at lunch with the other guests. The others were considerably older than Pat and were interested in what I had written. When she came to the part about naming the plane, she exclaimed "Oh they have a name for his plane," and she read: "It's 'Piccadilly Princess' and it's the only thing that can take on ten men at one time." The other guests could hardly contain themselves and, of course, Pat was slightly embarrassed. I was told she did not read any more of my letters aloud.

CHAPTER 19

MISSIONS SIX AND SEVEN—THE DUTCH COAST

Huls Synthetic Rubber Plant—June 22, 1943, 92nd Bomb Group—
6:00 hours flying total—235 bombers over target, 16 planes
lost, no escorts but Spit fighters to meet us on the way home.

We didn't fly another mission until June 22, when the 92nd BG dispatched 29 Forts, including 11 YB-40s, to take out the rubber plant at Huls, Germany. Huls provided a third of the entire Axis rubber production capacity. The plant was just north of the Ruhr area and was the second largest of its kind in Germany. Start engines was to begin before 2:00 a.m. on June 21, but fog closed down some of the bomber bases, so it was the next day, during our pre-dawn briefing, that they told us that this mission was the closest approach so far of the U.S. Army Air Forces to Germany's heavily defended Ruhr industrial region. It was only 300 miles from England, within easy reach of Forts, but it was also the first time our bombers had flown that far into Germany. We all understood that the farther we penetrated into Germany with no escorts, the more vulnerable we were to enemy fighters.

We were part of a force of 235 bombers comprised of a number of groups; although by the time we reached the target we were down to fewer than 200 due to aborts. Lt. Colonel Reid and Lt. Shaefer were leading us. At 6:00 a.m. the weather en route and over the target was pretty clear, so we were cleared to go.

Again I did most of the flying because of our position in the formation. The various groups, flying on converging courses, were to be brought together at bombing altitude at around 8:45 a.m. Then we were to turn south to the target while a small decoy force kept the German fighters busy in the northwest. Each of our Forts had a dozen .50-caliber machine guns, so flying in such a large formation provided a lot of firepower, but in actual combat, we were pretty vulnerable.

As soon as we crossed the Dutch coast, about thirty German fighters launched an attack, surrounding our formation and weaving in and out, but then they broke off with no success. While we had no fighter escorts, we did have the 11 YB-40s deployed throughout the formation undergoing their first real combat run. The idea was that these YB-40s could protect us during deep penetration by Jerry fighters. It didn't work. They added nothing to our defense and they didn't have bombs, so they added nothing to our offense.

Once we crossed the North Sea and headed over land into the Ruhr industrial area we faced fifty more German fighters, which approached us from the rear, once again without success. They attacked from above at about 11:00 a.m. and from below at about 6 p.m. They tried hard to break up our formation, but because they didn't seem to want to give battle close in, they were unsuccessful for the most part. Some of our gunners were disgusted that there weren't more targets to shoot at. Once we were directly over Huls, the battle in the sky was a sight to see. There were clouds of smoke and large red flames billowing up at least ten thousand feet from the rubber plant, and enemy fighters all over the sky. The tracers from our planes made huge arcing patterns and combined with the flak coming up from the target area. It was an unforgettable sight.

The gradually thickening cloud cover over the target was a concern. Blind-bombing equipment didn't exist then. Our bombardier had to take visual aim if the clouds beneath him covered as much as five-tenths of the sky. We were concerned, but we caught a break. The clouds parted as we turned into our bomb run around 9:40. We were going about 250 miles per hour and I could hear the wind blowing through the gun hatches. It was about 30-degrees below zero. Ray dropped our bombs while the others watched columns of smoke and steam towering 7,500 feet into the air above the main target. We later found out that there had been no warning at the

Huls plant. Workers stepped outdoors to see the amazing formation, which they thought was composed of German planes. No alarm was sounded. As a result, 186 workers died and there were more than a thousand other casualties.

On the way back home we got some friendly fighter cover at the Dutch coast at Sliedrecht—twenty-three squadrons of RAF Spitfires and three of RAF Typhoons that stayed with us back to the English coast giving high, level, and low support. Out of our group we only lost one plane, a YB-40 that was last seen going down under control near the Dutch frontier. We later found out the crew were all taken as prisoners.

By the time we got to the Channel, for the first time in hours I felt myself breathe. One ship had a feathered prop and a second engine that was smoking. The Spits had just joined our formation, so they protected this ship from the Jerries all the way in.

During our post-mission interrogation, everyone expressed joy to report that the bombing results had been good. One more raid down.

Eating and relieving

A number of people have asked me over the years about what we ate and drank on our missions and how we handled relieving ourselves. After our early morning breakfasts, which usually took place around 2 a.m., we seldom ate again until returning from the mission. No one wanted to "toss their cookies" while wearing an oxygen mask for one thing, and once we were in the plane, we were pumped so high on adrenaline along with the fear that accompanied us on every flight that we all lost our appetites. The last thing I wanted to do was eat or drink. As far as relieving ourselves, since we were unable to move about, the pilot and co-pilot actually had a funnel contraption that led from between our legs to outside the plane. The spray from our "relief" would often blow back and hit the glass of the ball turret window. For the men in the back there was a portable toilet but there were plenty of times that a helmet or the floor was also acceptable.

Becoming a first pilot

Lloyd Eves was the pilot on the plane we had trained on in the United States and he was the pilot on my first seven raids. I had let it be known at the squadron level that I wanted my own crew, and if the opportunity should arise, to give me consideration. It was during the raid over Huls that I was given the opportunity to sit in the left seat with Lieutenant Colonel Todd acting as the co-pilot, checking me out to see how I handled the crew and combat when we had both flak and fighters to contend with. All went well and after one more mission, my seventh, I became a First Pilot.

My crew was made up of replacement personnel and crewmembers who had been on other crews and wanted to complete their tours and get home. My advancement to first pilot after the mission on the Paris Air Depot also meant that Lloyd Eves had to find a new co-pilot.

Prior to the United States' entering WWII, many Americans volunteered to train and fight with the RAF. Once the U.S. joined the war, most of these volunteers were transferred to the 8th Air Force. We had three officers in our squadron who had experience with the RAF or RCAF, and had been transferred as warrant flight officers. One of these flight officers, Red Morgan, was to win the Medal of Honor for heroic efforts in completing a raid under the most difficult circumstances. Another flight officer by the name of Sullivan was to become Lloyd's co-pilot.

Early in March 1944, Lloyd's crew was scheduled to make a raid on Berlin. Berlin probably had more antiaircraft guns surrounding it than any other German city. It would be a long flight, about four and a half hours to the target, and of course, the German fighters would do everything they could to stop the 8th. While on the bomb run, with very heavy flak, a piece of shrapnel entered the B-17 Lloyd was flying, coming through the instrument panel and hitting Sullivan in the shoulder. It cut off his arm. At the same time, Lloyd was hit in the leg. Sullivan's wound was so close to the shoulder that a tourniquet could not be applied and he bled to death in the cockpit.

If I had not been so determined to become a first pilot, in all probability I would have been in Sullivan's place and dead. Sullivan's bad luck was my good luck.

*Paris, June 26, 1943, 92nd Bomb Group—6:00 hours flying
total—56 bombers over targets, 5 planes lost, 130 escorts.*

My last mission with the 92nd Bomb Group and as a co-pilot under Lloyd Eves was on June 26. Our secondary target was the airdrome at Poissy, France. The primary target, Villacoubly Airdrome, was obscured by cloud cover (although it was bombed by one group, not ours). The rest of us turned left and proceeded to Poissy by flying directly over Paris, while other groups bombed other targets.

We started out uneventfully until we hit landfall on the French coast. At that point we encountered about 40 single-engine German fighters, FW-190s and BF-109s. Determined to do as much damage as possible to our small formation of 56 Forts, the Germans stuck with us throughout the entire mission and back again. They even followed us ten miles out to sea on our way home. They were operating in groups of 2 or more, and more than once I observed them attacking the leader in a vertical dive and then climbing back up to attack the leader's wingman from directly underneath. Occasionally one rolled through the formation from a 45-degree angle in an attempt to break us up. On two occasions we saw a Jerry playing around in the sun while a second fighter, acting as a decoy below the formation, drew our fire. Then the one in the sun dived to press home an attack. They knocked two B-17s out of formation this way. At least there was very little flak.

Once we got over the target, the weather went to 9/10 overcast, so it was difficult to see if our bombs were hitting the target. On our way home, the formation picked up fighter support near the enemy coast all the way to Alconbury. While I didn't see this, it was reported from different squadrons that enemy fighters were firing at our men in parachutes. The men had bailed out of a Fortress and about 40 bursts of what must have been 88mm fire was seen to explode around them. I couldn't help thinking, those poor bastards. Even if they made it to ground in one piece, they had to survive on foot. At least they bailed out over France and not Germany.

CHAPTER 20

PATHFINDING IN THE EIGHTH AIR FORCE

I didn't fly another mission from June 26 until September 27, three months later. Instead, I was assigned to Pathfinder training, which until then had been performed by the RAF. At the very beginning of this training I learned I had been promoted, but in an extremely roundabout way.

We were all commissioned as second lieutenants. This meant that there was a lot of room to move up through the ranks. Co-pilots were all second lieutenants, pilots were first lieutenants or captains, majors were operations officers, and so on. The army had a table of organization that identified each job with a specific rank.

The 482nd Bomb Group was activated at Alconbury on August 20, 1943. I was assigned to the new unit to train as a "Pathfinder" first pilot. No one at my level quite knew what we were in for. On August 26, Lieutenant Colonel Bill Cowart, the 482nd Group's operations officer, called me to his office and told me I had been recommended for promotion to first lieutenant. He said that this promotion was the reward for my contributions in the development of the 482nd into a Pathfinder organization.

The order promoting me was issued on September 16 and we had a party at the officers' club that night. On October 2, I was told to report to Colonel Cowart as soon as possible. When I walked into his office, he said, "Ray, who have you crossed?" My reply was that, to the best of my knowledge, no one. Cowart then told me that my promotion orders had been canceled. He gave me a copy of Special Orders 274, dated October 1, 1943 from ETOUSA, the headquarters for all American forces in Northwestern Europe, which revoked my promotion. I was upset. Colonel Cowart told me to take a couple of days off and go to London and try to track down what had happened.

I left by train that afternoon, but I was not able to get to the ETOUSA headquarters in time to check on this very important problem. At least, to me it was important.

The following morning I went over to ETUOUSA, and following a considerable runaround I got to the right office. I explained my problem to a colonel who had been commissioned in the cavalry. I knew this because he was wearing riding trousers and boots. From the way he treated me, I don't think he liked second lieutenants in the Air Corps. Anyway, he was gone for a little while with the papers I had given him, and when he came back he told me that nothing was wrong with the orders canceling my promotion because I had been promoted back in the United States prior to coming overseas. This was the first time that I heard of that earlier promotion. He gave me a copy of the orders that had promoted me to first lieutenant on March 15, 1943. This was the surprise of surprises, and of course I would now get the back pay, which made it even nicer.

Unbeknownst to me, Captain Dick Ezzard and Major Fred Crimmins had processed the paperwork that upgraded me to being first pilot. Being a first pilot made me eligible for promotion, and these two officers had taken care of the promotion paperwork at the same time. We left the United States before the paperwork had gone through the proper channels and before my orders were published. Why these two veterans did this for me I'll never know, but I will always be grateful for their actions.

When I returned to Alconbury, the first person I went to see Colonel Cowart. I showed him the copy of the earlier promotion orders, and he was relieved. He said "You have been a first lieutenant long enough for me to recommend you for promotion to Captain within 30 days." He lived up to his word. I was promoted to Captain on November 23, 1943, one year and two months from the time I was commissioned as an officer. I might add that it was a long dry spell after this promotion.

Pathfinder training

We depended on clear weather so the Norden bombsight could pinpoint the target and release the bombs. In occupied areas like France and the Netherlands, if you could not see the target you would normally bring the bombs back home to England. This was to save innocent lives. No crewmember liked to do that, but it was the right thing to do. In many cases, we dropped the bombs over the ocean just to get rid of the damn things. Over Germany, many bombs were dropped just in the hope of hitting something, even a cabbage field.

Unfortunately, we did not have a very advanced weather forecasting system; there were no satellites and no worldwide reporting of weather conditions. The poor weatherman at each of the group bases would get extremely limited observations and barometric pressures at different locations, sometimes many hundreds of miles apart. In England, reports would come in from Iceland, Greenland, Scotland and Ireland, but most of these were from ground observers with limited experience and crude equipment. Sometimes pilots of planes noted the weather at a given point and forwarded it to a radio station. Ships in the Atlantic had to be careful about reporting weather because the German submarines would then know the ship's location and subject it to attack.

I remember the weatherman working over his charts and joining reported barometric pressures with a line using the latest information he had and then forecasting what he *thought* was indicated by these charts. As a pilot, I was very hard on the weatherman. We depended on the advice he gave, but if it didn't work out, we took it out on the poor guy. We had weather reconnaissance planes, normally a specially equipped P-38 or RAF Mosquito, but early in the war they did not penetrate very far into Germany or the occupied areas.

On one mission I was flying on the right wing of the leader of the 1st Air Division, and, when we arrived at the coast of Germany, a bank of clouds covered the area, maybe as high as 30,000 feet. The leader ordered us all to turn to the south and our formation changed course. While this was going on, the leader of the 3rd Air Division, who was leading his formation to another target, ordered his groups to turn north. All of a sudden, we had two full air divisions on a collision course. At the very last moment, we were told "Everyone for themselves." Several planes had midair collisions and their crews were lost.

The RAF had been fighting weather problems starting in 1939 when they were first bombing Germany, but after 1940 they were able to develop instruments that permitted aircrews to bomb through clouds. The first was a system called "Gee," depending on radio signals, which the Germans had used early in their bombing of England. The British adopted a similar system and, in the 8th Air Force, we used it primarily as a navigation aid.

H2S

It wasn't until January 1943, when they were almost exclusively bombing at night, that the British developed a radar set called "H2S," which was the system ultimately installed in Pathfinder aircraft. H2S was a method of determining the location of a reflecting surface by analysis of an electrical echo. This equipment gave the navigator a picture of the ground beneath the plane, with its distinguishing landmarks. The H2S radar system improved the number of successful night raids the RAF carried out. Radar made it possible to define industrial areas because of the metal used in construction. It was also possible to define docking areas of ships where the reflection of water and land differed. And, most important of all, as far as the 8th Air Force was concerned, with radar, cloud cover did not inhibit locating targets.

Bill Cowart

The driving force to develop a Pathfinder organization for the 8th Air Force was Lieutenant Colonel William S. Cowart, our squadron commander. Cowart had graduated from Virginia Military Institute, joined the Army Air Corps pilot training program and was sent to Harvard to get his master's degree in electronics. He became General Ira Eaker's aide and was with him when Eaker arrived in England to direct the buildup and operation of the new 8th Air Force. When the 92nd Bomb Group was being formed in England, Cowart became one of the squadron commanders, and I was lucky enough to be assigned to his unit.

Cowart was a leader. He flew combat instead of taking the easy missions, which many commanders elected to do. He had the imagination to think about adapting the H2S to our B-17 aircraft, and used his close relationship with General Eaker (which was not appreciated by some senior officers) to advance this concept. On August 26, 1943, Special Order No. 230 from Headquarters, 1st Bombardment Wing, formed the 482nd Bomb Group with the mission to become the Pathfinder unit for the 8th Air Force. This same special order transferred many of the people of the 325th Bomb Squadron of the 92nd to the 482nd, and I was lucky enough to be among them. Shortly after the 482nd was organized, Bill Cowart was sent to the United States to sell the concept of radar targeting. Armed with a lot of information accumulated by the RAF, he was successful. He was sent to M.I.T. where the university was given a contract to develop the American version of H2S.

The first Pathfinders

The 482nd was the only US Air Force Group to be activated outside of the United States based on Pathfinder equipment installed in certain B 17s to be used during periods of cloud cover. Of course the primary goal of missions we flew as Pathfinders was always to destroy a particular target, but as we experimented with the development of blind bombing it became clear that of equal importance was the mission to refine our radar techniques. This responsibility was necessarily broad and vague since until then no specific radar equipment had proven itself capable of reliably locating targets hidden from sight by overcast, and no procedures for attacking these targets had been created for daylight bombing. The Group began working at the Alconbury base, which was also enlarged to accommodate more planes and crews. There was even a visit by the King George IV and Queen Elizabeth to honor our efforts, which impressed us all.

Five B-17s were sent to Wales, to an RAF depot where H2S systems were to be installed in them. The H2S, H2X, and later Eagle H2X were the main systems used by the Eighth Air Force. These radar systems were basically pilotage and target-finding units by which a beam of transmitted energy scanned the ground areas. The reflected signals gave a map picture on our unit screens with dark areas for water, light areas for ground, and bright areas for towns and cities. Then our navigator compared the radar picture with a map.

In the meantime, ground schools were started for us to learn as much as we could about radar and how the RAF used it on their night-bombing missions. It didn't take long to modify the Forts, so by August I was sent with another pilot to bring back one of these five newly equipped planes.

"Stinky"

The H2S and H2X, with centimetric radar technology, had far greater scanning ranges than the Oboe radar device, which was a completely different type of technology depending on two radio beams intersecting at the drop point. However the H2S, in particular, often didn't work as well as advertised (including for us when we were trying to "sell" it to Bomber Command). Once Pathfinder crews started using H2S in the fall of 1943, we gave it the nickname of "Stinky" because of its unexplained power failures and because, for those of us who knew a minimum of chemistry, H2S was the formula for Hydrogen Sulphide, that same rotten egg gas I released in the movie theater back in Dividend. We were told by the Brits that H2S stood for "Home Sweet Home" or H-S-H (H2S).

We were on a lean budget to say the least. Our orders stated: "Reimbursement for actual and necessary expenses not to exceed $4 per day for quarters and an allowance of $1.25 per day to cover excess cost of subsistence is authorized where government quarters and rations are not furnished or available while traveling."

As soon as we arrived at the RAF Depot in Wales, we checked out the first Pathfinder B-17 and noted a large bathtub-like fiberglass structure underneath the nose of the plane. This "bathtub" housed the antenna and the mechanism for operating the H2S. The fiberglass had been molded to fit the fuselage of the plane. After a routine walk around the plane, we prepared for a test flight.

Everything checked out and we taxied to the runway. Upon getting a clearance to roll, we proceeded down the runway while the co-pilot started calling off the airspeed. Normally, takeoff speed was 110 to 130 miles per-hour. We reached this indication long before we were halfway down the runway. I knew that we did not have flying speed by the feel of the controls, so we just kept rolling. At an indicated speed of 170 mph, the plane finally became airborne. We continued to climb away from the field and were amazed at the airspeed indications. I decided that the only thing to do was to run some flying tests and note the airspeed.

The B-17, depending on its weight, would normally stall out at about 100 mph, but when we purposely stalled this plane, the indicated speed was 140. We did this maneuver several times, sometimes with the flaps down in order to learn the approximate difference between the airspeeds we were dealing with. I advised the tower of our problem and they alerted the crash crews just in case we had miscalculated our approach speed. It was normal for the airspeed on the approach to be read off to the pilot, but we added the experience factor learned from stalling the plane earlier. Based on our flight tests, we decided to make our final approach at 160 mph indicated airspeed. We flew a normal pattern around the airfield and everything was set for the final approach.

I don't remember ever listening as intently to the called-off airspeed and maintaining it as I did then. As we crossed over the end of the runway, I pulled back on the throttles and we touched down without a bounce. But instead of the three-point landing the B-17 was designed for, this landing was on the two main landing gears, so we had to slow down before we could apply a lot of brake. We were about halfway down the runway before I could apply sufficient brake pressure to bring the plane to a halt. We were happy to be on the ground with our B-17 still in one piece. Taxiing back to the hangar was no problem. We were met by the rescue people and those from the operation tower.

The maintenance people were the first to ask if we had forgotten to take off the pitot cover. The pitot tube was located on the left side of the fuselage, just below the pilot's window. It was the instrument that measures ram pressure versus static pressure, which gives the airspeed reading. This was not the problem; the crew chief had the pitot cover in his pocket. The maintenance people checked the instruments in the plane and all the connections, and found nothing wrong. Something had disturbed the airflow over the pitot. Inasmuch as the only change to the fuselage was the addition of the H2S bathtub, they decided that the tub was the culprit. Tests were run in the hangar and, sure enough, the addition of the bathtub had impacted the airflow, causing the indicated airspeed to be in error. As long as the pilot knew of this error, the plane could be flown safely and adjustments made to the indicated takeoff speed and the cruising and landing speeds. After a couple more test runs, we felt confident with our new knowledge and how to compensate for it, and we flew the plane back to Alconbury, our home base. As I landed the plane I might have noticed (but didn't since at that point I was simply trying to land the plane while compensating for the new air speeds) that I had just become one of the first five original Pathfinder pilots to use the new equipment in the US air war effort.

Rumors

We didn't anticipate all the misinformation concerning Pathfinders that sprang up during those first weeks we were training on them at Alconbury. There was the rumor that Pathfinders were only going on missions when there was extreme cloud cover and that we would go ahead of the rest of the group, drop down real low to bomb the target and then send up flares for the rest of the planes to use as markers. While there was real danger in being the lead plane in a formation, another rumor that passed from crew to crew was that Pathfinder crews were basically "dead meat" because we would be out in front and therefore be taken down by Jerry before we could reach our targets. The logical corollary to that rumor was that we only had to go on five missions since we'd never make it to number six. All these rumors were false but they didn't make our job selling the technology to the Command any easier. Of course it was true that if the Germans took out the lead plane the second plane would have to take over, and that would cause some confusion in the formation.

CHAPTER 21

TIME OFF

In between missions there was a lot of down time that was often taken up with marathon poker games always played for stakes. It wasn't long before I learned what a mediocre player I was. This was way beyond shooting craps in the back of that school bus during my high school days. After losing too much too many times I wised up and stopped playing altogether. There was a small library available but most of the time all of us, airmen, ground crews, enlisted and officers alike went out into the countryside, either by bicycle to nearby towns like Huntington for an evening, or by train or bus to larger cities like Cambridge or London for weekends. Alconbury was very small and had only one pub so most of the time the men wanted to leave town.

I took my marriage vows very seriously, which made me a poor companion for many of the single men on leave. I was a "stick in the mud", I'll admit it. Plus, I didn't fraternize with the enlisted men and had only a few officers as close friends. But that doesn't mean there wasn't temptation everywhere I went. There were pubs in every town, on every corner where more often than not you could find young women waiting to meet American service men. As the saying went: "Americans were over paid; over sexed and over there." Every Brit assumed we were well off financially and usually asked if we were from Hollywood.

Huntington was a medium-sized town five miles from Alconbury, which meant I could get there by bike. There was a movie theater, a Red Cross Club that served Coke and donuts, some pubs and a drug store.

I remember getting film developed at the drug store because while we couldn't take photos of equipment or planes, we could take photos of each other to send home.

Everyone frequented the pubs, smoke filled rooms where friendly locals would offer to buy us a pint of bitter as often as not. This generosity on the part of our hosts often went beyond a pint or two. When in London I used to have dinner at the Savoy Hotel which was an extravagance even for "rich" American flyboys, and more than once my entire meal tab was picked up by a fellow diner, always British, as a "thank you" for defending their country against the Nazis. Most pubs didn't serve hard liquor, although each one was supposedly given a fifth of scotch for special occasions. Everyone smoked (it seemed except me) and a sure fire way to meet an English lass was to offer her a cigarette. English cigarettes were expensive and said to be of poor quality. The only downside to the pub was the 10 p.m. closing hour, although we sometimes sneaked a pint outside under our jackets to enjoy "one for the road".

R&R

In between testing the pathfinding equipment and getting everyone "on board" once we got back to Alconbury, I was able to take a few weekends off. London, Cambridge, and Nottingham were my favorite cities to visit. It was in Nottingham that I bought most of the English china we have in the corner cabinets in our home.

The first time I visited Nottingham, I did not have a hotel reservation and, when I went to the desk of the Blackstone Hotel I was told there was no room available. Two middle-aged ladies were behind the desk and I asked them to put me on the list if a room became available. They assured me that they would but that I should look for another room someplace else in the city. As I left, I placed a couple packs of cigarettes on the desk. I did not smoke, and we were issued or could buy American cigarettes for 15 or 20 cents a pack. They were very good to use as a tip or to barter. In about an hour, I went back to the Blackstone. Would you believe that a room was available?

The room was a typical 1943 hotel room in England, with a washstand with towels on each side, a very small mirror over the washstand, and a very, very small light above. The toilet (WC) was down the hallway and next to it was a bathroom where one could take a bath. The bed had a down comforter and the room had little if any heat. There was no window, so the room was rather dark. Of course, this was wartime; everything was controlled or rationed. I couldn't complain. I had a room.

On one of my walking tours of the city, I passed an expensive looking china shop and stopped long enough to see many beautiful objects. The shop was about two blocks from the hotel. On the bottom of one of the pieces of Coalport I bought is the following address: C. Darby, 30 Market St. Nottington. I went in the store to just look at all the beautiful china and an elderly lady offered to assist me. After spending considerable time looking, I bought two pieces. In retrospect, I must have been very optimistic. I still had many raids to make over Germany and the odds were not in my favor. At that time, the chances of finishing my 25 raids were still about 50 percent since the 8th Air Force had still not committed to fighter escorts in any substantive way.

I took the two pieces of china back to Alconbury and placed them in a box that was addressed to my wonderful wife back in the United States. I'm not sure the box would have ever been shipped back if I had been shot down, but that was a chance I was willing to take.

I was back in Nottingham sometime later and went back to the Blackstone Hotel. The two Irish ladies recognized me this time and I had no trouble getting a room. This time four packs of cigarettes were left on the desk as I registered. While the room was about the same, it was definitely a little larger. The two Irish ladies seemed to like me but they did not like the British and felt they were being treated as second- or third-class citizens. They did say they liked the RAF and the 8th Air Force.

It was on this trip that I went back to the Darby store to look again at different beautiful pieces of china. An elderly gentleman came into the store and spoke to the ladies. When he noticed me, he gave me hell about buying beautiful pieces of china and said something to the effect that Americans were taking advantage of the fact that the locals did not have the money to buy it. With that, he walked out of the store and the two ladies apologized for his "being so rude."

I purchased two more pieces of the Coalport and was at the counter when the gentleman came back into the store. He came up to me and said he was sorry for what he had said. After a few more minutes of talking, he asked me if I would like to come to his home for lunch. Having nothing else to do, I accepted. The two lady clerks said they would keep the packaged china for me and I could pick it up later.

At this point, the gentleman introduced himself as Mr. Fisk. He told me he had some more errands to run prior to going home. We walked down a street that had fruit stands out in front of the stores. As we approached one of the stands, Mr. Fisk saw some lemons and we stopped to buy as many as they would sell since, like everything else, they were rationed. He told me that these lemons were the first he had been able to buy since World War II started in 1939. We were allowed two lemons.

After completing the errands, Mr. Fisk hailed a taxi and we went to his home. While in the taxi, he told me his wife was not well and was confined to a wheelchair. He also had a daughter who was working for the government as a translator of books from the nations we were fighting.

Mr Fisk's home was a large red brick house, set up on a hill. The Union Jack was flying from a pole atop the roof. When the taxi stopped, a man came out of the house and took the parcels Mr. Fisk had purchased. The home was filled with large pieces of furniture and the rooms were large. Mr. Fisk took me on a tour. We started at the top, where a small door opened onto a deck, a sort of Widow's Walk, where the flagpole was located. From this vantage point, I could see much of the city of Nottingham. The next floor down was the smoking room, with paneled walls and a billiard table in the center. Along the walls were racks of billiard sticks.

On the floor below was an area where many long thin drawers lined the wall. It was then that I learned that Mr. Fisk was in the business of manufacturing lace; in each drawer were select pieces of lace his company had made. He opened a couple of the drawers to show that each piece of lace had been very carefully placed without a single wrinkle. Today, this would be a collector's dream. The pieces of lace stored in those drawers must have been in the hundreds. I was impressed.

We continued the tour of this lovely old home, coming down to the main floor. It was here that I met Mrs. Fisk, a lady dressed in black, sitting in a chair that was placed so she could see her garden. She did not say much, and Mr. Fisk explained to her what had happened earlier in the day and that he had asked me to have lunch with them. In the meantime, we continued the tour of the Fisk home. The paneled rooms on the main floor were large, and at each of the windows were blackout curtains in addition to the drapes. This made the rooms a little darker than they would have been normally.

Mr. Fisk took me into the china and silver closet. I had never seen so many different patterns of china and so many pieces of silver hollowware. The china and the hollowware were displayed like one would find in a large department store. It was here that I saw a complete set of black china with a gold band around the edges. I thought it was beautiful and from that day on I wanted a set of black china. (We have one now, but it is not the quality the Fisk family had, and it sure does not have any gold band.)

When we passed through the kitchen, I saw that in addition to the gentleman who met us at the door and took the parcels from Mr. Fisk, there was a lady standing over the kitchen stove. Mr. Fisk asked if I liked rabbit, because this was the menu for lunch. I could not remember having had rabbit, but I assured him that it would be very special. The kitchen was very large and had white tile covering most of the walls.

When we left the kitchen, we went outside to see the garden. Mr Fisk explained to me that the garden was nothing like it used to be and that it was now a garden to grow vegetables. Nevertheless, rose bushes provided a border. Off to one side was a hothouse that permitted the Fisks to grow vegetables during the winter months. I'm sure the family had never grown vegetables in the garden prior to the start of the war, only flowers.

In time, we were called to lunch and I was seated between Mr. Fisk at one end of the long table and Mrs. Fisk at the other. I don't recall our table conversation, but I'm sure it dealt with the progress of the war and discussions of my family as well as theirs.

After lunch I excused myself, thanking them for the special hospitality they had shown me. Mr. Fisk called me a taxi, and I went back to the china shop where this experience had all started. On later visits, I did try to get in touch with him but it never worked out.

I did go back to Nottingham several more times. By then I was leaving a full carton of cigarettes at the desk of the Blackstone, and the room improved with each visit.

The three-handled mug

Another time I went to Nottingham with my navigator, Doug Cunningham, who had become a good friend, my only really close friend from the crew. We wandered into a curio shop and both of us took a fancy to a three-handled "Toby Mug." Since it was one of a kind and expensive (for our budgets anyway) we decided to split the cost and buy it together. The deal was that if I got shot down, Doug would keep it and if he got shot down, then I obtained ownership. Of course this was a bit ridiculous since we were both members of the same "Brim Crew," but it seemed fair at the time. When it turned out that I completed my 25 missions before Doug finished his and was assigned to a different crew, we had a dilemma. I wanted to take the mug home with me. I ended up trading my radio that had been rewired from 110 to 220 watts accommodating English voltage requirements to Doug for his half of the three-handled mug.

When I completed the required 25 raids over Europe, I packed the china in wooden boxes, took some RAF maps that had a linen base to them and wrapped the boxes with the map inside. I hand-carried these boxes on my return from England by ship to the United States and from New York City to Salt Lake City by troop train. I then gave them to my bride of three months some fourteen months after leaving her to go to England.

Selling the value of Pathfinding

Back at Alconbury, we were faced with the problem of convincing some of the staff and crews that the difference in indicated airspeed and real airspeed could be accommodated. Our concern was determining a comparable scale to use when leading formations and flying the modified B-17. Again and again, we flew over known distances, using the bombsight to insure time over the measured distance, and recording the indicated airspeed. In time, we were able to get a trailing airspeed instrument that was on a long cable attached to another speed instrument. This trailing instrument gave the correct airspeed and we recorded the difference. We also flew formations with other aircraft and compared their airspeed against our indicated airspeed.

All this test flying was not only necessary but critical because the five B-17 Pathfinders would be leading other formations of aircraft. Airspeed for most of the combat B-17 formations was set at 150 mph. In a very few cases, the Pathfinder was used to lead B-24 formations, and B-24 combat formations flew faster than the B-17s. We needed to convince the other group commanders that the airspeed on the Pathfinder was off and that the indicated airspeed we were showing was really 150 mph, and not the 180 or so shown on our instruments.

There were two enlisted men who were absolute geniuses in maintaining the radar. They had a little building on the flight line and worked night and day to keep this very temperamental equipment working. The building they worked in was jammed with equipment and spare parts. They were among the first to greet a crew following a mission to check on how the radar equipment had worked and what problems had been encountered. These two men did not get the recognition they should have. I am sure that in the civilian world, they would have been at the top of their field.

In time, our position was accepted and the first mission to use H2S was scheduled. We wanted the ideal contrast for radar reflection—that being water and land. Our target was Emden, a city on the west coast of Germany.

CHAPTER 22

MISSION EIGHT—FIRST AS A PATHFINDER

*Emden Industrial Area, September 27, 1943, 482nd Bomb Group—6:00
hours flying total—246 bombers over targets, 7 planes lost, 262 escorts.*

My crew

A B-17 crew flying mission after mission together becomes as close as
you can get to family. My "band of brothers" was no different than any
other crew; we had to trust each other with our lives. As the highest
ranking officer and pilot I was their leader, and I tried very hard to
inspire their confidence and respect, even though I was only 21. I had
been bitching and moaning about having my own crew ever since I'd
been flying co-pilot for Lloyd Eves so I was determined to be deserving
of getting what I had asked for. At the same time, I tried to have confidence in these nine men and to show them that respect went two ways.
I'd have given any one of them the shirt off my back, and I made it a
policy to never bawl them out in public if they slipped up.

I just assumed we knew what we had to do; we'd support each other
to the death; and hopefully we'd get our bombs dropped and return
home in one piece. I think most pilots were like me when it came to
encouraging words. The most any of us ever heard that was close to a
pep talk was at the end of the briefing when the briefing officer said
"good luck". Nothing more than that. On every crew we all had the

same fears; we all knew our jobs and we were aware every moment we were in the air of how dependent we were on each other.

My co-pilot was Lt. Frederick (Fritz) Hintz. He was a quiet fellow but he did what he had to do. When we were flying with the formation to our left, I did most of the flying. When the formation was to our right, Hintz often flew. If something had happened to me of course he would have taken over. My navigator was Lt. Dudley (Doug) Cunningham, smart as a tack, and as I've said before we became great friends. He was a helluva nice guy and a little older than I. In order to use the H2S Pathfinder technology Doug had to sit next to the "radio room," his head covered with a black shield so that there would be no reflection on the cathode ray tube used to scan the landscape below. Since he couldn't see to write, he couldn't take notes and would have to dictate to Sergeant Allen, our radioman, whatever he needed to record.

Lt. Nick Dear, who was my bombardier, was part Native American and part Mexican. Near the end of my missions I had an issue with Nick. He was the only member of my crew that I had to remove because of his drinking, and quite honestly, overall character. After a while I realized he just didn't perform his duties well, I think, because he was often hung over. Now that we were flying with the Pathfinder radar, the navigator was in charge of when to drop our bombs and all Nick had to do was throw a switch to open the bomb bay doors, but I still wanted a functioning bombardier, particularly since the bombardier was also one of our gunners. After I had him removed from the crew, he and I never spoke again.

Master Sergeant Davis was our engineer and top turret gunner. He was the oldest noncommissioned officer, being in his late twenties. When Davis had his .50 caliber guns pointing forward to shoot Jerry as he flew right at us, it was impossible to talk on the intercom, the noise was so loud. As our engineer he also had to watch our instruments and see if anything was out of the normal. Technical Sergeant Allen was a gunner, shooting the .50 caliber machine gun from the radio room and was also our radioman. He was the only person other than Hinz and myself who could communicate with the ground and Command. It was highly un-likely that he was ever called upon to shoot the gun since the Germans rarely attacked from that angle.

Staff Sergeant Robert Burry was my ball turret gunner, a short and stocky fellow—the right body type since he had to curl up in the ball turret for hours on end. Burry was an amateur boxer, although I never saw him in the ring. In later missions, after I had completed my 25 in March 1944, H2X radar, or radome, was located in the ball turret position so there was no ball turret gunner. But until then the H2S radome was slung under the nose of the plane so Bob Burry flew with me every time I flew. Staff Sergeant John Ford was my tail gunner. After we had finished our missions we became friends and even corresponded when we returned stateside. John was often in a position to defend our plane because Germans fighters often attacked us from the rear. My two waist gunners were Staff Sergeant Kline and Staff Sergeant Baun, both excellent brave gunners and nice guys. In the excitement of combat every one of the gunners claimed they had shot down a fighter, but there was no way you could prove it, which is why, as I have already pointed out, the number of destroyed German fighters was so hyper-inflated after our missions.

A historic day

The first Pathfinder mission, which was my eighth raid, was over Emden, September 27 was a day that went down in history. I was set for the first American Pathfinder mission against Germany. Four sets of three Pathfinders in each set were dispatched and three sets failed, all except mine. This was essentially a practice mission because of the contrast between water and land as it showed up on the new radar systems. There was a lot of activity on the night of September 26. We were alerted that we would fly the next day, so we loaded all our bombs and the rest of our equipment into our Fort and took off over blacked-out England to our designated base. We bedded down for a few hours and then got the call for a predawn briefing. After all our months of training and preparation, three of us from the 482nd piloted the PFF Fortesses that led the two air divisions on the raid. Lt. Gurney, Lt Collins and I were the pilots.

The new equipment worked effectively through a solid cloud cover and the 1st and 3rd Air divisions released their bombs on the flares of the new PFF aircraft. And, while we couldn't see the results because of the undercast between us and the target area, the mission was believed to be a success. Pilotage points were picked up, which indicated the formations had passed over the target with the help of our three PFF planes and dropped their bombs spot-on. Five hundred and five tons of bombs were dropped.

We were using the H2S "Stinky" equipment, which proved to be not so "stinky" this time around.

There wasn't much flak, but we did encounter thirty to forty enemy aircraft, mostly BF-109s. They attacked in pairs and in fours, focusing on the lead aircraft—the Pathfinders—using the sun and vapor trails to their advantage. Our briefing and interrogation was done at Bassinbourn and Knettishall before we returned to Alconbury. Even though our raid was deemed "successful," it was decided to return to Emden a few days later.

Photo reconnaissance showed that in actuality the bombing was scattered throughout the city due to cloud cover. The difference between what we initially reported, usually upbeat assessments based on our sighting of smoke from the ground where our bombs hit, and the reality of poorly placed bombing even with the Pathfinder technology, was not uncommon.

MISSIONS NINE AND TEN— EXPERIMENTAL FLYING

*EMDEN INDUSTRIAL AREA, October 2, 1943, 482nd Bomb Group—
6:00 hours flying total—339 bombers over targets, 2 planes lost, 227 escorts.*

Lt. Gurney and I flew the two Pathfinder planes leading 339 1st and 3rd Air division Fortresses to Emden. The attack repeated the profile of our raid on September 27. I flew to Bury St. Edmunds to lead the 3rd Air Division and Gurney flew to Grafton Underwood to lead the 1st. This was the first time that more than 955 tons of bombs were dropped on a single target. While our equipment worked well, the bombing results were not considered satisfactory in that a sizable number of bombs fell short of the target. This was because bombardiers released their loads too early.

We were still experimenting with the best way to use the Pathfinders to mark the targets. When we dropped the flares and then the bombs to mark the targets through the undercast, everyone in the succeeding formation would try to hit the same target. The problem was that, in trying to anticipate exactly where they should drop, each bombardier dropped his bombs a little bit earlier than they should have on these first Pathfinders runs. As a result, the bombing pattern moved backwards towards where the formations were coming from. This "target creep" was only natural when I think about it, since we all wanted to drop our bombs and get the hell out of there as soon as we could. On later missions it was worked out that the flares would be released only with the bombs. Parachute-marker flares were the only target indicators being used to show the following groups where to bomb.

The enemy opposition was slight to moderate. Only four or five single-engine fighters were observed by the bomber crews, three of which made an attack on the low group of the formation. Our P-47s gave us terrific fighter support. The long-range escort fighters downed six Luftwaffe fighters over the Netherlands and Germany during our withdrawal. However, the flak was extremely accurate, with many large white bursts about 100 feet in diameter being reported.

This was a "red letter day" for our fighters, and therefore the bombers our fighters were protecting. Thanks to the retrofitting of the P-47 with additional larger fuel tank capacity, they could finally escort us to the bomb site as long as it wasn't too deep into Germany. Our longer escorted missions would start in the spring of 1944 when the P-47s and P-51s were equipped with even longer-range fuel tank capacities. But I wasn't complaining. After those maiden missions in the spring, any escorts over enemy territory made a difference.

The bombing results were good and every crew received a commendation from Winston Churchill via teletype.

DUREN INDUSTRIAL AREA, October 20, 1943, 482nd Bomb Group—
6:15 hours flying total—97 bombers over targets, 9 planes lost, 360 escorts.

This was the first "Oboe" Mission, and our target was the city center of Duren. There were four Pathfinder planes leading the mission. My crew was dispatched from Kenettishall leading the 3rd Air Division. I was leading a combat wing and we were having equipment problems.

Oboe was the first of a series of radar beacon bombing technologies that the Brits had been using. We had practiced the technique of using Oboe over special ranges in England and knew it worked best with short-range distances. It was a circular beam that was transmitted from stations near Dover. From another transmitter in England, approximately 75 miles to the north, signals were transmitted along the circular beam that told us when to start the bomb run, when to open the bomb bay doors and when to drop the bombs. The system could be jammed by the Germans so it was only turned on for short periods. Nonetheless the 482nd tested it in close to fifty day raids and 16 night missions. It didn't compare to the H2S or the H2X in terms of distance. Oboe's average instrumental bombing error was 400 yards while H2S's average was 200 yards. But still the Brits used it throughout the war.

About three minutes before target there was an erroneous release and we dropped the bombs early. We later figured that the equipment failed and gave us the faulty signal. The weather was terrible and it forced some of the formations to turn back to England even before they dropped their bombs. One entire combat wing bombed in the vicinity of the Gilze-Rijen aerodome in Holland, while returning home, "a target of opportunity."

When the formation was exact, our crews could actually see each other. A good friend was flying off my right wing. He was one of the better pilots in the unit and it was just a matter of assignment that he was flying off my wing and not leading, since he too was a Pathfinder. He flew formation very well, and had tucked in the left wing of his plane nice and tight. We had made the turn at the IP and started on our bomb run with the bomb-bay doors open. As I described earlier, German fighters seldom attacked us on a bomb run because the flak was heavy and they did not want to be shot down by their own guns. On this raid, the flak was very heavy. Black puffs of smoke were everywhere as the shells exploded, sending jagged pieces of shrapnel in all directions.

I never flew a mission where the plane was not damaged by flak. This time there were holes all over the wings and fuselage. Most of the flak went through the plane and out the other side. Every time it hit I'd feel myself tense up. I was worrying; we were all always worrying about the gas tanks. If flak punctured a tank and the tank leaked fuel onto a hot engine you more often than not had an explosion. Another scenario was flak puncturing the bomb bay before we could get rid of our bombs. And that is exactly what happened next.

All of a sudden, my plane pitched sideways as I saw a flash of fire off my right wing, my friend's plane. One of the waist gunners called out on the interphone, "Their plane's has been hit!" Suddenly there was a terrific explosion. Within a matter of seconds, pieces were flying in all directions. Then the right wing folded up and the Fort went down in flames. We had to keep going toward the target to get rid of our bombs, but we knew what had happened to the crew. No chutes were seen. The plane was a ball of fire going down.

Getting back to Alconbury, our home base, seemed to take hours. We were anxious to check with other crews, to hear if they had seen any chutes from the plane. No chutes were reported. My plane had been badly damaged by shrapnel, but as far as the ground crew could tell, no damage had come from the explosion of the plane next to us.

If that projectile had been 50 feet to the left—the length of our right wing—our crew would have gone down and my friend would have taken my place in the formation.

I felt sick to my stomach. Anger, sadness and guilt. Ten men gone, all of whom I had known, including a man I'd gotten to know well between missions. I couldn't get the image of that plane going down in a ball of fire out of my head. Fifteen missions to go. I'd been flying in combat for less than a year but it felt like there had never been anything else but this. All I wanted to do was hit the sack and hope to God that I could forget what I'd seen and go to sleep.

Based on the explosion that took place and the fact that several crews witnessed it, we all concluded that the German round had penetrated the bomb bay of the B-17 and exploded there, causing the bombs to detonate at the same time. No member of the crew was ever reported as a prisoner of war, and I am sure they had all been killed.

Waiting

It was a month before our next mission. Too long. We were all impatient to get on with it. As nerve wracking as the missions were, and as chancy as the odds were for returning alive, we all wanted to fly. That was what we were there to do. When it wasn't raining I'd hop on a bike and go to one of the neighboring towns. When it was wet and cold, I'd take a train to London or Cambridge mostly by myself. We were coming upon the holiday season, and guys starting getting homesick. I missed Pat like the dickens. When a few days past and there was no letter from her I'd start to get low. I'd try not to show it. I could tell that there's nothing worse than young men trained and pumped up to do a high stakes job sitting around waiting, twiddling our thumbs. There was bickering over minor stuff like someone not sharing a particularly lavish package from home with the other members of the crew; someone taking too much money off another in poker; a joke at someone's expense that became a grudge; it seemed that the Eighth was always about hurry up, hurry up, hurry up and then wait. Then we got orders for our next mission, over Gelsenkirchen.

CHAPTER 24

MISSIONS ELEVEN AND TWELVE— JOHN FORD GETS WOUNDED

GELSENKIRCHEN, GERMANY, November 19, 1943, 482nd Bomb Group—6:05 hours flying total—130 bombers over targets, 1 plane lost, 130 escorts.

Six "Oboe" Pathfinders including my plane were assigned to lead 167 B-17s of the three combat wings of 3rd Air Division over the western region of Germany against Gelsenkirchen. I led the 45th Combat Wing.

We flew at about 27,000 feet with a briefed course, across the Dutch coast and the Zuider Zee to Meppel. From this point to the Dutch–German border in the vicinity of Arnhem-Nijmegen we flew an exceedingly irregular course until "bombs away". The assigned targets were the iron foundry and railway marshalling yards at Gelsenkirchen in the Ruhr.

We proceeded to the control point but were unable to pick up the proper signals. No one could determine the exact cause of the complete failure of the equipment. Three of our aircraft dropped their bombs near Emmerich and the remainder either brought their bombs back home or attacked targets of opportunity in Germany and the Netherlands, which was what I always did.

Enemy fighters, mostly FW-190s, were seen in the distance, though none approached close enough to attack our planes. There was almost no flak. Two hundred eighty-eight VIII Fighter Command P-47s provided escort and support for the B-17s.

The failure of the Oboe equipment on this mission ended its use as primary guidance on high-altitude bombing missions for the 8th Air Force. Although I still used it on occasion in later missions. The Oboe equipment, which relied on radio signals from ground stations in England, was transferred to the Ninth Air Force, whose medium-altitude work did not interfere with the Oboe guidance technique. Meanwhile, the Eighth Air Force fell back upon H2S and H2X airborne ground-radar equipment, which provided much better results for high-altitude work.

I knew it wasn't a successful mission in terms of bombing our targets, thanks to Oboe, but after four weeks of sitting around doing nothing we were flying again, and we'd only lost one Fort.

BREMEN PORT AREAS, November 26, 1943, 482nd Bomb Group—6:45 hours flying total—440 bombers over targets, 25 planes lost, 361 escorts.

After being scrubbed twice in a row we were finally cleared to hit Bremen. Then, before taxing out, we were ordered to sit tight. I can't describe the tension of waiting in your Fort to see if the delay would turn into a complete scrub or a live mission. But sit there we did, engines rising and falling, the plane quivering. Then we were told to go. The brakes came off and we crept out onto the taxi strip. Before we knew it, I was flashing the tower's message over the intercom: thirty-minute delay. At the end of thirty minutes we started the engines again. There were roars all over the runway and the planes taxied out a little farther. No go. I got the next message from Combat Command: Another thirty-minute delay. The problem was, the more delays the more problems down the pike in terms of plans for attacks, timing of diversions, and fighter escort. You can't imagine how tight nerves were when this happened. Then they scrubbed the mission. This dance happened time and again as the season advanced and the weather systems over Europe grew increasingly unpredictable.

But this time, on November 26, there were no delays or scrubs. I was one of fourteen Pathfinders using H2X and H2S radar leading the raid. Eleven of us attacked the target. And in spite of 10/10 clouds, we believed we were successful. It was the biggest show put on by the Eighth Air Force to date, 440 heavy bombers. We dropped more than 1,600 tons of bombs on the primary target and we hit the city. There was enough haze, cloud, and smoke to show that the target was hit and heavy damage was inflicted. One of our Pathfinders aborted and in the other the bombardier was seriously wounded.

Right before we dropped our bombs I saw a fighter coming straight at us. I never heard such cussing as went across the intercom when we'd see Jerry heading our way. You could tell when they were going to attack by the way they cocked their wings. Then they'd sort of crab in sideways and start shooting. But instead of sideways this guy came at us head on. I was piloting and Hinz was on the intercom and without even thinking I took the plane down. That 109 passed right over us but then turned and started shooting at our back. We didn't know for sure if it was him or another fighter but my tail gunner, John Ford, took a bullet in his side. I think it was a 109 that approached from the rear, firing its 20mm nose cannon because it actually hit our tail guns. When it was all over, he said to me—I won't use the language that he used—"You know, that so-and-so fighter pilot was a better shot than I was. I was trying my best to get him, but he got me."

We lost twenty-five planes on that mission…250 men. When I got out of the plane Hinz said I looked as angry as he'd ever seen me. One of crew had been wounded on my watch. That's the way I felt about it.

Christmas 1943 at Alconbury

Everyone at Alconbury tried to make this Christmas much like the ones we had at home. The cooks served a traditional Christmas dinner: turkey and stuffing, mashed potatoes, vegetables, and apple and mince pies. Our gifts from home increased morale. Special religious services were held on December 24 with a midnight mass celebrated in the movie theater. There were decorations hung everywhere in the combat-crew mess hall. And a Christmas tree. In the early afternoon of Christmas Day, families from in and around Alconbury were trucked in for a party. We had Santa Claus and the airmen and the children played games, got presents from Santa, and enjoyed refreshments.

I was in the doghouse with Pat regarding Christmas. She had sent a large box of gifts in late November to make sure that they arrived in time. The moment the box arrived I opened it. I couldn't wait. Beautifully wrapped in Christmas foil and bows were Christmas cookies, socks, books, and a lovely framed photo of her. I immediately went out and did my Christmas shopping for her, in a hurry to get a box off to the

States that would arrive in time for the holiday, just as she had. To save money, I wrapped my gifts in her wrapping paper and bows. When she received her box, she immediately realized that I had already opened my gifts. Boy, was my next letter from her a scolding. I think it was our first argument, luckily long distance, and soon forgotten and forgiven.

CHAPTER 25

MISSION THIRTEEN—THE BLOODY HUNDREDTH

LUDWIGSHAFEN OIL REFINERY, December 30, 1943, 482nd Bomb Group—
8:20 hours flying total—658 bombers over targets, 23 planes lost, 169 escorts.

The limited number of Pathfinder aircraft in the 8th Air Force during 1943 required that we fly combat missions with different groups. We were normally briefed about the mission at Alconbury, and then flew to the base of the group we were to lead on the combat mission. Sometimes, this resulted in little sleep for my crew, maybe two to three hours, because we also attended the mission briefing of the group we were leading on the raid.

On December 30, 1943, my 13th mission, I was assigned to fly with the 100th Bomb Group. When one was assigned to the 100th, he realized that his chance of survival was even less than with the rest of the 8th Air Force. The group was known as the "Bloody Hundredth" and "Clay Pigeons" because of its high losses.

The story about the 100th's bad luck goes back to a much earlier raid, when, purportedly, one of their B-17s was in trouble over Germany. We had all been told that if we lowered the landing gear of a crippled plane—a sign of surrender—and got out of the range of fire from the formations, the German fighter planes would escort the crippled plane to a safe landing in Germany or occupied countries. This custom was in respect of one air crewman to another. It seems that one of the planes from the 100th lowered its gear when German fighters were on each side of the plane. Suddenly the B-17 gunners opened fire and the two German fighters were shot down. The B-17 was immediately attacked and also shot down. Because of the distinctive markings on the tail of the B-17, the Germans knew what group had shot down the fighters. This group then became a special target of the Luftwaffe.

Early in the morning of December 30, 1943, I flew my Pathfinder to Thorpe Abbott's, the home of the 100th. After checking in with the operations people, we got some sleep, but were awakened early with the other crews to go to the briefing. A major came in and unveiled the map, which showed the tape running to chemical plants in Ludwigshafen, Germany. It was a long haul. We were to have fighter protection about one-third of the way in and Spitfires to meet us on the way out—as far as their fuel capacity would allow. Our bombing altitude was to be 28,000 feet. A Major Reed was assigned to go with us on this raid as a representative of the 100th. He would act as the co-pilot.

We were the lead plane, so we were the first off. We were carrying 500-pound bombs. In time, 18 other planes from the group formed up around us in normal combat formation. I got reports from the tail gunner, Sergeant Ford, that the formation appeared to be fairly tight and, by the time we left England, all members were doing very well. As the other formations proceeded on the course over Germany, we watched flak come up around them. German fighters attacked the formations.

Just prior to our starting on the bomb run, German fighters attacked us from all sides. About 40 of these FW-190s, BF-109s and 110s jumped on us. Those fighters that I could see executed a frontal attack. I could see their 20mm cannon rounds explode as they approached our formation. The Germans had loaded their belts of ammunition with armor-piercing shells interlaced with explosive shells. It was the exploding ones that I could see.

We took some evasive action, but with a formation following our plane, that action was very limited. The exploding projectiles seemed to walk right at us as the German fighters swept through the formation. The crew continued to report fighters attacking from all directions.

Once we were on the bomb run, the enemy fighters pulled back to avoid antiaircraft fire, which became intense. The explosions of the

88mm and 105mm antiaircraft projectiles from the ground batteries made a dark black cloud.

We completed the bomb run, the bombs were on the way, and we had just turned toward England when all hell broke loose in the cockpit of my plane. A piece of shrapnel from a flak explosion had come between number-three engine and the cockpit. It entered the plane and went through the main oxygen tanks on the right side of the cockpit, ricocheted off the post of the upper turret, punctured the oxygen tanks on the other side of the cockpit, and fell to the deck beside the upper turret. With the sudden release of oxygen from the tanks, there was an explosion in the cockpit. Dust was flying all over. Then, suddenly, I was facing something dark green in front of my eyes, which made it impossible for me to see what was going on. I thought I was passing out. But what I finally realized was that the sunshade over the pilot's seat had been blown loose and was hanging down in front of me.

I was greatly relieved. All I had to do was reach up and jerk it loose. Then I could see the rest of the crew in the cockpit as well as the instruments. The explosion had not only torn the soundproofing away from the sides of the plane but it had also stirred up the dust and dirt that had accumulated since the plane had left the factory in the United States. After I checked to see if anyone was hurt, I studied the instruments on the panel. Everything was working except the main oxygen system. But we were still leading the formation and that demanded we continue on course, back to England.

I got on the intercom and told the crew what had happened and that they had to get on their walk-around oxygen bottles at once. As I recall, the walk-around bottles contained no more than an hour's worth of oxygen, so it had to be conserved. We still had about two hours to get to the coast, where we could let down to an altitude where oxygen was not required. On this particular mission, we had been assigned to a flying altitude of 25,000 feet after bombing, meaning that we were 15,000 feet above the altitude at which we could remove our oxygen masks. It was impossible for the gunners to use the walk-around oxygen system while manning the guns, so I told them to sit down or stretch out on the deck of the plane and expend as little energy as possible to save what oxygen they had.

It was extremely important that the pilot have oxygen because he was responsible for getting the plane and the formation home. We had to depend on the rest of the formation to provide firepower to protect us. I called the deputy group leader on the radio, told him of our condition, and advised him of the possibility of our having to leave the formation. I then called our friendly P-51 escort fighters on the common frequency and asked for their cover. If the Germans had known of our problem, they could have concentrated their attacks on us, and we already had enough problems. We were still under attack. In fact, two B-17s from our formation had been lost on the way out.

The crew was told to monitor one another, to watch for signs of passing out because of the lack of oxygen. I made the decision to gradually lose some altitude as we proceeded towards the coast. The formation remained with us. I think we were down to about 20,000 feet when I noticed Major Reed looking rather pale and shaking. He had tried to save his oxygen so that I could be sure of having enough. I talked him into turning his portable tank back on and we continued on as Reed responded to the increased oxygen.

When the coast of France came into view, a number of friendly fighters joined our formation. The fighters were much faster than our B-17s; they made sweeping turns above our formation to provide the protection we needed. With this fighter protection and the coast in view, I called the deputy group commander to tell him that I was leaving the formation for a lower altitude and that he should lead the group home. We continued down to 10,000 feet, the safe altitude to take off our oxygen masks. As we crossed the English Channel, we knew we had it made. We had all been very cold on this return leg of the mission, but that did not matter now that we no longer worried about running out of oxygen.

We were all very lucky. Perhaps the luckiest person on the crew was Sergeant Davis, the top-turret gunner. If his turret had been turned in any other direction than it was when the piece of shrapnel entered the plane, it would have hit him rather than the turret post. He kept the piece of shrapnel as a good luck charm.

I heard later that Major Reed was killed in an aircraft accident in Florida. He survived his tour with the Bloody Hundredth, but his luck evidently ran out.

Later, on the first raid to Berlin by the 8th Air Force, the 100th lost 15 of 18 planes, the most any one group lost on one raid up to that date—March 6, 1944.

CHAPTER 26

MISSIONS FOURTEEN AND FIFTEEN—THE MILK RUN

*KIEL AND MUNSTER, January 4, 1944, 482nd Bomb Group—6:40
hours flying total—486 bombers over targets, 17 planes lost, 112 escorts.*

Superstitions

We all had our superstitions about the missions. Fellows carried lucky
coins, some carried tokens from their wife or girlfriend, a cross or rosary
beads. I carried a Navaho Indian beaded rabbit's foot that my mother had
picked up on a summer trip after I'd left home. She was the last person
to believe in that sort of thing but she gave it to me and I always put it
in the pocket of my flight jacket before a mission. For me, the previous
mission had combined two unlucky numbers, number thirteen and flying with the Bloody 100th, so five days later when we were called up
for mission fourteen to target the U-boat pens at Kiel, I should have
felt relief. But as we were waiting to take off the familiar fear sat in my
stomach like a coiled snake.

The pattern was always the same. All the pacing around the plane and
going over every detail with the ground crew and the weatherman and
of course talking to Cunningham was a way to handle the strain...the
fear of death. The fear would stay with me as we flew over the Channel
with the noise of the engines but no one really talking much. Just silence.
Then, when we'd get into combat and the flak and the fighters started
coming up something would change and my fear would be replaced

with excitement and disappear entirely. The worst of the strain was over. Might as well finish the job. After landing, we'd pile out of the Fort cussing and bitching and grumbling because the worst of the tension was over. Then mixed with relief would be the tiny beginnings of the fear again. But I never, I like to think, let my crew know what I felt inside. This was the first mission of 1944 and I was determined to lead it with all the skill I could muster.

Fifteen combat wing formations of the 1st, 2nd, and 3rd Bombardment divisions were led by ten Pathfinders, including me. It was a massive attack. Even though our bombing was done through heavy cloud cover, our Pathfinder equipment functioned well and all the PFF crewmen I spoke with afterwards believed that we hit both Kiel and Munster hard. But the raid took a toll: We lost 17 planes, and 170 crewmen were reported missing in action.

We took off from Alconbury to our base where we had breakfast. Fresh eggs and hot coffee. During our briefing, when we found out that Kiel was the target, everyone was impressed. It was a long trip and a hot spot. There were a total of 300 German twin- and single-engine fighters within interception range and we anticipated a considerable amount of flak. We were to fly at an altitude of 29,000 feet at a temperature of minus 52 degrees.

We started our engines at around 6:30 a.m. and lifted off the ground, the whole formation banking eastward toward Germany. We leveled off at about 24,000 feet. I felt sorry for Burry, the turret gunner; it was cold up there even with his electric heated suit on. We saw no opposition across Denmark and over the Baltic. Then we turned south and bore down on Kiel. Our Fort was one of three Pathfinders in the lead group.

When we arrived over Kiel, we encountered only moderate flak but it was very accurate and of heavy caliber. German fighters dived into our formation. We had lots of P-38s and P-51s for fighter cover, and they just couldn't be beat. I thought back to our initial missions in the spring of 1943, when we had no escorts whatsoever, and no Pathfinding equipment. Things change quickly when you're at war.

As soon as the bomb bay doors opened, flak poured up at us. We lost one brand-new aircraft on its first combat mission. It was hit by enemy fighters and left the formation, ditching into the North Sea with the loss of the crew.

The night raid

DUREN INDUSTRIAL AREA, January 23–30, 1944, 482nd Bomb Group—4:10 hours flying total—1 bomber over target, 0 planes lost, 0 escorts.

It seemed to me that the taxiways at Alconbury were always being repaired. I have a photo in which a section of the taxiway had been removed and the cement machine is mixing the cement to be poured into the hole. There are seven laborers, most of whom were Irish at that time, repairing the taxiway. It was a cement machine like the one I hit on my return from night mission number 15, over Duren, Germany.

In January 1944, we were on "select crew status" because the 482nd Bomb Group was the only 8th Air Force unit equipped for "blind bombing." Night raids were uncommon for the 8th, which was out to prove that daylight bombing was the best way to damage the Germans. The RAF concentrated on night raids, and the combination of day and night raids kept the Germans busy. But because we were experimenting with different kinds of equipment, we also had the opportunity to make a few night raids. The 482nd had already made three raids before I got my turn. The three raids prior to mine had been what were called "milk runs," with no problems of any kind. That is, they were short in duration with no interference from enemy fighters or flak. We all looked forward to this kind of a mission. For this reason, people not on combat status volunteered to go along. Our group flight surgeon joined us for the Duren nighttime "milk run."

Sour milk

When I say "milk run," that does not mean that we were not afraid. There is no such thing as "getting used to combat." Every combat mission placed stress on an individual, and each one of us handled it in his own way.

I had made many night landings without landing lights. The RAF had developed a lighting system that assisted us via the use of three lights set at an angle on the final approach; they told the pilot if he was lined up correctly and coming in at the right angle. If you were high, a yellow light would be the most visible. If low, the pilot would see a red light. At the right angle, he would see green. It was a simple but very effective aid to night landings. You did not want to use your landing lights because German night fighters had been known to wait for someone to turn on his landing lights and thus make an easy target to shoot down. One aircraft turned back due to "Gee" radar equipment failure, the other dropped on estimated time of arrival due to the special equipment failure.

Our takeoff was scheduled to be at 7:05 p.m., so we had plenty of time to check out the plane with each crewmember having assigned responsibilities. We were all to be at the plane no later than 6:00 p.m.

This extra time gave Major Schumacher (Doc) and me time to go to the hospital and pick up some new experimental flying equipment that we wanted to take on the flight. On the way to the plane, we stopped at the parachute hut and got our chutes and other flight gear. From there, I went to the tower to get additional information regarding the mission. I also picked up the colors of the day (flares) and the location of various pundents along the route in England. (A pundent was a light beacon that flashed a code that could be seen at night. The code was changed at different hours each day, so we had to know the time of change, the code and the pundents' locations to help us get back to our home base, which in our case was Alconbury.)

Doc and I got into our jeep and rode out to the plane to be met there by the flight crew and ground crew. The crew chief who was in charge of maintaining the plane advised me that number-four generator had caught fire during pre-flight, and Supply did not have a replacement. With no replacement in Supply, the ground crew removed a generator from a hangar queen (a plane that was not operational and was slowly cannibalized for spare parts) and replaced the defective number-four generator.

I checked Form 1-A, which is a written report on the condition of the airplane, signed it, and gave it back to the crew chief. Then I checked with each crewmember regarding his equipment and what he had observed about the plane. It was during this time that I gave Doug Cunningham the pundent list and locations, which would prove to be very important later on in the mission. The crew chief then told me that an extra 200 gallons of fuel had been put in the tanks. My attitude about extra fuel was that you could never have enough. I took one last walk around the plane and climbed aboard.

Hintz and I started the engines at about 6:45 and I tried to contact the tower. For some reason, the radio was not as clear as it should have been, but I got a green light from the tower, which was all the clearance I needed to taxi. With that, I gave the ground crew a high-sign, released the brakes, and we were on our way. At the run-up pad at the end of the runway, we went through the pre-takeoff checklist and run-up. Again I called the tower for takeoff clearance, but no luck. Then the traffic control van at the end of the runway gave us a green light and we turned onto the runway for takeoff. Both Fritz and I thought the reason the tower had not wanted to reply was because of the mission and for security of all concerned.

Fritz and I had been flying together long enough that it was a pretty routine takeoff. We always had plenty of speed on the runway before I would pull back on the control and we would lift off. I left the superchargers on until we had additional airspeed and altitude. After adjusting the power to maintain our desired climb rate, I switched over to the interphone for a crew check and to confirm the departure heading of 235 degrees with Doug.

We ran into clouds at 8,000 feet, but broke out of them around 10,000. We went through more clouds at 14,000 feet, and it was then that Nick Dear, the bombardier, called to ask if we could see the sparks around the nose of the plane. I looked then and did see a few sparks jumping across the astrodome. This was nothing more than static electricity that we were picking up; sometimes a blue hue would also form around the astrodome.

Doug called several times to ask if we could increase our rate of climb because we were falling behind our schedule and were not where we should have been at that point of our mission. By increasing the power of the engines, we did improve the rate of climb so that by the time we left the English coast, we were behind by only 1,000 feet. All lights were turned out as we left the English coast; even the instruments in the cockpit were turned down to minimum. On this mission, we did not test fire our guns because the muzzle flash would have revealed our position.

We were about halfway across the Channel when Doug called to ask that I hold a tight heading and airspeed so he could get a good reading on the direction and speed of the wind at our assigned altitude. We crossed the French coast at 26,000 feet, and I then started to carry out evasive action to avoid German fighter pilots who could be coming up on the plane. No sense in putting the tail gunner, Sergeant Ford, to work this early in the mission.

We knew the Germans had picked us up on their radar just about the time we left the English coast. The German radar would also identify the fact that we were a single plane. The question that bothered us was whether the German command would send up fighters for just one plane. I could not take a chance. Evasive action consisted of turning 10 degrees to the left for a set time and 20 degrees back toward the base course, changing altitude a few hundred feet during the time on each heading. These course changes kept Doug busy making sure that we averaged out to the course necessary to get us to the initial point for the bomb run at the right altitude and heading.

Disaster

Even though we had the cockpit lights turned down low, I noticed that they would go out for a short period of time and then come back on. I knew we only had three generators (the generator on number-two engine had been removed to be replaced by an alternator to operate the Oboe equipment), but we had operated on as few as two generators before and had completed the mission on the practice range. We also knew that we were having an electrical problem because the heat suits for the gunners were not working. The heat suits were like an electrical blanket and were critical for the gunners in the back of the plane, where the temperature could be minus 50 degrees.

Just about this time, the number-two supercharger regulator started to freeze up. I worked the controls back and forth to get warm oil circulating to the supercharger. I turned this job over to Fritz while I flew the plane. After a short time, Fritz was able to get sufficient oil into the regulator and the surging stopped. The problem of surging superchargers at high altitude where the temperature was extremely cold was not uncommon.

We arrived at the waiting point four minutes early, so I made a 360-degree turn and activated the Oboe receiver at the same time. Upon completion of the 360, I received a course from Doug and went off interphone so I could concentrate on the Oboe. The lights on the instrument panel went out again. I had picked up the signal from Oboe, but it was very faint. The signal faded, so I asked Doug for another course to the target. Doug gave me a heading of 51 degrees, and with the help of a flashlight held by Fritz, we tried to maintain that course. I tried Oboe many times but with no success. It was then that I made the decision to drop the bombs.

I knew we had big problems, but they were dwarfed when, as Nick attempted to open the bomb bay doors, the landing gear light on the instrument panel came on. With the aid of the flashlight, I checked the amp meters, which were down on a panel by my left leg. There was very little current, none by the generator on number-four engine. Sergeant Davis cranked the bomb-bay doors open. Nick then called and said that the plane didn't have enough power to get rid of the bombs, so he had to manually salvo them, one by one out the doors. To this day I don't know what we hit with the bombs, and the Germans never reported damage, so maybe we hit some poor farmer's field or barn.

Trying to get home

The tail wind that had caused us to arrive early at the coast and at our waiting point for Oboe, and that had had such an impact on the climb schedule, was not working for us as we tried to get home. We continued our evasive action, adding to the time en route. It always seemed to take a lot longer getting out of Germany than going in. I was becoming concerned about our fuel at this point and wanted to get as much fuel in the main tanks as possible. Sgt. Davis came down from the top turret and transferred as much fuel as gravity would move to the main tanks.

The extra 200 gallons that had been put aboard prior to the mission certainly relieved some of the concern.

While we had had only a few searchlights sweeping the sky when we were inbound to the target, they seemed to light up the sky on our way back. My tail gunner was worried that fighters might be coming straight for him at any moment, breaking through the clouds and sweeping the sky for us. Once caught, we would have been a good target for a fighter.

The clouds did break up as we approached the coast, and we looked down on what appeared to be an airfield, which would have been in Belgium. I'm sure the Germans would have liked us to land there, thinking we were in England. Confusion under stress can lead to strange decisions, and this could have been one of those times.

The first good fix on a position that Doug could give me was just off the Belgian coast. We were south of our planned course but not in any trouble, and shortly we would be over the Channel, which would give us some relief. At least I could stop our evasive action so we could face our other problems. We were still at 26,000 feet and the crew was getting very, very cold. We were all using flashlights to get around and to see what instruments had been frozen in the off position or the last reading before they lost power. In fact, the only instruments I had were the needle ball and airspeed plus the magnetic compass. I sent a note back to the radio operator to turn on his IFF to try to get a fix for us from a DF (directional-finding) station, but this was wishful thinking and a waste of time.

The clouds finally broke and we at last found ourselves over England. We started the letdown, and when we got below what appeared to be the lowest clouds, I had a flare fired in the hope that some airfield would turn on its runway lights, or that searchlights would give us some aid. During the briefing prior to the mission, we had been told that the searchlights in England would point toward an airfield if we were in trouble.

We fired another flare at 6,000 feet. Several searchlights did come on, but they were some distance away. As we approached them, they went off. Then luck was on our side because Doug located a "pundit" that was flashing a code we had been given and we now had a much better idea where we were. All the messages between Doug and me were carried by Nick, while Sergeant Davis held the flashlight on the four basic instruments I had left. At this point, I had the crew put on their chutes, because by now we were more than an hour overdue and I could only estimate how much fuel was left. I passed the word that if even one engine quit, they were to be ready to jump or to go ahead and jump since we were over England.

Doug had given me a heading of 300 degrees from the pundent, with an estimated time to Alconbury of six minutes. At the end of six minutes, we could see no airfield or anything we might have recognized. The searchlights came on again and moved in a northerly direction. At last, the crew and I thought we had someone's attention, but just after we turned toward them, the lights went out again. Turning back to a southerly course, we noticed lights on the ground, and, while we were not sure, we thought it was the city of Peterborough.

We were sure enough that it was Peterborough that I started to let down to 2,000 feet. At the same time, I had Sergeant Davis crank down the landing gear because that took considerable time and I didn't want to find an airfield and not have the gear down. We continued to fire flares until a flare was shot from the ground and the airfield perimeter lights were turned on. We could not see the runway so I flew toward the perimeter lights knowing that in time I would be lined up for both the runway and the glide lights mentioned earlier. While still flying to the perimeter lights, I had Sergeant Davis go back and crank down the flaps.

As we were led into the final approach, I started the letdown for the landing with Fritz calling off the airspeed of about 110 miles per hour. Minutes later, we were on the ground and the runway was long enough for me to stop the plane using the emergency brakes as well as the normal brakes.

In time, a spotlight from the tower shined on the plane and we could see a jeep coming toward us. As we waited for it, some of the crew got out of the plane. They had had enough of the sick airplane and were just happy to be on the ground.

Rendezvous with a cement mixer

With all the confusion and relief, I failed to think about the braking system, so when the crew chief in the jeep told us to follow him to the parking area, I just did. If I had been thinking, I would have shut down everything on the plane. Fritz unlocked the tail wheel, and I started to follow the jeep. As we approached a turn in the taxiway, the plane turned to the left. I applied the brakes hard only to find that I didn't have any brakes. I reached for the emergency brakes, but they too were out. I had forgotten that the brake pressure accumulators were electrically operated. I had drained the accumulators on the landing stop. I tried to control the plane with the engines but it was too late. I knew I was in deep trouble when the spotlight that had been leading us to the parking spot picked up some construction equipment in front of the plane. As I pulled the master switch to shut off the engines, the plane hit a cement mixer between number-three and number-four engines. The propellers chewed up the cement mixer. The cement mixer pieces were going in all directions, but all I could do was sit and watch this ending to the mission. When I finally got out of the plane, I was shaking like a leaf. I went back for a debriefing, and they gave me sleeping pills.

We had arrived home, but not the way I wanted to. No one was hurt, the plane was a mess, and I didn't volunteer for any more "milk runs" at night. At least they never sent me a bill for the damage I did to the plane (or the cement mixer).

Doug Cunningham and I were required to write up this mission the following day, and I kept a copy of my notes. The accident investigation revealed that the hangar-queen generator shorted out and, with the gunners using their heat suits, the two remaining generators could not support the demand.

In a letter dated January 17, 1991, our tail gunner, John Ford, sent me these comments: "Back to the mission over Duren, Germany. It might have showed, but you had one extremely cold, terrified tail gunner. With a probable temperature of 40 to 50 degrees below zero at that altitude, and the electrical system out, it was extremely frigid. To admit that I was not afraid as you say, I would be a liar. I recall staring out into the darkness, seeing imaginary shadows of German night fighters. I too recall the probing searchlights and also the blinking lights on the ground of flak guns trying to shoot us down."

CHAPTER 27

MISSIONS SIXTEEN THROUGH TWENTY—COUNTING DOWN

*BRUNSWICK STEEL INDUSTRY, January 30, 1944, 482nd Bomb Group—
7:00 hours flying total—742 bombers over targets, 20 planes lost, 635 escorts.*

Fifteen of our Pathfinders were dispatched to lead combat wings of the 3rd Air Division in an attack on the aircraft factories in Brunswick. I was deputy leader of the 1st Combat Wing, 1st Division. One of our PFF planes turned back because of mechanical failure and another led a combat wing to Hanover, bombing this target of opportunity through full cloud cover. Haze and contrails had made formation flying impossible for this combat wing.

The rest of us led our formations to Brunswick and, even though there was 10/10 cloud cover, we bombed the assigned targets. Our pathfinder equipment was working so well that we were able to spot smoke rising through the undercast. We encountered more than a hundred enemy fighters of different types as well as captured B-17s flown by the enemy, some of which were equipped with rocket firing capabilities. The Germans attacked vigorously with cannon and air-to-air bombs.

They came in from all angles of the clock firing everything you could think of, barrel rolling through our formation, shooting lead in all directions. My intercom was a cacophony of gunners calling out fighters they were targeting. The sky was full of flak bursts, bombers on fire, parachutes, pieces of planes and bodies. It was hell up there. There wasn't a moment when I wasn't dodging something. Men would jump from planes but slip through their parachutes or a chute would open too soon and catch on fire. Suddenly a Fort up ahead caught fire, dropped a couple hundred feet and exploded as though dynamite had been cram packed into it. 10 men lost. The attack continued and flak poured up. A few minutes later, although it seemed a lot longer than that, P-47s showed up and the Luftwaffe simply peeled off and disappeared. Only 8 more missions to go.

FRANKFURT AU MAIN MARSHALLING YARD, February 8, 1944, 482nd Bomb Group—8:00 hours flying total—633 bombers over targets, 13 planes lost, 553 escorts.

Eight of the 482nd PFF aircraft were dispatched to lead the 1st and 3rd Air divisions over Frankfurt. Four attacked the primary target, three bombed Wiesbaden, and one of our Pathfinder planes was shot down near the French coast on the way over to Germany. While three of our squadron's Forts were dispatched on this raid, only two of us flew. On this mission, our plane was the deputy leader of the 45th Combat Wing, 3rd Division. We were lucky enough to achieve accurate bombing, even though the flak was intense over the target and we encountered about 25 Focke Wulfs on the way in. Soon it started to get rough. The flak bursting all around us, the roar of the engines and the rattling of fire from every gunner pouring it to Jerry made it impossible to hear a thing. The 190s seemed to be zeroing in on us with good reason. It was like they knew that if we couldn't drop our bombs the whole wing could fail. We were all swearing and shooting and I was doing my damnedest to keep us airborne. Then it was bombs away and we were out of there.

Five of our planes had minor battle damage, including ours. The Pathfinder plane we lost was piloted by Lt. Joe Gold and was observed going down about twenty miles east of Le Treport, France. We saw seven parachutes before the plane broke into two because of rocket fire, but ultimately the entire crew was killed.

His last flight

An incident concerning the loss of my good friend Lt. Rip Collins took place on February 4. It illustrates how the best-laid plans before a mission could go astray.

Prior to going on a raid, we normally placed our wallets in a large envelope and the squadron intelligence officer put each envelope in a safe. The purpose of doing this was to deny the Germans any additional information about you as an individual, and also to preclude them from using any money you might have had with you to subsidize their intelligence efforts.

On one occasion we were scheduled to go on a raid and I made the decision to put my wallet in an inside pocket of a jacket that was hung up in my closet. We aborted the raid for some reason and came home. When I went to get my wallet, it was gone. Someone had gone through my clothes and found it while we were out. Now if we had made the raid and been shot down, no one would have known about the wallet. Whoever took the wallet was playing the odds.

I reported the loss to the military police, but they could do little other than report it to the local British police department. This was required because our barracks was built on a farmer's land, and the Brits still had police authority for incidents like stealing.

I got a partial payment so I would have spending money and did not hear from the police for about a month. One day, a British Bobby appeared at my door and said he had some information regarding the missing wallet.

It seems that on the day of the robbery, the Collins crew was not scheduled to make the raid. While we were away from the barracks, the bombardier on the Collins crew, Fred S. Bell, had gotten a three-day pass and had gone to London. Other Collins crewmembers reported to the police that Bell had lost a lot of money gambling during that weekend, much more than he would normally have in his possession. When the police questioned Bell, he denied everything, but it was the Bobbies' opinion that Bell had been the individual who took the money from my jacket. They were not happy with his answers or attitude regarding the stolen wallet. The Bobby also told me that the casino staff remembered him because he was in uniform and they confirmed that Bell had lost considerable money on that weekend. He would be under scrutiny from now on. When the word got out about my loss, other crewmen said they thought someone had gone through their closets as well.

It was just a matter of days before Rip and his crew were shot down, and Bell was among the missing. From that day on, when I went on a raid, my wallet was in the yellow envelope. My experience was used by the intelligence officer as a good reason to follow instructions and leave one's wallet in the safe. It was bad luck, but also my fault to have been robbed.

Routine Missions, 18–20

BRUNSWICK AVIATION INDUSTRY, February 29, 1944, 482nd Bomb Group—8:00 hours flying total—633 bombers over targets, 13 planes lost, 554 escorts.

Eleven of our PPF planes were dispatched to lead 213 3rd Air Division B-17s on February 29, in another attack on the aircraft manufacturing plants in the Brunswick area. One PPF airplane turned back over Holland when its oxygen system failed, but the other ten of us bombed through heavy cloud cover. Our Pathfinder equipment worked well and, although we couldn't see the results, we thought they were pretty good. There were no enemy fighters but there was plenty of flak.

Occasionally I'd hear the ripping of metal when a piece went through the fuselage. There was just a wall of black puffs of flak and I could feel the plane lurch from the bursts beneath us. They could really put it up there! Ironically, since we usually flew in bad weather, sometimes our fighters couldn't fly to protect us but this day they were in the hundreds. A plane to my left lost two of its engines and the gas tank on its right side. Then a third engine went out and it broke formation trailing white and black smoke. We saw chutes before it disappeared, but none of us could tell the number. But I came to realize something: Every time a Fort went down it went down with its nose pointing at the target if we were over the target. Somebody was in that plane still aiming by God and it made my heart ache inside from pride, anger and sadness. Ultimately the bombing results were pretty good but we paid the price in those 13 lost Forts and 130 good men.

LUDWIGSHAFEN, March 2, 1944, 482nd Bomb Group—7:40 hours flying total—375 bombers over targets, 9 planes lost, 244 escorts.

Our crew was alerted on March 1 that we were going on our next mission the following day. We came to find out that the raid was a repeat mission to Ludwigshafen and its marshaling yards. Since it was winter, the forecast was for 10/10 cloud cover over the target. It was cold and cloudy when we took off. On our way in there was some flak, but the bad weather over Germany actually helped us keep Jerry fighters to a minimum, even though it in no way hindered the heavy flak we encountered. Our bomb drop was guided by radar through an extremely heavy cloud cover with varying degrees of success.

It was one of those bomb runs where the flak was so thick you could step out and walk on it. I kept thinking: just follow the radar to the target. Forget the flak; forget the fighters; just get over the target and drop the bombs. If we don't drop our bombs, our mission is wasted. In some respects, I felt a lot of pressure as a Pathfinder pilot. I knew that the enemy wanted to knock me down to break up the bombing of the whole group. If I veered the plane even five degrees we could be 700 feet off target. If I or Hinz messed around with the throttles and changed the speed, we'd throw the bombing off. Changing just a few miles per hour at 25,000 feet altitude could mean we'd miss the target entirely and so would everyone else. When all was said and done, no Eighth Air Force Group was ever beaten back from a target by flak or fighters. Ever.

WILHELMSHAVEN OIL INDUSTRY, March 3, 1944, 482nd Bomb Group—
7:15 hours flying total—79 bombers over targets, 11 planes lost, 730 escorts.

Ten of our PFF aircraft were dispatched to lead combat wings of all three air divisions to Erkner, Kleinmachnow, and Annahof, Germany. Seven hundred forty-eight B-17s and B-24s took part. With the clouds reaching to 29,000 feet, with persistent dense contrails and extremely cold weather, it was difficult for me to keep to our formation flying, a real challenge. The combat wing commanders ordered the mission abandoned after we had crossed into Germany, but I opted to continue on while leading a combat wing of the 1st Air Division over Wilhelmshaven. When our bomb bay doors failed to open, we signaled the combat wing to drop their loads on the town. Another of our Pathfinders leading a combat wing of the 3rd Division broke through the clouds with only three aircraft and visually bombed a town named Ulvesbull on the Jut-land Peninsula.

We encountered no enemy fighters, except for one combat wing that was attacked vigorously by 25 to 30 BF-109s and FW-190s. There was no flak except over Heligoland, where it was intense and deadly accurate up to 28,000 feet.

By now we were prepared for flak on every mission, but even when it was predicted it was always a jolt. Wham, ratta-tat-tat, like a lawnmower on our wing. And if it penetrated the plane you'd feel the cold wind rushing through first one hole and then another and another.

CHAPTER 28

MISSION TWENTY-ONE—THE BIG "B"

BERLIN OIL INDUSTRY, March 8, 1944, 482nd Bomb Group—9:10
hours flying total—539 bombers over targets, 37 planes lost, 252 escorts.

If asked before March 6, 1944, any Eighth Air Force bomber crewman would have told you that his personal goal for the war was taking part in a mission over the Nazi capital, Berlin. For a host of technical, tactical and strategic reasons, Berlin could not be reached or would not be targeted until March 1944. Indeed, a P-38 fighter group commander, ranging ahead of the massive Berlin-bound bomber formation my crew and I were leading on March 3, was the first American to spot roofs in the city proper. However he had to pull out of the area when the more than six hundred heavy bombers he was escorting had to abort in the face of execrable weather only a short way from the Berlin aircraft factories they had been sent to pulverize. Three days later, on March 6, 730 American heavy bombers—the mightiest 8th Bomber Command formation to date—braved bad weather to finally reach the sky over Berlin and its immediate surroundings. We missed being there, but we were actually giddy when we heard the news.

Our turn came two days later, on March 8.

Berlin week

The March 8 mission would prove to be one in a series of U.S. heavy bomber daylight attempts and actual attacks on Berlin over a period of days in early March. In fact, 8th Bomber Command had determined that March 4 through 10 would be "Berlin Week," and four missions were mounted in that period of time. As the capital of Germany, Berlin was supposedly immune to bombing by American planes because of its heavy duty flak guns and squadrons of fighter planes, which we naturally took as a challenge.

The 95th Bomb Group had flown the first Berlin mission just two days before, on March 6, with disastrous results. It was clear weather and the German fighters defended their capital with ruthless accuracy. Worse, there was highly accurate flak. The total losses for the mission were 69 bombers and 11 fighters, the highest single mission loss of the entire strategic bombing offensive during the war. Our group, the 482nd, lost a Pathfinder piloted by Major Fred Rabo, who was a friend of mine. His co-pilot, Red Morgan, who had received the Medal of Honor for heroism on a mission before this one, was another close friend of mine. When their B-17 was hit by three bursts of flak, the engines caught fire and the plane exploded. Rabo and Morgan and the two waist gunners were able to pull their parachute rip cords and survive. Morgan was just able to get his parachute opened in time before hitting the ground. All four were prisoners of war until liberated in 1945.

It was very cold and very dark when we boarded our Fort in the early hours of March 8. Previous missions, starting with the raid on March 4, reported that 414 heavy-caliber flak guns and a lot of German fighters were posted in the Berlin area. Nevertheless, Germany was having a day of bad weather, which made it doubtful if many of their fighters could be launched. We hoped that was the case. I was scared during every mission I flew. You had to be an idiot not to be afraid that you were going to die up there, one way or another. But that day I remember looking around at the planes lined up on the runway waiting to take off and thinking we had been stripped lean of everything except being crewmembers of these great machines—these Flying Fortresses—and maybe we were making a little history.

Ten Pathfinder aircraft were dispatched to lead combat wings of all three air divisions. After the briefing, everyone went to their regular duty stations. I picked up the latest weather reports, communications procedures, exact times for control points, and where we would fly in the formation. My co-pilot took care of the escape kits, candy bars, and extra equipment issued for each mission. Our navigator got his flight plan ready, the bombardier drew his bombing kit and went over the targets, and the gunners went to the gunnery room to check out and load the .50-caliber machine guns aboard the planes.

We were worried about the weather because, as so often happened, a deterioration would force us to chalk up another canceled raid. But the weather held. Along the runways, our bombers waited for the flare that would signal the lead aircraft to start its takeoff. For heavy bombers, joining a formation in small groups was tough in good weather and very dangerous when the weather was poor, so we were lucky that there were no mishaps flying over England on our way to our next control point, the coast of Holland. As we approached Holland, I ordered the gunners to test-fire their weapons. We flew into solid cloud cover over Germany, then climbed to 29,000 feet, the maximum altitude for formation flying. We couldn't get any higher, and yet the cloudy conditions made flying wingtip-to-wingtip extremely dangerous. When we got to Hannover, we encountered the heaviest fighter attacks imaginable, vigorous and relentless, with German planes diving back and forth through our formation. Our Forts sent out a hail of lead, but the fighters persisted. It was like a dust storm when bullets from one of their machine guns hit the side of the plane, I could only thank God that their exploding 20mm cannon shells missed us. The intercom was full of noise and chatter as the gunners made comments to each other about the fighters heading straight for us. "Get set. Look at those bastards. Here they come. 12 o'clock. Come on get him. He's gone. Here's another one; another noser. Come on now, get the bastard."

Some of our own P-51s were waiting for us but so were the Jerries. "fighters, four o'clock low; fighters eleven o'clock high" I was dodging fighters right and left then got enough respite thanks to the P-51s to settle down and drop my bombs. As the bomb bay doors opened those Jerries were still trying go in for the kill, little flashes of light as they fired their cannons. One fighter passed so close we could see the pilot but then he got hit with a hail of lead and went straight down.

Over Berlin

At last we reached the city of Berlin and commenced our bomb run. Eight planes bombed the Erkner ballbearing factory, one bombed the Tempelhof district, and one was forced to turn back because of severe damage caused by enemy fighters. The flak over Tempelhof was intense enough that six of our bombers suffered minor damage and two crewmen were wounded. Ultimately, the Pathfinder equipment worked very well on my aircraft and one other, seven sets worked well enough, and one didn't operate at all.

We were so worn out when we finally got home that we could barely crawl out of the plane. The mission wasn't over until we had reported to interrogation and given a complete rundown of the entire mission. These interrogations required input from every crewmember for details.

CHAPTER 29

MISSIONS TWENTY-TWO THROUGH TWENTY-FIVE— THE HOME STRETCH

MUNSTER MARSHALING YARDS, March 11, 1944, 482nd Bomb Group—
6:05 hours flying total—124 bombers over targets, 1 plane lost, 140 escorts.

There is not a lot to say about this relatively small mission by 124 B-17s. Eight of our Pathfinder aircraft were dispatched to lead combat wings of the 1st and 3rd Air Divisions to Munster. We attacked the city's rail yards through 10/10 cloud cover using radar, which worked well in four of our Forts including mine, but only fair to poorly in the other four. We couldn't see the results, but later photos showed that we made some hits near the yards. There were no enemy fighters to be seen and very little flak, although two of our planes did sustain some battle damage.

BRUNSWICK INDUSTRIAL AREA, March 15, 1944, 482nd Bomb Group—
8:00 hours flying total—330 bombers over targets, 3 planes lost, 259 escorts.

Eight PFF B-17 Forts and four PF4 B-24 Liberators were dispatched to lead combat wings of the 1st and 3rd Air divisions on a mission to bomb Brunswick. I piloted one of the Pathfinders. The cloud cover was too heavy to observe the accuracy of our bombs, but one of the B-24 crews saw smoke and fire in the city through a break in the clouds. The enemy fighter opposition was meager to the point of nonexistent. At the same time, more than a hundred enemy planes were seen by our crews, but they were quickly driven away by friendly escort fighters. We did encounter flak, moderate but with deadly accuracy and intensity. It was of the barrage type emanating from large motorized trailers between Ymiuden and Egmond. Two of our aircraft suffered minor battle damage, but no one was wounded.

During this raid my waist gunners would throw strips or even bundles of aluminum foil called "chaff" out of the open window. The idea was to reduce the exposure of the Forts to flak by jamming the radar equipment of the AA batteries. I didn't let myself think about what it was like leaning out of the window throwing strips of foil but I do think it helped. I was more worried about the flak than the fighters because we stood a chance again the Jerries with our gunners and the P-47s, P-38s and the more modern P-51s.

AUGSBURG MUNITIONS INDUSTRY, March 16, 1944, 482nd Bomb Group—9:20 hours flying total—401 bombers over targets, 23 planes lost, 868 escorts.

Less than 24 hours later, we were dispatched on a mission to Augsburg, but by then I didn't care. At the briefing, I looked around me and saw basically, when I think back on it now, a bunch of young men, kids really, my own age who would go on this raid and the next and the one after that until they were either shot down or completed their missions. I was getting so close to completing my 25 missions that I couldn't go on a raid fast enough. This time, twelve Pathfinder Forts were dispatched to lead the combat wings of all three Air Divisions to airfields and aircraft manufacturing plants at Oberpfaffenhofen, Lechfeld, Landsberg, Augsburg, Gablingen, Lowenthal and Friedrichshafen. I was one of nine Pathfinders who led combat wings to Augsburg.

I wanted to get these last two missions over and done with. They were long, each over nine hours. Now my ground crew would sneak in a little extra fuel, which went against the philosophy that there was no point to carry gas to and from a target and not use it. But if I could talk the ground crew into adding another 100 gallons it might save the plane so I always gave it try. The engineer (and top turret gunner) could transfer gas from one tank to another. We lost 23 Forts on this mission. We saw a couple of Forts leave the group formation and dip down to cloud cover. I had hoped they made it back to Britain but they were counted as lost.

It was once again difficult to see if our bombs were on target due to the extreme cloud undercast at the target. In general, the radar equipment worked well, although three of our aircraft bombed on flares of the preceding combat wings because of equipment failure over Augsburg. There were some vicious enemy fighter attacks by as many as 200 enemy aircraft of all types. The twin-engine BF-110s fired rockets. Our friendly fighter support was good and only two of our Forts were damaged. We encountered some flak of the barrage type, which started out meager and inaccurate and then grew more and more intense and accurate as the last planes flew over the munitions plant.

OBERPFAFFENHOFEN, March 18, 1944, 482nd Bomb Group—9:25
hours flying total—480 bombers over targets, 43 planes lost, 925 escorts.

On March 18, 1944, I was on my 25th mission, the pilot of the leading bomber force, flying with the 91st Bomb Group, one of the bomb groups of the 1st Division. The commanding officer of the 91st accompanied me.

I had flown from Alconbury to Bassingbourn the night before with my B-17. After the briefing that outlined the three targets of the day, we were told that the B-24s would bomb Frankfurt, the 3rd Division B-17s would bomb Munchen, and our 1st Division would bomb Oberpfaffenhofen. After assembling the bombing formations over England, we headed out for the targets, scheduled to cross the coast of Belgium at 9:51 a.m. Oberpfaffenhofen hosted a German airfield and a BF-109 factory near Munchen. This was the Dornier Aircraft Company, makers of bombers and Germany's oldest aviation plant.

If all went as planned, and it never did, we would reach the I.P. at 11:53 a.m. to start the bomb run on the target. We experienced many fighter attacks en route, most of them coming from the front in an effort to knock out the leaders of the formation. The German fighters swept through the formation, firing their cannon, and doing as much damage as they could. Of course, the rate of closure with the B-17 formations flying at 150 miles per hour and the German fighters coming at us at 250 miles per hour was very fast. After each pass, the fighters re-formed and attacked again, sometimes from the tail end of the formation. It was one attack after another, and being in the lead aircraft during the frontal attacks, I could see the tracers from the 20mm rounds the fighters fired as they flew head-on toward our formations.

We didn't get much flak until we got to the I.P. when the sky literally darkened with bursts. This continued until we had dropped our bombs and were headed home. Once we were out of the target area the German fighters would attempt to knock out of the sky those of us who were left. For another two and a half hours we would be over Germany, under attack but on our way home. We also had friendly fighters with us most of the way who continued to harass the Germans and protect the bomber force as much as possible. Our losses would have been much higher without this support of the P-51s, P-47s and P-38s. Seven hundred and thirty-eight bombers and 913 fighters from the 8th Air Force attacked Germany that day with a loss of 43 bombers and 13 fighters. We were in the air 9 hours and 35 minutes.

I became very emotional when I landed back at Alconbury knowing that I had survived my last raid. John Ford, the tail gunner, and I hugged each other since we had both made it through 25 missions. The crew always walked around the plane to check how much damage the flak and fighters had done, and on this raid it was considerable. Holes in the wings, fuselage, and one elevator showed again what a great and survivable airplane the B-17 was. As was the custom, photos were taken for the group file of those who had finished the required 25. The commanding officer of the 91st stated that he would fly with us on any combat mission and wanted to know if we would transfer to his organization and fly more missions. John and I both said no thanks. I'm sure the colonel understood. We wanted to go home.

The 482nd Group was the only Pathfinder Group in the Army Air Force. Pilots from this group led 80 percent of the 8th Air Force's missions from November 1943 through March 1944, the period I served with them. From March until VE Day the group trained all the 8th Instrument Bombing Navigators as well as the radar ground crews while continuing to make a few special operational flights and reconnaissance missions. The Pathfinder Group received multiple commendations for its outstanding performances of duty.

Of the 25 raids I made, 6,827 bombers participated with a loss of 298. While I made six raids without fighter escort, 4,204 fighters accompanied the bombers on the other 19 raids.

CHAPTER 30

SPECIAL ORDERS

The first name on Special Orders No. 60, dated March 23, 1944 from Headquarters Eighth Air Force, was Capt. Raymond E. Brim 0730358. These orders stated that I had completed an operational tour and was now assigned to the 12th Replacement Continental Depot for return to the United States. It was on March 25, 1943, that we had left the U.S., going overseas. But this time, instead of flying, I was to go home by ship.

The *Mauritania* had been a passenger ship that had been converted to a troop transport; she was bringing troops back to the States after unloading a greater number of troops in preparation for the invasion of Europe. I was assigned to a stateroom with three other officers. They were very tight quarters with four bunk beds, but we couldn't have cared less.

Much of the time aboard the ship, once it was underway, was spent playing poker, bridge and bingo, and doing emergency drills. The *Mauritania* moved right along, but she did not maintain a straight course; she zigzagged from one heading to another to avoid German submarines. Because of the speed of the ship and the frequent changing of course, the wake left behind was beautiful.

Once docked in New York, we were assigned to Fort Dix, New Jersey, to be processed and organized into different groups, all going in different directions. It was during those few days at Fort Dix that I went to New York City and took J.P. Clarendon's things to his father. It was from the

Clarendons' home in Hackensack that I called Pat to let her know that I was back in the U.S. and would be home in a few days.

Train travel was finally organized in such a way that select cars would be filled with "returning heroes." These cars would be dropped off at the depot closest to their homes. I was in charge of two cars that would be dropping off returnees in Utah. Part of my job was to be certain that each individual got off at the right place. I was carrying my box of English china that I had bought during my time in England. The box looked like a box kite, and if I had not been in charge of the two train cars, it might have been lost or at least put in the baggage compartment. I was bound and determined to get it home to Pat.

Home at last

Our arrival in Salt Lake seemed like a dream. After being married for just three months and then being gone for a year, I could hardly wait for the train to stop. At first I did not see Pat, but then she called out. What a beautiful sight she was. I was so excited that I put the box of china down and after a wonderful greeting, I almost forgot it. Someone called out and reminded me that the box was some distance from where we were and not to forget it.

The two families gathered at Pat's home for a drink and to hear about my experiences. I don't remember ever having the attention of the two families as I did this day. We had been together for about an hour when Pat asked me to come out into the kitchen. I thought she wanted to be romantic and was only too happy to be with her alone. How wrong I was. I did not realize that my language was now laced with many swear words, so she was concerned that I was shocking my folks as well as hers. When we talked about the Germans when I was in England, it was not in endearing terms. There was not anything bad enough we could say. After a year of this, I had gotten into the habit of calling them the lowest of low humans. Pat told me that I had to clean up my language, and I did. So much for romance.

Pat had made reservations at the Hotel Utah for our first night together after all those months apart. Romance and love were both all that one could expect. It was a night that I remember to this day. We looked back on it as one of the most wonderful nights we ever had. Being back together, holding each other, loving each other, and just being alone with one another made our reunion very, very special.

My leave in Salt Lake disappeared with parties, visiting relatives, more parties, and just being with each other. My family was greatly relieved that I had returned home without any physical scars of war and was with my new wife. They had learned to love Pat while I was overseas, and now our being together was all they could and did ask for.

The orders that arrived too soon sent me to Santa Monica, California, to another replacement center. We left Salt Lake with 13 suitcases that included a record player and albums of classical music. When we arrived in L.A., Pat's uncle met us, and when he saw all those suitcases, he suggested that we learn to travel light. I was so happy that if we had had even more suitcases, it would have been fine with me.

We went to a very nice hotel on the coast and had a room that overlooked the ocean. Duties for me were very limited; I just had to report in and await orders to my next duty station. Pat and I walked on the beach and went out to dinner at some of the finest places every night. We could hear the ocean breakers from our room, which added to the romance of being together. Finally, a honeymoon.

Assigned to home

When my orders arrived, I couldn't believe it. I was assigned to the 9th Service Command in Salt Lake City—to the public relations and recruiting division. We called the folks to tell them we were coming home. My job was to help sell war bonds and to encourage young men and women to join the service. Each of the services had similar offices in Salt Lake, and when we had a walk-in who could not pass the minimum test, we would suggest he or she try the Marines. Of course the Marines did the same to us.

A war bond stand was set up on Main Street and 2nd South in Salt Lake, and on occasions I would tell my story about flying in the 8th Air Force and encourage people to buy bonds. I talked to women's groups, the Town Club, men's clubs and groups, schools, the Civil Air Patrol—any group who would listen.

Pat and I found a little apartment on 12th East and 2nd South and furnished it with things from both of our families. Pat's mother did a great job in bringing these three rooms together to make a comfortable home. We frequently had a group, mostly young ladies, at the house, many of them looking for an officer to date. My cousin, Peg Pearsall, met a young officer and they seemed to hit it off to the extent that Peg's father became a little concerned. In fact, he had Vincent investigated because he was from the South. No prejudice there…

The 9th Service Command had several planes assigned under the senior Army Air Forces officer, Lieutenant Colonel Johnstone. To get my flying time in, I went out to the Salt Lake municipal airport and flew one of the several airplanes that were available. It was here that I flew the Navy SBD Dauntless dive-bomber, with its strange perforated flaps. It was designated as an RA-25. A Navy torpedo bomber, the TBF Avenger, was designated the RA-24. Both of these aircraft had their rear guns removed, which gave the passenger in back of the pilot more room. Checking out was not very formal; Johnstone would point out a few controls, explain how to lower and raise the flaps, the landing gear, the fuel gauges, and, on the RA-24, how to unlock the tail wheel. Other than that, it was kick the tire and get out of here. My flight records show that I got about 25 hours in these two planes.

The home front at war

Upon completion of a three-month tour in Salt Lake, we were ordered to Maxwell Field, Alabama, which was another replacement depot for the Training Command. Prior to leaving Salt Lake, I bought a second-hand car, a Studebaker President coupe, which was the best-looking car we ever had. The body was a cream color with a black top. The engine was a straight eight-cylinder with a synchronized transmission so you could shift without using the clutch. It had retreaded tires, which proved to be a problem, but new tires were impossible to get. The car had a very large trunk, and when we left Salt Lake it was full, as was the back seat.

Upon checking in at Maxwell Field, I was offered an assignment of recruiting aircrews to fly B-29s. I was to be checked out in the B-29, and then travel from base to base to encourage airmen who had completed a combat tour to retrain into the B-29. At that time, however, the B-29 had a dubious record—engine problems and several crashes. I was concerned that if I became qualified, I would become eligible to go overseas for a second tour, so I turned the assignment down. I was then sent to Sebring, Florida, to become an instructor pilot on the B-17.

While in Sebring, we had to live in a hotel that was infested with cockroaches and ants. Not much had changed from the time we were in Salina, Kansas, when I was getting ready to go overseas.

Even though I had several hundred hours flying the B-17, this did not matter to the Training Command. Everything had to be done by the numbers, and you did it their way, period. Of the class I was in to become an instructor pilot, most of the students had completed a combat tour, and we all thought we could fly the B-17 as well as the Training Command instructors.

A meeting was called one day by the operations officer, Major Long, and we were given a lecture about our attitude and told that we had to realize that the Training Command knew what was necessary to survive combat. At the meeting I made the mistake of asking Major Long how much combat time he had, and of course he did not reply. Two days later I was reassigned to Laredo, Texas, to fly gunners who were in training. This was about as low a job as one could get and it was in payment for my asking an embarrassing question. The Training Command commandos knew how to take care of smart guys.

Laredo

We loaded up the car again and took off for Laredo. After checking into one of the two hotels in town and being told we could spend only four days there, our first priority was finding a place to live. We did find a nice looking neighborhood where Pat took one side of the street and I took the other. We would ring the bell of the home, explain our problem, and ask if they had a spare room they would rent to us. At one home, a lady met me at the door and, after listening to my appeal, told me they did have a spare room but she would have to discuss it with her mother, sister and brother. Also, they wanted to meet Pat. This was encouraging and a time was set for the next day when the two of us could meet the

Murphy family. We passed the test and now had a roof over our heads. During our interview, one of the ladies said that I looked like one of their sons, and that might have had some influence.

Our room was upstairs, and we were to share the bathroom with the rest of the family. This was the first time I had seen an all-metal bathtub. A schedule was worked out to use this common facility.

The Murphys were wonderful people. The brother was in the business of buying and selling hides from cattle, some coming from Mexico and some from Texas. The oldest person, the mother, was confined to a chair and said little. One sister was a retired schoolteacher. The other lady was just great. She had been married and one of her sons was in the Air Corps while the other had a ranch near Laredo. They all took a great liking to Pat, and that made it easier.

I reported in to the gunnery school at the base and asked if I could take the gunnery course that the enlisted men were taking. I felt that I would do a better job by understanding the training they were receiving, and if I was going to fly with them, I would just feel better and maybe even help them some. My request was approved and I started the school. Among other skills, I learned to assemble a .50-caliber machine gun blindfolded. How ridiculous. I was able to bring a gun home, and in drilling me Pat got to know the parts as well as I did.

We started looking for a house as soon as we could and in time found a small four-room house that an officer had rented until he had been reassigned. We just lucked into it. We rented furniture, and although we had little choice, we found enough to get by. But I had to build an icebox out of ammunition boxes I brought home from the base. It worked pretty well but was very small and could not be sealed sufficiently to keep things cool for any length of time or to keep the ants out. But we were happy and as comfortable as anyone else under these conditions. One of the nicer things about the house was the grapefruit and orange trees in the yard. We had never had such great, tasty grapefruit and we ate them twice a day. Just to go out and pick a grapefruit from the front yard was an experience for both of us.

I was able to get enough gasoline ration tickets to make a trip to Salt Lake. Pat and I thought it would be nice to take some grapefruits to the folks. I had built some boxes that fit in the trunk of our car and we loaded them with grapefruit. All was fine until we hit the border of Arizona, where we were stopped by state agriculture inspectors. They asked if we had any fruit with us and I had to say we did. After one look, the inspector told us that all the grapefruit had a disease called scale and had to be destroyed. They took the grapefruit out behind a building and poured oil over them and set them afire. I was less than happy. I did have one box of grapefruit in the car that I did not tell them about, and we got at least a few home to our families in Salt Lake.

Going to the opera

One day I came home from flying gunners and Pat told me that she had seen an ad for the opera "La Boheme." She thought it would be great if we could see it. It was being presented by a troupe from the New York Metropolitan Opera with the famous soprano Grace Moore in the lead. I agreed, but the problem was that the opera was being presented in San Antonio, 150 miles from Laredo. Pat called the opera office and was able to get tickets for a Saturday night. It was a very dressy affair, the newspaper said. At that time we were not supposed to go farther than 100 miles from the base. We agreed that we would take off for San Antonio in time to have dinner there, Pat would change into her formal dress in the car, and then we would go to the opera. But I did not want to be more than a hundred miles away for the night so we would head back towards Laredo after the opera.

All went as planned and we had a wonderful dinner at the Gunter Hotel. Our problem then was to find a place for Pat to change into her dark green velvet formal. We drove around San Antonio until we found an isolated area behind a warehouse. Pat got into the back seat of the car and changed into her formal while I kept a lookout for anyone walking, or in an approaching car. She finally made it with a little help from me to zip up the back of her dress. By then her hair looked as if it had never been combed, so that became the next project. In time she had her hair arranged and we took off for the opera house.

We were running a little late but got to our seats just before the curtain went up. The lady sitting next to me complimented me on having such a beautiful wife and how nice she looked. I did not tell her that Pat had changed into her formal in a back alley of San Antonio. Following the opera, we returned to Laredo, arriving just prior to sunrise. It had been a long day.

I was not happy flying gunners in Laredo. When I think back on it, it could have been what they call PTSD today but the constant firing of .50-caliber guns at targets placed on the grounds around the countryside made me anxious and jumpy. I decided to check out what specialists were needed for the Air Corps and found that a shortage existed for aircraft maintenance officers. Their school was at Chanute Air Force Base in Rantoul, Illinois, which is not too far from Champaign, Illinois. It did not take me long to fill out the paperwork for the transfer to Chanute.

After checking in, we were back to the old problem of finding a place to live. The base at Chanute had a list of housing that was available, but most of the time it was unacceptable. We became desperate as the school was about to start. We eventually found an annex to a fraternity house that was renting their upstairs.

Pat wanted to go back to school, so she enrolled at the University of Illinois at Champaign, taking classes in political science and music. Pat was an accomplished pianist and wanted to continue her training while at the university. The university had practice rooms, but we thought it would be easier for her if she had a piano in our apartment. One of the downtown music companies rented us a piano and agreed to deliver it to the second floor. Pat began to practice her music during the day, all of it classical. The piano was an upright and even though it had been tuned after being moved, it would not hold the tuning. We learned why this instrument was being rented.

In the meantime, I was going to school at Chanute, doing classroom work in the mornings and labs in the afternoon, taking engines apart and putting them back together. The course was very intensive, covering everything that went into keeping airplanes operating. I still have some of the tools we made that I turned out on lathes in the machine shop.

To save gas, several of us started a car pool and would pick each other up on select days of the week. This made it possible for the wives to get out of their houses, and it also led to social activities after school and on weekends. Pat met some of her sorority sisters who were officers' wives and going through the same adjustments she was, like having to move into temporary housing every few months. Most of the husbands had returned from overseas and were in the same situation we were in.

One day, Pat asked some of her friends in for a lunch and bridge. I'm sure her guests were not impressed with our apartment. It happened to be the end of the month, and when I got home, I took a check down to the landlord. He started laying into me about the wild parties being given with a bunch of women and the damn piano practicing classical music. He said that if the piano was going to be played it had to be at least boogie-woogie music. He then told me: "Lieutenants were O.K., and majors are great, but captains are smart alecks and a pain in the ass." I was able to get the check back only on the condition that we would move out right then and there, that night. I went upstairs and told Pat we had to move and to start packing.

A friend of Pat's who had been at the luncheon that day said they had two army cots in a spare room and that we could use them until we found another place to rent. I started taking things down to the car and Pat was in tears as she packed our suitcases. I called the piano company and asked them to come and get the piano and we left with a loaded car and an ironing board partway out the back window and Pat holding a card table on the running board. In a couple of days, with the help of friends, we found a three-room apartment in Urbana. Pat continued with her classes and used the University of Illinois practice rooms. I went back to school at Chanute.

It was in Urbana that we learned of President Roosevelt's death. What a shock it was to all of us. How were we going to win the war without his leadership? Who was this guy Truman? The death of President Roosevelt put even more pressure on the military and it was felt in the school. Suddenly we were moving along faster in our class because we still had the war in Europe to win and then the Japanese to deal with.

We were finishing our schooling, me at Chanute and Pat at the university, when we learned of a new bomb called the "atomic bomb" that had been used against Japan. No one seemed to know much about it other than one fellow student, who advised us that in time we would be using atomic energy to power our cars with an engine about the size of a shoebox. With the event of the second atom bomb and the ending of the war shortly thereafter, our life changed dramatically. We had to make some decisions that would impact the rest of our lives, and it was not easy. The aircraft maintenance school was drawing to a close. I could stay in the Army Air Forces and perhaps go overseas, but there was no guarantee that Pat would be able to accompany me. She had just finished a semester at the University of Illinois, so at least the timing was good.

In time we made the decision to get out of the service, return to Salt Lake City, and go back to school. I would go to school on the G.I. Bill, which paid $75 a month and school expenses. As I look back on the experiences we had during World War II, I see myself as very lucky in many ways. I was not injured during combat and I was lucky enough to have a wife who put up with many moves and very trying conditions. We were not the exception, as many young people put up with less. We were young, and the future was ours.

PART III

AFTER THE WAR, 1945–1975

CHAPTER 31

THE BLACK DAYS

I had been out of the Army Air Forces for two years, and the experience had not been what Pat and I had hoped for. In the fall of 1945 we both returned to the University of Utah, me on the G.I. Bill, and with money saved by Pat while I was overseas. We took a small three-room apartment on Second Avenue in Salt Lake City. We were so happy, but I was not able to concentrate on my schoolwork. In retrospect, I was still mentally in the military and having an extremely hard time adjusting to my new civilian life.

We did not have much money, but I did yard work around the apartment building to get a reduced rent. That winter, I shoveled snow at different places to earn additional cash. The folks helped out as well as they could, but they had limited funds. Dad gave us a 1936 car so we could get to school and around the city. Pat made most of her clothes. For Christmas 1946, she gave me an empty golf bag and I gave her two books. Our living room furniture was hand-me-downs from the families. I made the one overstuffed chair we had by tying old springs together to form the structure. It was upholstered with drapes that had been used at the Condon's at one time. The couch came from the basement of my folks' home.

We had a little washing machine that sat on the counter when in use. It was all we could find or afford after the war. It would wash one sheet at a time. We had a rack that held the washed laundry so it could dry, but it was an all-day job just to finish the washing. Pat did all the cooking and cleaning of the apartment—all the things that made our living comfortable. If I attempted to assist in any way, she would say, "Stop trying to take over. I'm going to take care of this apartment. If I need help, I'll call you." Even with all her walking problems from her polio, she never complained.

A baby on the way

I think it was during the month of May 1946 that we went to Dr. Russ Wherritt (a distant cousin), who ran tests and told us we were to become parents. Three and a half years after we were married, the news that we were going to have a baby made Pat and me very happy. At the time, we gave little or no thought about the impact of an addition to our family; the thrill far outweighed the concern of how we would manage financially.

After talking to Russ, we went directly to my folks home to tell them that they were about to become grandparents. They were thrilled. Dad never thought he would be a grandparent; he was seventy years old and not well. We then went to the Condons to tell them the same news, and it was like Old Faithful exploding. Pat's father was pleased, but Geneal went into hysterics with comments like, "I was afraid of this." She talked to Pat like she was a child. She then gave me hell and said it was all my fault: "Don't you know better and don't you know Pat can't have a baby. She's had polio." This experience took much of the joy out of the day and our prospects of a new baby. Pat was in tears and I was pissed off. But we eventually gave up the apartment and moved in with Pat's family to save money.

To some degree, it was very reasonable to be concerned about our future and how we were going to support a family. For a short time, I became a salesman and attempted to sell costume jewelry in California. It was on a return trip to Salt Lake that I rolled the car after hitting a horse at about 4:00 in the morning. When the state police came by, one of them said, "I can tell you are married and expecting a baby with all the diapers and nursing bottles you have spilled around in your car." The car would still run, so I drove it on into Salt Lake with the windshield half gone where the horses head had come through. We decided that being a salesman was not my calling and, besides, I wanted to be with Pat during her pregnancy. I then took a job at Geneva Steel, in the production planning office, which required that I carpool for the 30-mile trip to and from plant. It was a long drive to a job—not a career—and I hated it, but at least I was out of the house and not exposed to my mother-in-law's harassment about me getting Pat pregnant.

Civilian life was turning out to be a disaster. I felt like there was only one path to take—submit an application to go back into the military. I had kept up my reserve officer commission after getting out of the service, which meant that once a month I attended a meeting at Hill Air Base outside of Salt Lake and flew AT-6s for a few hours.

With the arrival of our new baby daughter, Cecilia, our life changed and, of course, we were so proud and happy. She became the center of our very limited activities and was worshiped by her grandparents on both sides of the family. I continued to work at the Geneva Steel Plant during this time as we waited to hear back from what was no longer the U.S. Army Air Forces, but the new U.S. Air Force.

Captain with flying pay

It was on October 1, 1947, that I received a telegram from the Air Force headquarters offering me the opportunity to come back on active duty with an assignment to Eglin Field, Florida. I was to come back as a captain, on flying pay. I had one week to accept the opportunity. Captain's pay was $500 a month plus flight pay. It took Pat and me about thirty seconds to accept their offer. All of a sudden, we had some sunshine in our life. The dark days faded away.

CHAPTER 32

PROJECT SANDSTONE

At Eglin Field I was assigned to the 1st Guided Missile Group, where I would be flying B-17s again. I couldn't have been happier. Eglin Field was about 50 miles east of Pensacola, Florida, and we stayed at the Santa Rosa Hotel in Pensacola. I went out to the base, checked in, and inquired about housing for my family. I was told it was my problem and they would give me some time off to find a place. Pensacola was a big naval airbase, so competition for any available housing was immense. Housing around Eglin was already taken up and, at best, it was limited in many ways. Pat and I decided to look for housing in the town of Pensacola. I could drive back and forth to work.

One day, while we were still looking for a place, I met an old friend who was the comptroller of the Air Proving Ground at Eglin. Dick Ezzard had checked me out to be a first pilot in the B-17 while we were at Salina, Kansas, prior to my going to England during the war. He told me he knew of a house near his, in Pensacola, and we should check on it. The house was on Bobe Street (pronounced Boobe) and the owner lived in a small house behind the unit for rent. Upon checking this lead, we found a small house with a front porch, two bedrooms, a kitchen, and a living room. Getting to it was a problem because the streets in the area were unpaved and we had nothing but red clay as roads. We took the house, sent for the few pieces of furniture we had stored in Salt Lake, and considered ourselves lucky.

Training for atomic testing

My work at Eglin consisted of re-familiarizing myself with the B-17 again and taking an instrument check. The mission of our organization at the time was to prepare to fly radio-controlled B-17s or drones through the cloud that developed after an atomic test. I was a safety pilot on the radio-controlled plane; my job was to take over if the radio controls did not respond. It was not the easiest job in that I had to trust the ground controllers until I, as a pilot, decided the plane was not under their control. We practiced day and night in anticipation of the next atomic tests out in the Pacific.

Drone B-17s had been used to collect particulate debris from the clouds of atomic tests during Operation Crossroads, the first atomic test to take place in the Pacific. My group had been alerted that additional tests would take place in 1948 and that more planes would be required. It was because of this that I was selected to participate, because by then I had over 1,000 hours of flying the B-17. Experience counted.

The selection of the B-17 to be a drone aircraft was an excellent choice since it was very stable. The biggest challenge was training the ground crews to take the plane off and land it using radio controls. Once in the air, it was a rather simple operation as long as the "mother" plane remained close enough to the drone to maintain radio contact. The mother plane was also a B-17. The modifications to the B-17s were rather crude, but they worked.

For the basic flying of the plane, the autopilot—"George"—was used. The control for this was very similar to the controls used to fly model airplanes today. The four throttles that were normally free to operate each engine were clamped together and moved by an arm attached to a servo motor located in the nose of the plane. Brakes were controlled by two buttons on the control box, one for each brake. The autopilot, throttles and brakes had different radio frequencies, and all had to work to get the airplane launched. A very primitive television picture of the instrument panel of the drone was transmitted to the ground controllers and the mother aircraft.

The sequence for launching one of the drones went something like this: The mother airplane took off and circled near the end of the runway to await the drone. The ground controller, using a surveyor's sextant (the controller could pick up any deviation from the centerline faster with this instrument), would line up the drone on the runway and then check the radio control of the plane. When he was confident that all controls were working, he applied the power and released the brakes, all the time watching the plane through the sextant. As it proceeded down the runway, he had to judge what the airplane was doing and control it. Behind the ground controller was a technician who watched the television and called out the airspeed. This was necessary so the ground controller would know when to send the radio signal to move the elevators to get the plane off the ground. Once the plane was airborne, the mother plane took over and the mission was on its way.

My job was to be sure that the ground controller kept the plane on the runway and got it airborne, and that the control was transferred to the mother plane. It was our responsibility to let the ground controller go as far as he could in controlling the plane, but if the plane appeared to be out of control, the safety pilot took over. This job could be—and was—often harrowing. We trained day in and day out at taking off and landing the drone. The takeoff in the Pacific would be at night, so we also practiced at night under large spotlights that helped the ground controller visualize what the plane was doing.

One night, the ground controller lost control shortly after we had started down the runway. I took over just in time to miss colliding with the ground-control approach shack. Another time, when the controller locked the brakes after we had landed, both tires were blown out. We earned our flight pay. While I was actually piloting the drone, my role as safety pilot would be on the ground when the drone when through an atomic cloud.

In due course, we were advised that we would be going to Eniwetok, a small atoll in the western Marshall Islands, to participate in atomic energy tests.

Pat did not want to stay in Pensacola while I was gone for the estimated three months, so we decided that she would return to Salt Lake and live with my folks. Her folks had gone to Athens, Greece, on a job for the U.S. State Department. I made arrangements to take the few days of leave I had accumulated to drive my family back home. I would then fly to San Francisco and pick up the plane to continue the flight to Eniwetok.

The old Plymouth would be put to the test again and we took off knowing that we would be crossing the mountains of Colorado during early spring. To prevent cold drafts coming into the car, I put tape around three doors and we all used the passenger side door to enter and exit. It looked as if we were holding the car together with surgical tape, which, to some extent we were.

Shortly after we got to Salt Lake, I hopped a bus to Travis Air Force Base near San Francisco, met the rest of the crew, and took off for Hawaii the next night, a 10-hour flight at 150 miles per hour and a head wind to fight all the way.

From Kwajale to Eniwetook through an atomic cloud

Our next destination was Johnston Island, where we refueled, had a bite to eat, and continued on to Kwajalein in the eastern Marshalls. We would live in tents there while the atomic testing took place in Eniwetok Atoll. On the approach to the runway of Johnston, the tail of another plane protruded from the ocean floor about 100 feet from the end of the runway. Someone unfortunately had landed short, but thereafter the submerged plane provided us an aid to line up with the runway and also to make it to the island. Project Sandstone was about to begin.

Background of Sandstone

Few people remember the early testing known as "Sandstone." I guess I'm among the last participants, based on my age of 93 in October 2016. I was involved in the collection of the particulate matter within the cloud following the three tests: (1) X-Ray, a 37-kiloton bomb on April 15, 1948; (2) the second test, Yoke, on May 1 with a yield of 49 kiloton; and (3) Zebra, an 18-kiloton device on May 5, 1948. That was three atomic tests within a month.

At that time, individuals' exposure to radiation was given limited consideration. The B-17s that had flown through the cloud were contaminated and had to be scrubbed down in preparation for the next atomic test series. Bluntly, the pressure that was on us at the time meant that little or no consideration was given to the exposure of the airmen who cleaned the planes of radioactivity. These airmen were issued dosimeters that were entirely different than those worn by the officers. The dosimeter would normally be carried in the pocket or attached to clothing; it measured the number of roentgens the individual had absorbed. The dosimeter given to each airman could be zeroed out with just a quick snap of the wrist. This alone could account for the low dosage reported by the Defense Department Nuclear Agency.

It should be noted that the radiological specialists assigned to evaluate the amount of exposure to individuals and structures had limited experience in their duties. I had a friend, Dr. William Crockett, who was the dental officer aboard one of the ships participating in Sandstone. All he had to conduct testing was a Geiger counter and a manual outlining the limitations of the instrument and the range to record of individuals and the surrounding area. The two bombs dropped on Japan provided some guidance, but few of the radiologists had been to Japan.

In 1985, a Congressional committee came to the conclusion "that the design of film badges, methods of film processing, and densitometric techniques and calibration were relatively crude." (See the Eisenbud Committee report in a 1985 NAS publication.) In my judgment, this is an understatement. As of this date, I cannot find anything on the dosimeters used in the early atomic testing program. Sometimes, it is easy to lose negative documentation.

It would be interesting to know how many men who participated in Project Sandstone are still alive. Based on my own experiences with the project, I have a difficult time accepting the so-called official report of exposure prepared by the Defense Nuclear Agency. For me, it is all a cover-up.

For example, after the project was over and I flew the last contaminated drone back to the States, why did they burn the uniforms they gave us? Why were we restricted from flying after landing at Johnston Island? Upon landing at Hickam Air Force Base, why were we parked in an isolated area with radioactive warning signs placed around the plane? Why was an armed guard placed at the site where the two planes were parked, other than to keep away anyone except crewmembers? The guards were stationed at the planes until we took off for the mainland.

The historical documents have sometimes been "lost"; the paper trail has been spread across our government agencies and civilian contractors. In other words: "Capitalizing on Ignorance."

During our free time, we were allowed to wander around Kwajalein, although it wasn't a very big island and there wasn't much to do. We were not permitted to go swimming because of the tide. After all the training they had invested in us at Eglin Field, they did not want to lose anyone. For entertainment we had outdoor movies to go to, and there was also a lot of bending of the arms at the officers' club.

I have a copy of an operations order that shows we had a strange schedule, but it did reflect what we would be doing at the test site. It reads as follows:

Time Schedule:

- Breakfast 01:30
- Operations 02:15
- Briefing 02:20
- H hour 05:54 [H hour was the scheduled time for the bomb to go off]
- Immediately after takeoff, pairs will climb using Visual Flight Rules (VFR) to stations altitude using the Standard Operating Procedure (SOP) climb procedure. SOP interception procedure will be followed.
- After completion of 3rd pass, all pairs will let down VFR over Kwajalein.

This training schedule continued at Kwajalein and at Eniwetok where the atomic energy tests were to be held.

Each drone was assigned an altitude to penetrate the mushroom cloud that developed after the bomb had been detonated. Scoops were attached to each plane to capture the debris from the cloud on filter papers contained in the scoop. The filter paper was turned over to the experts for analysis after the mission had been completed. It was hoped that the debris at each altitude would give some indication of the amount of radiation that was in the cloud, the dispersal of the elements that made up the bomb, and so forth. Both chemical and physical analysis was made of everything on the filter paper. The direction the cloud moved after the detonation was of little concern, because the test was hundreds of miles from any concentration of people.

The day before the first test shot, we were very excited as we flew the planes from Kwajelein to Eniwetok. What we were going to do had not been done before, and being a participant in this new world of atomic bombs was not only exciting, it was in the best interest of the United States.

Once again I found myself leading the way, so to speak. No one had talked about the dangers of being exposed to radiation. We had been told that we would have to wear special goggles to keep the bright light from hurting our eyes. We were all issued goggles that had a small slit in the black lens. We were also issued dosimeters that would measure the amount of radiation to which we were exposed.

Test one: X-ray

There were two kinds of dosimeters issued. One looked like a pen, and when the two leaves in the pen became separated you were to report to a radiation officer. The only problem with these instruments was that all you had to do was shake them and they would zero out again. As I mentioned earlier, those were the ones issued to the enlisted men who scrubbed down the drone B–17s. The other instrument was a small black badge. These were issued to officers. This difference in dosimeters proved to be a problem later on.

All of the tests were to be tower tests. That is, the device would be mounted approximately 200 feet in the air on a tower. On April 15, the first atomic test took place under the codename of X-RAY. It was a 37-kiloton shot (one kiloton equals the approximate energy release of a one-thousand-ton TNT explosion), and all the drones were launched and in place to fly through the cloud and pick up the particulate matter at the various assigned altitudes.

There was a twenty-minute interval between getting the mother plane and its drone off before the next pair was to be airborne. This meant that there was a lot of scrambling at the last minute with each pair at the end of the runway. I was one of the safety pilots who would line up the plane on the center of the runway and remain in it until all the controls had been checked out using the radio control system. When everything was ready, I left the plane and went back with the ground controller.

If something did not check out, a back-up plane would be launched after all other drones had taken off. If the ground controller lost control of the plane on the ground, he was to shut down the power and attempt to stop the plane.

Test two: YOKE

YOKE took place on May 1 and had a yield of 49 kilotons. After the plane was about a third of the way down the runway, the control team cut the power and stopped the plane half off and half on the runway. It was my job to get to the plane and taxi it off to a ramp so that the other planes could be launched as soon as possible.

Once aboard the drone, I had to disconnect the throttles that had been held together with a special clamp, turn off the autopilot and radio controls, and taxi the plane to the ramp. I remember very well running down the runway to get to the plane to disengage the controls. We had only two stand-by planes to cover the assigned mission.

To reduce the number of people on Eniwetok at the time of the explosion, all crews not needed to continue our mission were flown back to Kwajalein. I was the pilot of one of the B-17s flying back with the excess crews. We all wanted to see the explosion, so we took our time getting out of the area. We had our special glasses and could hear the countdown on the plane's radio. I don't remember how far away from Eniwetok we were when H-hour arrived, but I do remember how the cockpit of the plane lit up. Even with the glasses on, you could read the instruments on the panel.

The first light we noted was a kind of phosphorescent bluish purple that soon turned to a reddish yellow color. We could see the cloud start to form. Then we had to get out of the area and back to Kwajalein.

From all the reports we got back at Kwajalein, all had gone well with the drone operation and all the planes had been recovered. The people in charge were pleased with the debris picked up on the filter papers and no one had been hurt, or so we were led to believe.

The problem of getting ready for the next test was that some of the drones were by now very radioactive. They had gone through the cloud at different altitudes and brought back excellent samples. The procedure to reduce the radioactivity on the planes was to wash them down with water and "gunk", a special solvent used to clean planes. The engines and the area around the engines were the hottest areas on the plane. Any oil or dirt on the plane collected hot particles from the explosion. The enlisted men had the job of washing the planes until they were declared safe by a radiological officer.

The cowlings around the engines were removed so they and the engines could be washed time and time again. The run-off of water naturally was contaminated with radioactivity and the enlisted men were standing in that run-off as well as having it drip off the plane and onto them.

I flew back to Eniwetok to pick up a drone and fly it back to Kwajalein, but when I got there, the plane was still too hot to fly and had not been released by the radiological officer. Pressure to get the planes ready for the next test was building.

I talked to some of the enlisted men about how much longer it would be, but all they could tell me was that they would keep working on it until it was released. When I asked about the dosimeter and exposure, I was told by the enlisted men that it was not a problem since all they had to do to zero out the dosimeter was to shake it. No doubt, everyone in charge of getting the planes clean knew this neutralizing of the dosimeter was taking place.

There was a lot of talk about the impact radiation exposure would have on our manhood as well as other side effects. To offset our worries, Major General William Kepner decided it was time to have a meeting about this very subject. All Air Force personnel were required to attend. Kepner, who had aggressively commanded VIII Fighter Command in England in 1943–44, started the meeting with a statement that went something like this: "I understand there are concerns about your manhood after being exposed to the radiation that comes from these tests. Well, I have walked on some the hulks of ships used during Crossroads and I have been out to the site of the most recent test on Eniwetok. When I get home, Mrs. Kepner will not notice any change in our love making." We all laughed. General Kepner then introduced a radiological officer who outlined the limitations of exposure and answered some questions. The meeting ended with the comment from General Kepner, "Don't worry. We will take care of you."

Test Three: Zebra

The third and last test, Zebra, was an 18-kiloton shot. It took place on May 15. All went well on this one and the atomic energy tests were declared a success. It was now time to fly the planes back to the United States. One of the drones was presenting a problem, however: scrubbing crews could not get its radiation level down to a safe level. This was because after each test, it became more and more difficult to scrub down the drones to a safe level of radiation. But there was a lot of pressure to get the people and planes off Eniwetok, so the decision was made to bring the drone back to Kwajalein and continue to scrub it there.

I was selected to fly the drone back to Kwajalein, where a special building had been set up with showers and clothes lockers. We were now to check in with the radiological officers who worked in this building prior to and after each flight. This was a new requirement. The three of us assigned to pick up the plane (pilot, co-pilot, and engineer) went to the radiological building and were issued some summer uniforms to wear when we picked up the drone.

We were flown to Eniwetok in another B-17. On the flight back to Kwajalein, we brought back some of the enlisted men who had been scrubbing the drone. When we landed back at Kwajalein, we were directed to park the drone away from the operations center and to report back to the radiological building for evaluation.

All went well until the radiological officer started waving his Geiger counter around each of us. We were ordered to remove the clothes they had given us at the start of the mission and to go take a shower. The clothes were piled up at the end of the building to be burned. We were each issued a surgical scrubbing brush and told to wash down thoroughly.

Some of the men were cleared by the radiological officer after the first wash, but two of us had to scrub down for a second time before we were cleared to put our own clothes on. Our skin clearly showed the effect of two scrubbings with that surgical brush.

The planes from our group were starting to return to the United States. I would be flying back the same "hot" plane I had flown down from Eniwetok, but even after several additional scrubbings it was still too radioactive for us to fly the long hours back to the States. As a result, we were the last B-17 to leave Kwajalein.

Liquor was very cheap on Kwajalein. Several of us decided to buy a couple of cases apiece and take them back to Florida. Our liquor exceeded the authorized quota by a considerable margin. The bomb bay of the B-17s had been modified to carry luggage and anything else needed for our mission. I had the two wooden boxes for my liquor, painted in olive drab and stenciled with the word "Instruments." These boxes were placed on the bottom of the luggage container in the bomb bay. Everything else was placed on top of our investment.

Special treatment

We departed from Kwajalein, and following a long flight landed at Johnston Island. We were required to remain there for a period of time because if we had taken off right away we would have exceeded the permitted radiation dosage. The flight from Johnston to Hickam Field, Oahu, was short and we were all looking forward to spending a little time in Hawaii. When I radioed in for landing instructions, I was advised to follow a jeep to an isolated area on the field after landing. The first thing that crossed my mind was that the customs officials were going to inspect our plane for the liquor we were bringing in. There was not a thing we could do about it other than hope the customs folks would not unload the bomb bay.

I taxied the plane behind the jeep to an area that was rather open and parked next to another of our B-17s. I got out of the plane and asked the jeep driver why we were being parked so far away. He told me that it was because our plane had participated in the atomic tests. I noticed that "Danger, Radiation" signs had been placed against each of the wheels and tail of the B-17 we were parked next to. About 50 yards in front of the planes was a guard sitting on a chair, positioned so he could watch them. We were advised to take what luggage we needed for our stay in Hawaii and to leave everything else on the plane.

It was then that I learned what caused the special attention we were getting. It seems that the plane we were parked next to had some engine problems when it landed at Hickam a couple of days ahead of us. The mechanic who worked on the engine problem was a civilian employee of the base. When he had completed his work, he was advised to go wash up prior to being checked for radiation. The mechanic did as he was instructed, but word spread on the base that he had worked on a radioactive plane and had been endangered. The base commander ordered the plane removed to an isolated area. Then, because we too had been flying a plane that had participated in the test, we received the same treatment.

Those of us who had hidden the liquor were relieved because now we had radioactive danger signs around our plane and a guard posted to keep people away, but at the same time that danger was protecting our investment.

The last leg of the trip to San Francisco was routine and I left the crew there to go to Salt Lake to pick up my family prior to going back to Florida. A friend took care of the liquor for me until I returned to Florida.

After I retired, I read a notice to anyone who had ever been exposed to radiation to advise the Department of Defense. I sent a letter advising the concerned office of my experiences and in time I received what we used to call an "idiot letter." It stated that they had reviewed the records of personnel who had participated in Operation Sandstone and found no evidence that anyone had received an excess of radiation.

Perhaps I was lucky, but I'll never know. The enlisted men who had to scrub down the planes, who were splashed with run-off radioactive water, who stood in the water from the washings, who would shake the dosimeters to zero them out because of the pressure to get the planes ready for the next test, who had their clothes soaked with this same water… what about them?

CHAPTER 33

ALL OVER THE MAP

After I returned from Project Sandstone, I left the B-17 crew at Travis Air Force Base and took a commercial plane to Salt Lake. While I was on Kwajalein, I had grown a mustache but had not mentioned it to Pat in my letters. When she saw me get off the United Airlines plane and walk towards her, the first thing she said was, "If you expect to go to bed with me tonight, that thing comes off." The mustache was removed. After checking in back at Eglin, my goal was house hunting and in time I found a four-room apartment, again in Pensacola. It was on the main floor and the building had five other units. After Pat and Cecilia arrived we started our life together again.

Since I had returned from the Pacific, the Air Force found that they had more pilots than were needed. When the personnel officer saw that I had attended the aircraft maintenance school, I soon was assigned to be the assistant S-4 officer of the group. My boss was a lieutenant colonel who was looking for a job in the Strategic Air Command. In time, he got his wish and left to go to SAC while I became the S-4 for the group. The S-4 was responsible for the supply and maintenance of the organization and I was one busy guy.

Following World War II, each of the services established a guided missile organization in simultaneous efforts to capture the entire missile mission for all the armed forces. The success Germany had had with its V-1 and V-2 missiles during World War II had opened up a new means of warfare. Each branch of the services was fighting for the mission of fielding missiles. The Army had an organization at Fort Bliss, Texas, and the Navy's was at Point Mugu, California. The Air Force had its testing at Eglin. We were all doing the same testing of these old missiles. My unit, the 1st Guided Missile Group, had launched many of them into the Gulf of Mexico. On a couple of occasions they blew up on the ramp or shortly after leaving it. Events like this made it interesting. The three services had not tested these weapons in a cold environment, so we took on the task of taking the missiles to Alaska to try our luck.

I was tasked, along with Captain Duncan "Sandy" Sanderson, to develop a plan for this test. I would be responsible for the logistics, and Sandy for the operational side of the project. We took a B-17 to Wright-Patterson Air Force Base, Ohio, which was the logistics headquarters of the Air Force, and presented our intended program. We received a lot of interest and support from the people at Wright-Pat, and then we flew out to Seattle, Washington, to talk to the people at Boeing who were supporting the operational side of the project.

Upon our return to Eglin, we presented our findings and recommendations to the staff and were complimented by Colonel Kilgore on the fine work we had done. I had received several notes from Kilgore saying what a terrific job I was doing, and both Sandy and I were complimented with a note on the side of our report about the Alaskan project of "great work."

The Air Force required an annual evaluation report on each of its officers, prepared by his senior officer. This report had a great impact on not only assignments, but also on the individual's future and promotion. Kilgore prepared one on me. He did not expect me to see it, but when I did, I was less than happy. He had rated me down in just about every subject of the report. I made the decision that I would ask to see him and challenge his evaluation of me. I had copies of his papers in which he complimented my work. When the interview took place in his office, he told me that the report reflected his evaluation and that was that. I responded that I could not work in this environment and I knew who had to leave.

I went to the base education office and talked to the officer in charge to find out what schools were available in the Air Force to which I could try to transfer. I learned from this meeting that the service was in need of intelligence and photo-radar interpreters, and that the school was at Lowry Field in Denver, Colorado. I volunteered and had my orders within a week.

Pope Air Base, Fayetteville

Following my stint at intelligence school I was assigned to the Tactical Air Force at Pope Air Base in Fayetteville, North Carolina. My assignment was to the intelligence section of the Air Force organization that provided tactical support to the Army's 82nd Airborne Division. My boss was a Colonel Noyes, who had just returned from Japan where he had been on General Douglas MacArthur's staff. He was not a happy warrior in that he considered this assignment a downgrade.

A joint Army-Navy-Air force operation with the code name Portrex was scheduled to take place in the Caribbean, with the USAF operating out of Ramey Air Force Base, Puerto Rico. For years, the Navy had been using a small island called Vieques for target practice, and this would be subjected to bombing by both the Air Force and the Navy, as called for by the war plan. We played the game and it all went well until one day some private property was damaged by a projectile fired from an airplane. The head of the Air Force operation, a Colonel Meyers, came to us to account for where our projectiles had landed. It made a difference on who would pay for the damage—the Air Force or the Navy. We worked overtime accounting for the projectiles we fired and could account for all but one. We thought we had an impact area where a missile could have landed, but we could not be sure until Meyers gave us guidance that it was the Air Force's missing missile.

On top of this problem, I was called into the personnel office of the wing and told that there was an intelligence requirement in Alaska and I was just the man to fill it.

Assignment: Alaska

When I went home and told Pat that we had an assignment in Alaska, she was very upset because we had just gotten settled in a house. We had no choice if we wanted to stay in the Air Force, so we packed up our things and had everything shipped back to Salt Lake. We had been told that it would be an 18-month wait for housing in Alaska and decided it would be best if Pat and Cecilia stayed in Salt Lake while I did my tour in Alaska. We signed out at the base and broke our lease. This was not a happy event.

When we got to Salt Lake we bought a little house for $14,500. It had three bedrooms, two of which were very small; a living room that was 12 by 18 feet; a small kitchen with a bay window and room for a table and chairs; and a bathroom. The basement had a coal furnace that had been converted to gas, so it took up a lot of room, but it worked.

I spent only two nights at the house before I had to report to Camp Stoneman, California, where I joined other troops going to Alaska. The troop ship had not been retrofitted since World War II, and four officers shared a room. The enlisted men were in the hold of the ship with hammocks stacked to the ceiling.

CHAPTER 34

THE ALEUTIAN ISLANDS

Island one: Cold Bay

When I reported in to the Alaska Air Command personnel office in Seward, a colonel told me that a mistake had been made, that several other officers had also been assigned to the intelligence section. In addition to this, the officer whom I was to replace had extended. I asked about an isolated tour and he jumped at the chance to work with someone who would volunteer for such an assignment. It just so happened that the operations officer at Cold Bay, also known as Thornborough Air Force Base, had completed his one-year tour in the Aleutian chain and I was qualified to take his place. The position required that the individual be a pilot, a captain, and willing to go.

With the bombing of Pearl Harbor, the decision was made to prioritize Europe, the Pacific, and then Alaska, in that order. The demand for sea lift to Europe and the Pacific exceeded the resources available, so on February 6, 1942, construction of the Alaskan Highway was approved by the Army and authorized by President Roosevelt five days later. It was completed in October 1942.

In the meantime, military installations were built to provide protection against the Japanese. Starting with Adak, Nak Nak, Cold Bay, Umnak and Dutch Harbor, the chain became the defense line for Alaska and the United States. With the invasion of Attu and Kiska by the Japanese, these remote installations became vitally important in the war effort. During the construction of bases in the Aleutians, the engineers had to tolerate miserable duty. Throughout the year, the islands were plagued with fog, freakish gales called "williwaws" screaming in from the seas at 100 miles an hour, blinding blizzards and torrential rains or snows.

The C-47 transport plane, known to civilians as the DC-3, was going out on the chain and I was a passenger sitting in the back on a bucket seat with my gear. It was about a two- to three-hour trip at 130 miles an hour, straight west toward Russia, and most of it over water. As we approached Cold Bay, ice built up on the propellers, so the pilot de-iced them with alcohol released on each propeller. When the ice broke away, it hit the side of the plane and made a hell of a noise. I was not sure that this isolated tour was such a good idea after all.

I was met by the commanding officer, Joe Cronin, another captain, and assigned to share a two-bedroom tar-paper-covered house with Lieutenant Carr, the base communication officer. We had a bathroom and a small living room, all heated by a single space heater. My job as operations officer was basically to monitor the flying in and out of the base, insuring that communications with incoming and outgoing planes, military and civilian, was available, including radar-assisted landings.

One day, Joe Cronin received a message that his wife was in need of a serious operation and he took emergency leave to return to the States. I was the next ranking captain, so I became the commanding officer as well as the operations officer. I was 27, about to turn 28.

It was deadly boring at the base other than the civilian planes coming in, and our weekly support flight from Anchorage. There is nothing worse than having 100 men standing around with nothing to keep them busy. This is especially true when they are isolated from normal contact with city life where their energies can be diverted.

On each side of the runway, approximately 50 feet, was a drainage ditch that had accumulated all kinds of junk. I decided to keep some of the men busy by cleaning out these ditches. I had the officer in charge of base maintenance get details of men and bring out the heavy equipment necessary to do the job. All was going well until the communications officer came in and told me they had lost contact with the outside world, which included the land lines going to our headquarters.

Cleaning ditches and other controversies

It so happened that in the process of cleaning up the ditches, a road grader had cut the communications cable. It took us some time to find the break, which was in one of the ditches along the side of the runway. This cable had been installed during World War II and at one time had been covered with enough dirt that it was protected, but the blade of the road grader had cut so deeply into the ground that the cable had been cut.

The cable contained many communication lines and was covered with a lead insulator, but there was not enough lead to prevent the blade of the road grader from cutting through. The communication officer had never been faced with this kind of a problem, and it wasn't until the senior enlisted man in his section came to the rescue that we were able to get connected back to the world. I found a World War II communications map that showed where the cables were located and we had stakes placed over the cables to protect them from my brilliant idea of how to keep men busy.

A few days later I was sitting in my office when the federal game warden, Bob Jones, came storming in. It seems that in our cleanup efforts, one of the old buildings that contained his smoking house had been wiped off the map. He had been smoking game, mostly small birds from the tundra that surrounded our base. When I asked if he had permission to use the building, he told me he did not want other people to know about his smoke house since they might raid it for the game. He was less than happy about it, but there was nothing I could do for him since the building was already destroyed. It was just one less building to worry about in my opinion.

We had also been having trouble with the power system on the base, mainly because the generators were old and required constant maintenance. One day I drove down to the dock and was walking around the buildings when I notice a diesel powered generator that looked new and I could not understand why it was sitting in the dock storage building. Upon inquiring, I learned that the generator had been placed in salvage, in other words, beyond repair. I also learned that the generator was scheduled to be given to Mike Utek, an Aleut (a native of the Aleutians).

Mike had been a guide for General Twining, General Vandenburg, and General Armstrong who commanded the Alaska Air Command, and several other high-ranking Air Force officers, during a bear hunt. He had gotten the impression that he had the run of our base because he had been the hunting guide for these officers. He lived in a small fishing village about five miles away, reachable by boat. I also learned that our enlisted men had repaired the generator with parts that came from our inventory, parts that we could have used to keep our power in operation. I ordered the men to take the generator back to our power plant and put it on line while the other generators were being repaired, and to consider this generator to be part of our equipment.

One night while I was eating my supper at the little officers' club, in walked Mike Utek, like a bull running through the streets of Spain. He was yelling at me and using four letter words that even surprised those of us at the table. As I recall the conversation went something like this (without the swearing).

Mike: "You took my generator that was given to me by General Twining for my village and I want it back."

I replied that we needed it to keep our base operational and that I understood that he had directed the enlisted men, in the name of General Twining, to repair the generator with parts from our inventory. And since the parts were owned by the US Air Force and the labor was provided by Air Force personnel, the generator could not be given away. In addition, we needed it for the operation of the base.

Mike was not impressed with my reply and stormed out of the club, saying, "I'll get your ass. I'm going to get in touch with General Armstrong and Twining and tell them you took my generator."

The door almost came off its hinges when Mike banged his way out of the club. The officers at the table were left hang-jawed at this event but I meant to stick with my decision. If I had given in, Mike would have been running the base. I did not sleep well that night.

Then there was the day Sergeant Green, who was working in the base maintenance section, came into my office and said, "Captain Brim, we have a problem." One of the enlisted men, while watching bear feed off the salmon, had been charged by a bear and had shot it. While I had to take this report at face value, I had some reservations regarding the bear charging an onlooker.

Just off the base was a stream that was loaded with salmon. The bears would enter the stream, flip the salmon onto the shore and in time, go ashore and enjoy a fish meal. Sometimes they would roll in the remains of the fish to get fish oil on their fur. If Bob Jones, the game warden, had found out that someone had shot a bear, all hell would have broken loose.

I told Sergeant Green to get a couple of his guys and a jeep, go get the bear and take it to the refrigerated store building and then get the butcher from the kitchen to butcher it. I then called the mess officer and told him what he could expect and we decided that we would serve the bear to the men as steak.

Somehow Bob Jones did not learn of this adventure and if he did he chose to ignore it. One night the bear was served as part of a meal to all of us. It was a much darker meat, impossible to chew and had the smell of fish. Most of us left it on the plate. A couple of days later, the bear was ground up and served as hamburger with the same results. I am sure the enlisted men knew what was going on but they also knew the consequence of telling on one of their own. Bob Jones never found out.

Building a reputation, but what kind?

Another incident involving our federal game warden was with a Navy Admiral from the base at Kodiak. To the north of our base, towards the Bering Sea, was an area where birds came during the summer months to nest and reproduce. It had been declared a federal game preserve. As a result of the great number of birds, it was ideal hunting ground. We would provide a weapons carrier to the hunters to take them out to the tundra and the swamp. We had many senior officers from the Air Force as well as the Navy arrive at our base to go hunting.

On this particular day, a Navy version of a C-47 arrived from Kodiak with an Admiral and his hunting companions. I arranged for the weapons carrier to take them to the hunting area and wished them luck. I was later in my office when one angry Admiral entered and wanted to know who this "#@### game warden was and who did he think he was, challenging an Admiral." It seems that after the Navy group had finished hunting they were on the way back to the base when a flock of geese flew over the weapons carrier and the Admiral stood up and shot one. He did not know that Bob Jones was in his jeep following the group of hunters. Bob pulled his jeep in front of the weapons carrier and brought it to a halt.

Bob demanded to know who shot the goose and the Admiral stated he had. Bob identified himself as a federal game warden and told the Admiral that he had broken the law, since he was not in the area designated as a hunting preserve, and in addition he had fired a weapon from a moving vehicle which also violated federal laws. The Admiral went ballistic but Bob ended up taking his gun and the birds he had with him and issued a warrant for the Admiral's arrest. I was told later that the Admiral had to go to Anchorage to reclaim his gun and pay a fine. The moral of this story: don't pull rank on a federal game warden.

A few days later, I received a message that General Donald R. Hutchinson would be arriving at Cold Bay, and the first thing I thought of was that Mike Utek had been successful in getting to the higher command, and that my career was coming to an end. General Hutchinson was in charge of the manning and operation of the Aleutian Islands. When he arrived we toured the base, and when we entered the power plant, he brought up the generator. I explained what had happened and the logic of my decision. General H. did not take a position one way or the other but suggested that we go fishing. On the way out to the stream, he asked me many questions regarding the base and some of the major problems I saw that needed attention. I was concerned with fire protection, medical support, the long delays in logistical support and of course, communications with his headquarters. I did not realize it at the time but I was being tested.

Shortly after this visit, Joe Cronin returned from his emergency leave. The first thing he said to me was "You have sure got the attention of a lot of people; I had to go to a meeting with General Armstrong to discuss what had been going on at Cold Bay. The first thing he asked me was 'Who is this guy Brim?'"

Island two: Cape Air Force Station on Umnak

Within a week, orders arrived assigning me to become the commander of Cape Air Force Station on the island of Umnak, farther out in the chain. At the time I thought it was a promotion, but problem officers are often moved just to get rid of them.

On Umnak, I moved into a house that had been General Buckner's, the commander of the island when it was the Army Headquarters for protecting all of the Aleutian Islands from invasion by the Japanese. The house had been built up on a hill that overlooked the base. The outside appearance showed the impact of Aleutian weather and the inside showed it had been neglected since the end of WWII. But I had my own jeep for transportation and the furniture would do.

I still have a copy of a report that I sent to my headquarters telling of the conditions I found at the base and felt they should understand what our limitations were. The report reads as follows:

> In the weather section 14 men assigned.
>
> Radiosons now in operation. Last month they were able to get six out of nine successful runs. Old equipment gives the weather people the most trouble.
>
> Celometer still lacks parts before it can be considered operational.
>
> Helium down to eight cyl. At present time will just last for four days.
>
> Steam fitters needed to overhaul the heating system in the hangar. Since this is the center of operations and men live in the hangar, it is necessary that sufficient heat be provided.
>
> 36,600 gallons of oil drums were gathered up out of frozen ground and emptied into a tank. This was done in two days and almost a superhuman effort by the men. Made doubly difficult due to lack of trucks and equipment to handle the drums.
>
> Rigging crew to re-roof the hangar. Recent storms have made the ceiling leak like a sieve. If the rigging crew can't come out would it be possible to send a tar pot and we could take care of the wings of the hangar where the men live.
>
> We are trying very hard to get the vehicles running but the lack of parts is a major problem. One of the fire trucks is out with a broken axle and the foam tank needs replacing. This is a 125. (I don't remember what a 125 represented but it must have indicated a priority of some kind.)
>
> Refrigeration is a problem. At present time we are down to fifty pounds of Freon gas. Just a case of old equipment and orders not being filled for replacements. There is a good possibility of spoilage of some food if this condition is not corrected.
>
> Mobile motor pool crew made up of all GIs has done a fine job, limited only by the lack of parts and not by their lack of spirit. Several members have asked to be re-assigned to Cape.

Saddle for 6" water line needed for new Non-Com Club. It's for the take-off from the wooden pipe and tapers down to the 4" take off.

Ray-Oil burners badly needed. This request was sent back for more nomenclature and we just don't have anymore. These are needed in the Mess hall, quarters, hospital and theater. This included tips for the Ray-Oil burners that are badly needed.

Fork Lift engine is in need of replacement.

Picking up equipment on our records once they have been salvaged. I discussed this with Colonel Capen and Colonel Haros and we agreed that it was not necessary. We are now told to do so in some of the correspondences from the headquarters A-4 section. What is the policy?

Ray Schinder, the only civilian at Umnak, has been here for over two years and is needed badly. Its felt he should work 48 hours a week until the base is back in operational condition. It was granted at one time and then was shut off by a TWX. Since the mobile personnel get 48 hours a week, it's felt that he is more important than they at our base and that he should be given the same consideration.

We need about 300 gallons of paint to complete the job we have just started at Cape. In the last two months, we have used just about that amount and we really need all you can spare.

ROTATIONS:

The 54 men stationed at Umnak have been doing a wonderful job and if it wasn't for the attitude of these men, Cape would really suffer. I would like to convey this to all the divisions of headquarters.

PERSONNEL:

Williams case. Need guidance and action.

Sgt Du Raud, the Aero-medic does not meet the standards of the rest of the people assigned to Cape and should be replaced as soon as possible.

Promotions: Why is it necessary to have all the airmen who are eligible for promotion come to Anchorage for evaluation? This puts a strain on the personnel and the sections when they come to Anchorage and still do not get promoted. Could a system be put into effect like AACS and Weather have for all personnel on the Chain?

I heard later that this same report was one of the main reasons for closing the base.

The island had been the main posting for troops in the defense of Alaska, and many Nissen huts were still standing and rusting away. They were also spread out over the island just in case the Japanese bombed this concentration of troops. To the east of Umnak was a large rock separated from the base by a half mile of rough ocean, and the story was that "girls hung out there." Of course, since it was impossible to get to the island because of the rough sea, no one had confirmed the fact that the girls were there but it made a good story. Mermaids, perhaps?

One of the hangars had been converted to a barracks for the enlisted men, our offices and a place to park the plane. It was the center of all the activities that kept a base going. At one side of the hangar was a basketball hoop, and the plane would be pushed out of the hangar when people wanted to play.

I will never know what brought about the message from headquarters that arrived shortly after my report arrived on conditions at Cape, but we were ordered to shut down all support operations including the weather reports and communications that supported the air traffic along the chain. They were closing the base. Two days after this message arrived, I was ordered to Shemya, another island even father out on the chain that was even closer to Russia. Maybe someone was trying to get rid of the troublemaker, but Shemya ended up being a much more challenging assignment.

Island three: Shemya

With orders in hand, I caught the next C-54 aircraft that was out of Anchorage en route to Shemya. Word had arrived that Captain Brim would be taking command of the base, and this was received by the assigned personnel with reservations and, in fact, a challenging attitude by some of the island's old hands. You would have to expect this reaction with 13 other captains assigned to the base. I just happened to outrank them by the date of promotion. The former commander had left the base prior to my arrival so there was no exchange of information.

During World War II, the United States had several thousand troops on Shemya, which provided a base of operations to attack the northern islands of Japan. At one time there were three runways, the longest being about 8,000 feet. In addition to the quarters for the troops, the base included hangars, a hospital, support buildings, and a very large fuel farm. When the facility was capable of supporting aircraft, a B–24 group was assigned there and they flew long over-water missions to bomb Japan.

After World War II the decision was made to destroy the facilities on Shemya to keep them away from the new enemy, Russia. As a result, many of the facilities were in a poor state of repair when the Korean War started in June of 1950. Just prior to my arrival, drums of gasoline would be perforated with a pickaxe and rolled down the center of a building and then set afire. With the advent of the Korean War, this program had to be stopped and in fact reversed to one of restoration. Shemya became a very important base for the airlift of equipment and personnel to Japan and Korea since it was one of the bases on the Great Circle Route, the shortest way to get to the ongoing war.

Shemya in disrepair

My plan was to prepare an evaluation of the base as I had at Cape, and forward it on to headquarters. This proved to be impossible. I would be up to my ears in ongoing projects, but I did not know that until the wheels of the C-54 1 I had hitched a ride on touched down on the runway. Shemya had a million dollar contract with the Puget Sound Construction Company out of Seattle for the rebuilding of the fuel farm that held gasoline for the planes coming through there. In addition to this contract, a new docking facility had to be built. The island did not have a natural harbor, so docks were built and breakwaters installed. It was considered the most protected beach on the island. Shortly after these facilities were finished, a furious storm hit that lasted several days. The docks were reduced to kindling and a great part of the breakwater was washed away. The contract with Puget Sound had then to be expanded to rebuild the dock. The pounding of the pile driver could be heard all over the island.

In time, buildings were constructed to withstand the weather, and that included hangars for the planes as well as facilities for the operation of the base. Some of the Nissen huts that were half below the surface were still used, as were the quarters I would inherit as commanding officer.

The hospital had many wings and so the main barracks and offices had been moved to this facility. Two wings were reserved for the hospital but were also used for visiting officials. At the time, 300-plus military people were assigned to the island. In addition to the military, contract workers and a detachment of Northwest Air Lines personnel were on the island. One of the advantages of this assignment was that I had the only staff car on the base, though the passenger door had been sprung by a blast of wind making it difficult to open or close.

After taking my gear to my new quarters, I went to the office to meet with the airmen who did the administrative work, and then held a meeting with all the officers on the base. After introducing myself, I asked that they continue to carry out our mission and that I would be visiting them at their offices. I also asked that they advise me of any particular problems they might be experiencing. Following the meeting, I went back to the office to a stack of paperwork that had been left behind.

A morale problem

Worse than having nothing to do, which was the case at Cold Bay, is having a base where military people feel sorry for themselves. Morale was dissipated, duties were neglected, and frequently the men drank too much.

Shortly after arriving, I noticed that some of the officers were not reporting to duty during normal working hours. The operations officer, was missing several mornings when I visited his office on the flight line. When I brought this to his attention, it was easy to see the reason for his absence. He was hung over from the night before. After several occasions of advising him he had to be on duty, and finding his habits unchanged, I called him in and said I had no choice but to include this problem in his annual report. The enlisted men were covering up for him but his actions could not be tolerated. I called a meeting of the officers and advised them that their responsibilities had to be carried out, and if drinking at the officers club made it impossible to carry out their duties, I would close the club.

This threat went over like a lead balloon. I explained that they would all pay a price for the actions of a few. But they didn't believe me until a couple days later when he was again absent from work. I drove to the club and confiscated the liquor, taking it to my quarters for safekeeping. In only a few hours, several of the officers came to me and asked if the liquor could be returned if they policed the actions of their fellow men. I agreed, but on the condition that duties came first and they had to prove they would monitor their fellow officers. The booze was returned and they seemed to have gotten the message.

Soon after my arrival, headquarters put us on alert for a possible engagement with Russia. It was during the time that the Korean War was not going well for us, and headquarters was concerned that Russia would enter this fight against us. There was little we could do since the only weapons we had were rifles that were in storage. I had the rifles cleaned and made distribution to the men who stored them in their barracks. At the same time, I stationed some men along the west side of the island to alert us if they saw an invasion approaching. I also ordered the men who operated the radar system, used for landing aircraft in bad weather, to man the system 24 hours a day. The captain in charge of the radar was very concerned that this patched together equipment could not operate for long periods of time, so we limited it to nighttime only.

Air Force ground personnel have limited training in how to use a rifle or any other weapon unless they are on a combat crew. The base had a rifle range so we started a program to familiarize airmen with the weapon. The whole effort was rather futile in a lot of respects but we did not want to give the impression that we would just surrender. Frankly, we did not have a plan for how to defend the island and I'm sure any organized military force would have had little trouble taking possession. I needn't have worried. The headquarters in Anchorage didn't even notify us that the alert had been called off. We learned this fact when a passing flight crew told us. I sent a message to headquarters confirming this information and received a reply saying yes, it had been called off, and they forgot to include us with message traffic. This event made all of us feel that we could be sacrificed in case of real combat.

One day, some of the enlisted men came to me and asked if they could refurbish an unoccupied building (we had plenty of them) as a Service Club. They said they would donate the time to get it going and I agreed, on the condition that booze would not be served. After all, we had an officers' club, a senior NCO club with the hard stuff, and beer was available at the enlisted club. But they were able to make the Service Club a great addition to our base. They got the Northwest Airlines people to provide the paint; they had recorded music; and headquarters donated a couple of pool tables and some lounge chairs. All of this was done during off-duty hours but it turned out well. I could tell morale was on the upswing on this isolated, forgotten Aleutian island.

Headquarters wanted to make the opening a special event and offered to bring a planeload of ladies who worked at Elmendorf Air Base over for the grand opening. On the big day, the C-54 with maybe fifteen ladies arrived, and a couple of chaperones who worked at the Special Service Club in Anchorage. When they got off the plane, one of the chaperones told me they had a problem with one of the girls, who was drunk. Since they would be staying at the hospital, I thought we could put her in one of the rooms and let her sober up, but she had other ideas.

The chaperone and I tried to get her to the room, but she resisted, and I will always remember what she said: "Don't try to force me to go the hospital. I've slept with colonels." We finally got her to her room and the chaperone stayed with her. She did not attend the opening celebration. Later on, I received a letter from the Special Service officer in Anchorage apologizing for the actions of this one guest.

One day I was driving by the back dock of the mess hall and saw one of our trucks backed up to the dock with no one present except the driver, who was busy reading a comic book. I stopped and asked what the cargo was and he told me it was from the freezer warehouse. I went into the mess hall and asked why the food was not being unloaded, and was told that they did not know it was at the dock. Followed by several people working in the mess hall, we went out to the truck and they started to unload the frozen food. I could see no reason for the driver not to participate in this effort, and when I told him to help, he told me it was not in his job description and went back to reading his comic book.

An anti-comic book stance that backfired

This pissed me off and I told him to get his ass out of the truck and help unload the truck if he wanted to eat while on Shemya. He put the comic book down and joined in the unloading of the truck. I also told the mess officer who was in charge of the base exchange to remove all the comic books from the exchange, and tear off the covers so we could send them back to Anchorage and get credit for them. This he did and I thought I had taken care of the incident. Another misguided decision on my part, as I was soon to find out.

About two weeks later I received a message that Brigadier General Agee would be paying us a visit. When General Agee arrived, I gave him our standard briefing and he suggested we take a tour of the base. He was very quiet. When we got to the exchange, he brought up the fact that no comic books were on the shelf. It did not dawn on me that this could be the reason for his visit and I told him the story about the frozen food being left in the truck by the driver while he read his comic book. Agee said. "Ray, I have to answer a Congressional inquiry regarding your denying your men the right to read magazines. Ray, put the comic magazines back on the shelf and we will forget this ever happened!!!" With this guidance, the comic books were back on the self, some without covers. The power of a letter to a Congressman.

It was on the 9th of April, 1951 when we received a message stating that a C-121, from the Special Air Missions Unit out of Washington D.C., would be arriving at Shemya en route to Japan. Very important people were aboard and we were to insure that we provided all the support they required. They had the highest priority that could be assigned to a flight.

I called a meeting and told my officers about the message and we had to be prepared to refuel this plane as quickly as possible with our limited number of fuel trucks and anything else we could do to expedite the stopover. The weather officer, Captain Walker, was to be on duty, and of course the radar assistance for landing was to be up and running.

About an hour before the ETA, I went down to the operations office to check on any communications that might have been received from the plane, and to insure that everything I could think of to expedite the transition of this VIP plane was done. Unfortunately we were down to one operating fuel truck, so it would have to be refilled to meet the needs of the plane.

4-star visitors need the loo

The first message from the plane advised us that they were ten minutes out and would be in need of complete service. We watched the C-121 land and taxi to the operations hard stand. The mobile steps were pushed up to the front exit of the plane and I went aboard. In the front compartment were more stars than I had ever seen in my life. General Vandenberg, the Chief of Staff for the Air Force, General Collins, the Chief of Staff of the Army, Admiral Low, Chief of Naval Operations, and several others, all with four stars on their shirt collars.

The first question they asked was, "Where is the closest latrine?" It seems that shortly after leaving McChord Air Force Base in Washington State, their latrine froze up after getting to an altitude where it was about minus 50 degrees. You couldn't open a window and dispose of the waste because the plane was pressurized. With a high priority mission and a very tight schedule, the decision was made to continue on to Shemya, an estimated 8-hour flight. Now this presented problems in that nature's calls were on schedule, and of course there were no facilities to take care of individual needs. Soon all containers were filled, and they had been giving General Vandenberg a hard time since it was an Air Force Special Operations plane.

I'm sure they had been traveling with their legs crossed for some time. I told them that the closest latrine was in the operations building but it was very limited in capacity. I suggested that the crew and other passengers could use these facilities and that I had two bathrooms in my quarters and perhaps they could make it to my house. They wanted to know how far it was to the quarters and I told them about 3 minutes once we got in the car. It was agreed that the senior people would go to my quarters. General Collins told his aide to bring some booze.

Upon arriving at my quarters, stars were flying into the house to be first in line. No rank was pulled; it was first in line, first served, if you want to call it that. For some reason, they were all smiling when they found the way to the living room where I had set up the bar.

General Vandenburg asked me what my major problems were, and I told him that Shemya was far down the priority list, even though we were attempting to support the airlift for the war with Korea. He wanted examples, and I told him that we had re-acquisitions disapproved because priority for the war in Korea was higher. While we understood this, it was difficult to keep our vehicles servicing the aircraft that passed through operational. Today we had only one fuel tanker that could take care of the very plane they were on. The warrant officer who brought the booze was taking notes on the conversation, so I had to be careful not to say too much.

Several drinks later, the pilot came to my quarters and said the plane was ready to go. There was an immediate question regarding the frozen latrine and they were assured that it was now operational. As we stepped out of my quarters, a Willawaw (a horizontal snow storm) was taking place and horizontal snow, sleet, and rain greeted the VIPs. We got them aboard the plane, closed the door, and I was happy to see them take off for Tokyo. I then sent a message to headquarters stating that the plane had departed Shemya, but under instructions, did not mention who was aboard.

Two days later, we heard over Armed Forces Radio that General MacArthur had been relieved of his command by order of President Truman, and members of the Joint Staff were in Tokyo to support this decision. The very people who arrived in Shemya with their legs crossed had gone on to Tokyo to support the President in the firing of MacArthur.

My tour on the chain was coming to a close. I had spent one year at three different locations and had learned a lot. A message arrived stating that Lieutenant Colonel Padgett would be arriving as my replacement. Padgett's career had been in the Special Air Missions organization. Upon his arrival, orders came assigning me to Alaska Air Command Headquarters in the Manpower Division.

The reason for my assignment was that in those days, only so many promotions to a higher grade could be made on a selected date. I had been told that I was number two on the list to be promoted to major in the Alaskan Air Command, and I had to be in the command on the selected date to gain the promotion. This meant that I would be in Alaska for four more months, but it was worth it. If I had been assigned to another command, I could have been on the bottom of that command's promotion list.

The date for the annual promotion boards arrived and the director of personnel for Alaska Command told me that I would be reassigned to the States in the near future. That was fine with me. If I had been advancing my career, I should have volunteered for Korea right then and there, but I wanted to be with my family. We had been apart long enough.

About a week later my orders arrived. I was assigned to the ROTC staff at Purdue University in West Lafayette, Indiana. I called Pat and told her I would be home in a few days and that we were going to Purdue. What a change of life for both of us.

CHAPTER 35

AN AIR FORCE CAREER

As a major at Purdue University in Lafayette, Indiana from 1951 to 1954, I taught courses in the ROTC program, such as Air Science-I (first year basic), and I was the cadet squadron tactical officer. I meantime logged as much flight time as I could out of Chanute Air Force Base. I also took as many part-time courses at Purdue as I could in my major, political science. In August 1952, we welcomed our second daughter, Christine, into the world.

In a year, my position was advanced to senior instructor Air Science-IV (flight operations). In 1953, because of my prior experience, I supervised Air Science instructors in flight operations. Also in 1953, I was staff advisor to the student Chandelle Squadron, which doubled in size that year, and to the MARS program. By 1954, I was managing all aspects of instruction in Air Science IV for 115 students, and supervised other instructors.

The Pentagon

In 1954 I was finishing my tour on the staff of the Air Force Reserve Officer Training Corps at Purdue University. I was concerned about the annual change-of-station report that was due, because my immediate boss and I did not get along. His career had been mostly in Training Command, and what the Air Force had been doing for the last three years in actual operations was, in his judgment, all wrong. Unfortunately he was a lieutenant colonel, and I was a major, and when I had the gall to challenge him in front of other instructors, he remembered.

The closest Air Force base was Chanute, near Rantoul, Illinois. A fellow instructor and friend of mine, Dick Godsmith, and I were able to get a B-25 and fly to Andrews Air Force Base, near Washington, D.C. We then found our way to the Pentagon, where our records were on file. I was heartsick when I saw what had been written about me. I could do nothing about it, so Dick and I left the vault where the records were kept.

We were in the main corridor of the Pentagon, on our way out, when I heard my name called out. It was Mel Giles, for whom I had worked in Alaska. Mel asked me what I was doing in the "big house," and when he heard the story, he just nodded and took it all in. I was glad to see him but mostly still worried about that performance review.

Dick and I cranked up the two engines on the B-25 and headed for home. Three weeks later, I was called into the office of the Purdue ROTC office and told I was being assigned to the Pentagon. We moved the family to Arlington, Virginia, and I started my new assignment in August 1955.

My new assignment at the Pentagon was working for Mel Giles, then a lieutenant colonel who was with the Manpower and Organization Division, with responsibility for establishing the proper staffing to "ensure mission accomplishment to the air commands in Operations, Manpower & Organizations, Plans & Programming, Flying Safety, Air Mission, Joint Activities, and MAAG areas". Mel had come to my rescue. This translated to my preparing a lot of field manpower surveys and statistical reports, as well as my first experience at briefing higher-ups at the Pentagon. I had to learn a lot—fast—about both the personnel field and statistical analysis. And, equally important, I had an opportunity to learn how to negotiate diplomatically with other commands. This assignment, my first at the Pentagon, was a real turning point in my career—a make-it-or-break-it opportunity. I was determined to make it work.

Commanders always ask for plenty of manpower to meet the needs of any assigned mission. They normally paint a bleak picture of possible scenarios in order to justify using more people.

I was a manpower utilization analyst on the team that had been handed the task of developing the requirements for the new Air Force

Academy. In 1948, the service had appointed a board, later named the Stearns-Eisenhower Board for its chairmen, to study the existing military academies and to come up with options for an Air Force academy. We asked the Army and the Navy if they would give us a copy of their manpower requirements for West Point and Annapolis, figuring that would give us a good starting point. The Army was immediately cooperative, but the Navy flat-out refused.

We had the responsibility to insure the right balance. The Air Force Academy was officially launched in April 1954, and on July 11, 1955, construction began in Colorado Springs. The first Air Force Academy class of 306 men was sworn in at the temporary site, Lowry Air Force Base, near Denver. We ended up with two manpower plans, one for the temporary academy facility at Lowry and another for Colorado Springs.

One of the projects I initiated was a study of the personnel priority designator (PPD) system, which led to a new relationship between the PPD system and the manpower authorizations within each command. It was an experience that gave me a much broader understanding of personnel policies in the Air Force that I would put to good use in later years.

I continued my education with night school and correspondence courses in political science, as I had during every assignment. In 1957, I completed the jet qualification course at Craig Air Force Base, Alabama—part of my transition to flying jets rather than conventional aircraft.

Japan

My superiors had consistently recommended that my next assignment should be in operations, and I wanted to get back into the field myself. Headquarters must have been listening, because in July 1957 I was sent as staff maintenance officer to Japan, as part of the Military Air Transport Wing (MATS). Pat and I were thrilled—our first overseas assignment together! I was assigned to the maintenance management staff of the 1503rd Transport Wing at the Tachikawa Air Force Base in Japan.

My training back at Chanute as an aircraft maintenance officer in 1945 was part of the reason I was assigned to MATS in Japan. But that had been 12 years earlier, so I had a steep learning curve to catch up with current maintenance management procedures. As staff maintenance officer, I had to draw up plans for moving the maintenance capability from Tokyo Airport to Tachikawa Air Force Base, and to work closely with other wing and group staffs to prepare the plan for the move. And I had to learn about contracts management in order to get a contractor on board right away to handle turnaround maintenance of all aircraft. This was on-the-job training for me, every day.

A little background on the 1503rd MATS is in order here, and on the importance of Tachikawa at the time. MATS flights were a 24-hour-a-day operation, with pilots flying C-118s, C-121s, C-124s, and C-133s, to Hawaii, Alaska, Korea, Saigon, Bangkok, Pakistan, Guam, and Midway.

Aircraft maintenance was an urgent priority at Tachikawa. We had to keep all those planes flying—and also because four years earlier, on June 18, 1953, the worst air crash in Air Force history at that time had occurred when 129 people were killed in a C-124 crash. The plane had taken off from Tachikawa, and crashed in a field nearby. The cause of that crash was engine failure.

And now, four years later, I was tasked with planning and overseeing the transfer of the Maintenance Air Transport Service to Tachikawa while continuing uninterrupted maintenance operations.

Meanwhile Tachikawa, with all that traffic 24/7, presented another problem—a runway only 1,500 meters (4,900 feet) long. That meant that a number of aircraft types could not use it at all, including those required for jet transport and also strategic missions. Plans had been drawn up to extend the Tachikawa runway into Sunagawa, a neighborhood right next to the base.

The Japanese farmers living in Sunagawa were not happy with this decision, to say the least, and had been protesting since late 1956. The protests had become very divisive, with politicians from the Socialist and Communist parties joining in; putatively non-violent protests became pitched battles between police and hundreds of protestors.

I arrived on March 8, 1957, and in the following weeks I saw protestors with their political party flags attached to long bamboo poles demonstrating at both ends of the runway, which bordered on private land held by the Sunagawa farmers. Four months after I arrived, on July 8, 1957, protestors actually overran the Tachikawa base in what was called the "Sunagawa riots." The issue became so contentious that the Air Force finally shelved the Tachikawa runway extension plans. Later, Yokota Air Base, with its longer runways, would be used extensively for transports.

By 1958 I had been given a new job as executive officer for the maintenance group. I visited all four squadrons in the group and found that airmen housing was in bad shape and affecting morale. To get these buildings repaired, I worked with the unit commanders to prepare their proposals and cost estimates, and then argued their case up the chain of command. Those relationships with the unit commanders helped my work with them for the rest of the Japan tour.

My superior, Colonel Jules Prevost, had two jobs: he was group commander and wing director of material. We had a good relationship and I was able to act in his name on everything that didn't require a personal decision by him.

Meanwhile, in 1958, to keep up my flying time, I flew C-124s and worked to re-qualify in flying jets, which took up a lot of weekend time.

Making the most of an overseas tour

In the rest of my free time, Pat and I reached out to every Japanese person we met to make friends—an easy task, because they wanted to meet Americans and improve their English. We both worked with the English-speaking societies of local universities, and I received an award from Chuo University for my work with their English-speaking society. Pat and I gave regular English lessons a couple times a week for a number of Japanese students, ranging from high school to college, to a physician and other professionals, in our little homes in Grant Heights and Tachikawa.

By early 1959, my title was changed to match what I had been doing for the past year—Administrative Assistant to Deputy Commander for Material—and I continued to be an advocate for better living conditions for our airmen.

I was able to put my Purdue experience in training and education to work, too, when we had to create a maintenance training capability for C-133 aircraft "in a minimum of time," that is, under the very typical constraints of short deadlines, little-to-no budget, and an absolute requirement for meeting performance standards. It was our job to keep C-133 aircraft ready to fly and in the air.

I also had an opportunity to prepare the briefings to represent the 1503rd Air Transport Wing in budget discussions. We managed to convert a planned budget cut into a decision by the committee to give over half of all the proposed funds to MATS organizations. I can't help but laugh now at the phrase used in my evaluation describing my lobbying in that budget campaign as "diplomatically forceful." Might just be a euphemism.

Later that year, I inherited a new position as chief of Plans & Manpower for the wing, and my responsibilities expanded beyond maintenance to emergency planning, manpower programming, and management engineering. We were faced immediately with a reduction in manpower authorizations, which would have crippled our ability to do our mission. I made it my task to convince headquarters to reconsider, which met with a lot of resistance at every step, but I kept at it for six months and, in October 1959, we finally got word that we would be maintained at our current strength. I made several trips to Travis Air Force Base to represent the 1503rd to keep our operations funded.

My work from 1957 to 1959 in Japan had helped me build some great relationships with other commands in the area, and in the early fall of 1959 I organized a three-day area management conference for the Far East region, the first of its kind, to bring all the commands together, including the Far East headquarters.

My friendships also developed with many officers in the Japanese military, helped by the English lessons Pat and I provided. In April 1960, at my initiative, I briefed the Japan Air Staff College and Air Staff officers on MATS worldwide operations, in preparation for them to stay in the U.S. for military training and education.

I kept an eye out for problems our airmen were encountering. A major one was that the bank at the base served the officers but wasn't accessible to enlisted men. In my off-hours in 1959, I organized a small team, and we established the first credit union at the base. I was chairman until I was reassigned back to the States.

CHAPTER 36

COMMAND AND STAFF COLLEGE, AND AFTERWARDS

For several years my superiors had recommended me for the Air Command and Staff College at Maxwell Air Force Base in Alabama, and I finally got the assignment. We arrived in Montgomery, Alabama, in June 1960.

The Command and Staff College had a year-long curriculum geared to mid-career officers that required a great deal of analysis and writing. The goal was to prepare us to manage a rapidly changing Air Force at the height of the Cold War. Most of my classmates were majors or equivalent ranks. I made some great friendships and I acted as the seminar leader during the school term.

I was designated a distinguished graduate of the Command and Staff College, and am particularly proud of that accomplishment. I have always struggled with my writing due to poor preparation back in my early education, so I had to work particularly hard to compete and to improve, fast. Pat, a superb editor who would go on to teach English during our next assignment, helped every step of the way. I was even selected for a trip to Canada for a Canadian-United States officer-exchange program, to evaluate their different approach to officer training.

1961–1965: The unsung heroes

In 1961, following graduation from Air Force Command and Staff College, I was assigned to the personnel planning division of the Air Force in Washington, D.C. as Chief, Programs and Project Section, Career

Planning Occupational Development Branch. I was one of the many staff officers at the Pentagon who worked on issues that affected multiple commands.

My job was with Airman Promotions and the distribution of promotions to different ranks and skills to the major commands throughout the Air Force. This proved to be one of the most interesting assignments I had during my 30-plus-year career. Our office was not in the Pentagon but in a temporary building called T-7 just off Wisconsin Avenue in the District, a short commute from our home in Bethesda. The building was built during World War II and was still in use some 20 years later.

In my judgment, at the time, the Air Force was not promoting enlisted men as early in their careers as the Army and Navy, and this was a cause of discontent within the force. It also had an impact on retaining airmen whom the Air Force had spent thousands of dollars training and who then, after four years, would leave the service. In one year, I answered 1,700 Congressional inquiries regarding complaints by airmen not being promoted.

With the support of my boss, Lieutenant Colonel Ken Flavin, and a capable staff, I made it my mission to improve the promotion system for airmen. This met with considerable resistance, but I had learned how to persist in spite of opposition. I had also learned how to be, as one of my evaluations for this assignment stated, "pleasantly aggressive".

We were losing some of our top performers because we had quotas on promotions and a mismatch in skills and requirements. I was convinced we could do better. At the start, I was able to build on my prior work in statistics and trend analysis from my previous personnel assignment back in the early 1950s. One of the master sergeants on my staff had a gift for statistical analysis, and he did a lot of the heavy lifting on our calculations. Our first task was to improve our ability to analyze promotion trends for each specialty, then a very time-consuming and often inaccurate process that we were able to reduce from four hours to one hour for each promotion cycle.

Once we had improved our methods, I set out to improve our ability to allocate promotions. The Air Force had a long-standing problem of surpluses in many skills and scarcities in others, a problem shared with the other services and pretty much any large organization. Once we got a start on reducing those surpluses, we could get rid of some of the promotion quotas and increase opportunities. Our objective was to raise the enlisted grade ceiling, which affected thousands of airmen. We spent hours doing research to support our position and, in time, wrote a paper that was published in a bulletin that went to the staff of the Air Force within the Pentagon.

I later received a call that started out: "This is Ben Davis, and I would like you to come to my office and brief me on your paper." General Benjamin O. Davis had been commander of the Tuskegee Airmen group of Black officers who were fighter pilots during WWII, the 332nd Fighter Group, as well as commander of the 99th Squadron. He had flown more than 60 combat missions. He was only the fourth Black graduate from West Point, and was the first African-American Air Force general. He was at the time a Major General in charge of the Manpower Directorate in the Pentagon. I was smart enough to answer his call by saying, "When can I be at your office?" The time was set, I briefed him on my findings, and we discussed ways and means of improving the situation. He was one of the easiest people to brief that I ever encountered, a real gentleman.

A couple of days later, my boss, Lieutenant Colonel Ken Flaven, told me that General Stone had requested that I come to the Pentagon and brief him. Stone was in charge of Air Force personnel and had read the same paper that was circulating around the Pentagon. After I briefed him, he said he thought the "Chief" should hear what I had prepared, and he would set up an appointment for the briefing. The "Chief" was General John P. McConnell, the chief of staff of the Air Force.

I was operating at a level I never dreamed I would be and one that very few officers in the Air Force ever experienced. The day arrived when General Stone and I went to the "Chief's" office and were shortly reporting in for the briefing. General McConnell told his aide that he did not want to be disturbed during the session. About halfway through, the aide came into the room and said that a general was on the phone and insisted on talking to the Chief now. McConnell was less than happy but took the call, and General Stone and I left his office to wait outside.

Shortly we were called back into his office and the first thing he said to us was, "There is nothing worse than a f---king stupid general." Upon finishing the briefing and after a few questions, General McConnell thanked me and asked that General Stone remain. I packed my charts and saluted the Chief, and went back to T-7.

We continued to sell the idea to the major commands and air staff agencies at all levels for months, and we finally got a go-ahead. I developed the "Top Flow" program for additional promotions for airmen in the top six enlisted grades. We continued to get hundreds of queries on denied promotions every year from Congress, all of which my staff and I answered. We had become the focal point of reforming promotion opportunities for airmen. I was personally promoted to the active duty rank of Lieutenant Colonel, though still with the permanent rank of Major.

1965–1966: The Air War College

In 1965, I received the permanent rank of Lieutenant Colonel and was reassigned to attend the Air War College, the senior professional military education school of the U.S. Air Force.

Following graduation, I was assigned to an organization that was new to me, because it was classified: the Air Force Technical Applications Center (AFTAC). Although our activities were entirely classified at the time, shortly after I retired in 1975, AFTAC implemented a series of partial mission declassifications. Since then, extensive information about AFTAC, encompassing the information in this book, has previously been published online and in military magazines.

Air Force Technical Applications Center

AFTAC operated the long-range detection system to detect foreign atomic tests. It was a worldwide system of sensors that detected nuclear explosions everywhere—in outer space, in the oceans, deep underground, and in the atmosphere. Those sensors used acoustic, seismic, and radiological equipment to conduct surveillance on nuclear activities. In the 1960s and early 1970s, we tracked whether those countries were complying with the 1963 Limited Test Ban Treaty, which prohibited all nuclear testing except underground, and also prohibited the venting of nuclear debris or radiation from those tests into the atmosphere outside the country's national border. AFTAC's job was to differentiate between, say, an earthquake and a nuclear explosion, and to pinpoint the location of the latter. We advised the HQ USAF, the regional commands, and other agencies of our findings.

AFTAC had agreements with countries around the world to install surveillance equipment and, in several countries, to man the surveillance stations. The first station had been placed in Turkey to be close to where the Soviet Union was testing nuclear devices. That manned station in Turkey continued to be important to AFTAC activities when I took command in 1970 of the 1157th Technical Operation Squadron, based in Wiesbaden, West Germany. During my years with AFTAC, I traveled to stations around the world, from South Africa to Easter Island to Iran.

I worked particularly closely with the British. For a period of time during 1966–67, I was in charge of the collection of airborne debris generated from the explosion of atomic devices throughout the world. From the leaf of a tree downwind from the explosion, to the particulate matter in the mushroom cloud, all were important elements in the analysis of the device that had been exploded.

The problem for us regarding the Soviets was access, because they conducted their tests thousands of miles from where we could begin our collections. After each event, we monitored the weather over the test site and projected when we could make a collection near Japan or Korea. Because of the high priority of our mission, we had access to many aircraft to complete the collections. These included U-2s, B-52s, B-57s, C-135s, and C-130s. We also had ground collectors around the world to augment our airborne collections.

It was extremely important to get the samples as soon as possible to aid in our analyses. Each one of these aircraft had a scoop collection system. The special system operator or the pilot (depending on the aircraft) changed the filter paper behind the scoop and logged the geographical location with each change. This procedure was important for follow-up flights by other aircraft. None of these planes except for the U-2 could fly above the tropopause (60,000 feet), so the U-2 became our principle debris collector at or above that altitude.

While all these flights presented many problems, the most difficult problem was locating the air mass—the "plume"—that carried the radioactive debris. We knew to a second when the explosion had taken place, but projecting the time we could start our collection was extremely difficult. We could not afford to miss the plume carrying the debris, so with our best forecast, we would put a plane on station hours ahead of time in order to insure collection.

This was expensive, and with the limitations of the aircraft to remain on station, we had to have a backup resource of planes. Aircraft flew search patterns at various altitudes until they were able to locate the debris. Once they found it, our mission was simplified and we could make the required collections. Our goal was to find the most radioactive part of the plume, thereby getting the best sample possible.

I asked our technical people why we did not have an instrument to assist the aircrews in locating the plume. It seemed to me that, inasmuch as the plume was radioactive, we should be able to develop an instrument to record its location. Without such an assist, we could be missing the radioactive cloud by as little as a few hundred feet.

Whenever I broached this subject, several reasons were given why it couldn't be done. It was suggested that the instrument would have to be mounted in the aircraft, which would then require modification, or that it would be large and difficult to work with while the pilot or special-equipment operator was involved with other duties, and so forth. Anyway, we did not have such an instrument.

It is interesting to note that both the British and the French had been forced to move their atomic testing sites. The first British tests took place in Australia, and the French were forced to move their tests from North Africa when they lost control over Algeria. The French moved to a test site on several small islands in the Pacific. Early in the American testing program, we too tested on isolated islands in the Pacific, but for logistic and financial reasons we moved the tests to Nevada. Only the Soviets, the Chinese, and the United States tested atomic weapons within their own borders on a regular basis.

By 2006, more than thirty years after I retired in 1975, AFTAC had expanded to more than 800 personnel, with installations in 50 nations on six continents. In 2006, AFTAC's U.S. Atomic Energy Detection System (USAEDS) confirmed North Korea's claim of a nuclear test, which resulted in sanctions against that state. Today, AFTAC is part of the 25th

Air Force with nearly 1,000 people and ten detachments entrusted with the same mission we had back in the 1960s and 1970s:

USAEDS has sensors on global positioning system and defense support system satellites that monitor space and Earth's atmosphere for light flashes, radioactivity, and other telltale signs of nuclear explosions. The system's hydroacoustic sensors are microphones that listen for nuclear explosions under the sea. Infrasound sensors measure changes in the atmosphere generated by very-low-frequency acoustic waves that can come from above-ground nuclear explosions.

As part of the system, a WC-135 aircraft flies to the sites of explosions and collects air that scientists on the ground analyze for radioactive particles and radioactive gases. And the system's 40 seismic stations around the world—using the same technology scientists use to measure earthquakes—monitor the planet for underground nuclear explosions.

AFTAC was simply a great place to work, tremendously challenging and right on the scientific front lines of national defense. It was the height of the Cold War, and AFTAC squadrons operated with a sense of urgency and vigilance, day and night. I was honored to serve with some of the smartest scientists and technicians in the military, and all of us held ourselves accountable for the constant surveillance of nuclear testing worldwide, 365 days a year.

Retirement

The Air Force had a policy that after 20 or 30 years of service, depending on your rank, if you were not promoted, you were retired ("Up or Out"). With my time in the service before I was 21 and my service in the Reserves before being recalled in 1947, the policy was that, on the promotion list, my service started at age 21, not 19. Therefore, I lost the years from World War II. I had a total of 33 years' service. Not being promoted in 1975, I was advised the Air Force had no further use for me and it was time to retire. I was 53 years old.

EPILOGUE

As I reflect on my life, I am often amazed at how lucky I've been, the places I've traveled and worked, and the wonderful people I've known over my ninety-three years. Not bad for a kid from Dividend.

The people in my life have been a determined lot. I think of my parents, who were patient and cheerful in hard times, and who made a good life for us. I remember the hard-working mining families who were our neighbors in the tiny town of Dividend in the 1920s and 1930s, who gave me a life-long sympathy for the underdog in any fight. I think of my fellow warriors who fought at my side during the air war over Germany and how our goal for every mission was to bomb the target and bring our B-17 home in one piece.

Collecting these memoirs has brought to mind so many stories of my friends and colleagues during my decades in the Air Force. We had a few challenges along the way, but we stayed the course and got the job done.

Most of all, I will always be inspired by the determination and gift for happiness of my wonderful wife Pat, who overcame polio to travel the world with me, raise our two daughters, and pursue careers in music, teaching and writing. She is always in my heart and my thoughts.

APPENDICES

1. The Loading List for a Flying Fortress Prior to a Combat Mission

1. LOADING LIST FOR A B-17 F

    a. NOSE COMPARTMENT

        1 navigator's box. On floor at navigator's table. Remove Navigator's stool and place it in the radio room

        5 B-4 bags or parachute bags. Put heaviest bags in nose. Place one on RH of bomber place 4 bags between seat and navigator

    b. ON WALK WAY BELOW COCKPIT

        1 c-3 bomb hoist box at aft end of walk. Tie down

        2 boxes containing 20 B-9 bomb shackles. Just forward of bomb hoist box. Tie down

        1 5 gal. can of water.

    c. COCKPIT

        2 D-6 bomb shackles

        2 D-6 adapters. Place shackles and adapters between upper turret and forward of bomb bay bunk-head. Tie down Lot of extra bomb shackles. Any loose ones should be wired together and tied down to floor beneath upper turret

    d. BOMB BAY

        Hang up as many B-7 bomb shackles as possible before bomb bay tanks are installed

e. RADIO GUN STORAGE COMPARTMENT (ABOVE BOMB BAY)

    4 .30–cal rifles

    1 sub–machine gun

f. CAMERA PIT

    9 cots. Place at aft end of camera pit. Pack mattresses around them

    4 mooring kits. Place on bottom of pit

    4 engine slings

    4 engine tool kits

    1 tail hoist sling

    1 armorer's kit

    1 kit of special B 17 F tools

    1 lot propeller tools

    2 cans of hydraulic oil

    1 bombsight bracket

    2 crew chief kits. Place one on bench at forward end of camera pit. Place the other immediately aft and on top of other items

    18 mattress covers. Pack these in remaining space between tool kit and electrical connection on LH side of camera pit

g. RADIO ROOM RH SIDE

    1 B-17 emergency kit. Box 5 feet long. Place next to anti–icer filler. Push forward as far as possible

    2 outboard heat exchangers

    6 B-4 parachute bags. Place as many of these bags as possible on RH side of radio room. Do not stow to close to radio sets or on dynoamotor on floor

h. RADIO ROMM LH SIDE

    1 frequency meter

    2 emergency radio sets in cartons

    1 box documents

    1 radio man's kit

    1 bail out rations

i. BALL TURRET

1 flame suppressor for No. 3 engine

4 bed rolls

Remainder of baggage including barrack bags, parachute bags

4 engine covers. Place on floor and walk on them

j. IMMEDIATELY AFT OF BALL TURRET

1 B 17- F emergency kit. Tie down

2 yellow overseas boxes. Place one on top of emergency kit. Place other behind. Tie down

2 nacelle jacks

1 towing bar. Tie down

1 box heat exchanger hoods

1 SCR 578A Radio (in yellow canvas case)

1 5 gal. can of water

k. AT SIDE WINDOWS

1 box extra oxygen masks

1 G.I. bucket and brush

1 spray gun

l. AT ENTRANCE DOOR

1 auxiliary power plant

m. AMMUNITION LOADING

100 rounds per gun. Total of 1100 rounds

CAUTION: Do not load more than 200 rounds in the talk or more than 200 rounds at side guns

n. CREW POSITIONS AT TAKEOFF AND LANDINGS

NOSE – 2 persons

COCK PIT – 4 persons

RADIO ROOM – 3 persons

2. IN ADDITION THE FOLLOWING WILL BE NOTED IN THE LOADING OF ALL B-17-Fs

a. No equipment stowed in bomb bay

b. Crewmembers luggage figured at 100 lbs per man

c. All loose items securely lashed on place

d. AFCE box not carried

e. Bombsight box carried at discretion of bombardier. If carried place after of ball turret provided 2nd B 17-F kit is not carried.

3. THE GROSS WEIGHT AND CENTER OF GRAVITY FOR THE
   ABOVE LOADING WILL BE AS FOLLOWS:
       a. FOR SERIAL NUMBERS 42-29467 to 42-29530
           Gross wt – 58,300
           C.G. 29.1%
           C. G. with crew at combat stations – 31.8%
       b. FOR ALL OTHER B-17-F AIRPLANES
           Gross wt – 57,900
           C.G. 29.7%
           C.G. with crew at combat stations – 32.4%

2. Statistics

Name: Raymond E. Brim
Rank: Captain
Duty: Pilot
Squadron: 813th Bomb Squadron
Group: 482nd Bomb Group
25 Raids: Targets and Flight Hours

Mission #	Date	Group #	Target	Flight Hours
1	5/17/43	92nd BG	Lorient, France	5:30
2	5/19/43	92nd BG	Kiel, Germany	6:45
3	5/29/43	92nd BG	St. Nazaire, France	6:00
4	6/11/43	92nd BG	Wilhelmshaven, Germany	6:15
5	6/13/43	92nd BG	Bremen, Germany	6:30
6	6/22/43	92nd BG	Huls, Germany	6:00
7	6/26/43	92nd BG	Paris, France	6:00
8	9/27/43	PFF#1	Emden, Germany	6:00
9	10/2/43	#2	Emden, Germany	6:00
10	10/20/43	#3	Duren, Germany	6:15
11	11/19/43	#12	Western region, Germany	6:05
12	11/26/43	#13	Bremen, Germany	6:45
13	12/30/43	#27	Ludwigshaven, Germany	8:20
14	1/4/44	#28	Kiel, Germany	6:40

15	1/23/44	#34	Duren, Germany	4:10
16	1/30/44	#39	Brunswick, Germany	7:00
17	2/8/44	#43	Frankfurt, Germany	8:00
18	2/29/44	#49	Brunswick, Germany	6:45
19	3/2/44	#50	Frankfurt, Germany	7:40
20	3/3/44	#51	Wilhelmshaven, Germany	7:15
21	3/8/44	#54	Berlin, Germany	9:10
22	3/11/44	#56	Munster, Germany	6:05
23	3/15/44	#57	Brunswick, Germany	8:00
24	3/16/44	#58	Augsburg, Germany	9:20
25	3/18/44	#59	Oberpfaffenhofen, Germany	9:35
			TOTAL COMBAT HOURS	172:00

25 Raids: Bomber Statistics

Raid #	Target	Bombers Over Target	Losses	Escorts
1	Lorient	118	6	0
2	Kiel	103	6	0
3	St. Nazaire	147	8	131
4	Wilhelmshaven	218	8	0
5	Bremen	122	4	0
6	Huls	183	16	0
7	Paris	56	5	130
8	Emden	246	7	262
9	Emden	339	2	227
10	Duren	97	9	360
11	Western region, Germany	130	1	130
12	Bremen	440	25	361
13	Ludwigshaven	658	23	169
14	Kiel	486	17	112
15	Duren	1	0	0
16	Brunswick	742	20	200
17	Frankfurt	195	13	214

18	Brunswick	218	1	241
19	Frankfurt	375	9	244
20	Wilhelmshaven	79	11	246
21	Berlin	539	37	252
22	Munster	124	1	140
23	Brunswick	330	3	259
24	Augsburg	401	23	262
25	Oberpfaffenhoffen	480	43	264

25 Raids: Target Industrial Sectors

Raid #	Target	Industrial Sector
1	Lorient	Submarine Base
2	Kiel	Kiel Canal
3	St. Nazaire	Submarine Base
4	Wilhelmshaven	Submarine Yard
5	Bremen	Submarine Yard
6	Huls	Synthetic Rubber
7	Paris	Air Depot
8	Emden	Industrial Area
9	Emden	Industrial Area
10	Duren	Industrial Area
11	Western region, Germany	Unknown
12	Bremen	Port Areas
13	Ludwigshaven	Oil Refinery
14	Kiel	Port Areas
15	Duren	Industrial Area
16	Brunswick	Steel Industry
17	Frankfurt	Marshalling Yards
18	Brunswick	Aviation Industry
19	Frankfurt	Marshalling Yards
20	Wilhelmshaven	Oil Industry
21	Berlin	Oil Industry
22	Munster	Marshalling Yards

23	Brunswick	Industrial Area
24	Augsburg	Munitions Industry
25	Oberpfaffenhoffen	Air Field/Aviation Industry

3. Deploying to England from US flying a B-17 – 1943

Flight Log B-17 Tail Number 42-5406

Morrison Field	04:00	3/25/43
Arr. Trinidad	13:30	3/25/43
Leave Trinidad	08:45	3/26/43
Arr. Belem, Brazil	15:40	3/26/43
Leave Belem	08:00	3/28/43
Arr. Natal, Brazil	14:40	3/28/43
Leave Natal	05:10	4/3/43
Arr. Ascencion Island	15:40	4/3/43
Leave Ascencion Island	08:10	4/4/43
Arr. Roberts Field, Liberia	14:00	4/4/43
Leave Roberts	10:00	4/5/43
Arr. Dakar	15:00	4/5/43
Leave Dakar	09:25	4/6/43
Arr. Agadir, Morocco	17:05	4/6/43
Leave Agadir	14:00	4/8/43
Arr. Marrakech, Morocco	15:20	4/8/43
Leave Marrakech	01:55	4/11/43
Arr. St Eval, England	10:50	4/11/43